D1251015

Byron and His Fictions

Byron and His Fictions

by

Peter J. Manning
University of Southern California

Wayne State University Press   Detroit, 1978

Library of Congress Cataloging in Publication Data
Manning, Peter J., 1942-
  Byron and his fictions.

  Bibliography: p.
  Includes index.
  1. Byron, George Gordon Nöel Byron, Baron, 1788–1824
—Criticism and interpretation.
2. Byron, George Gordon
Nöel Byron, Baron, 1788–1824. Don Juan. 3. Myth in
literature. 4. Heroes in literature. I. Title.
PR4388.M28   821'.7   78–7943
ISBN 0-8143-1600-X

Contents

Preface

A book as long in developing as this one incurs many obligations, and only my wish to avoid the kind of preface in which an author implicates everyone he has known since childhood checks my desire to thank all those who contributed. I first wrote on Byron as a graduate student at Yale University, with Cleanth Brooks and Maynard Mack. Portions of this manuscript were read and improved by Janet Adelman, Frederick Crews, Morton Paley, Robert Tracy, and Alex Zwerdling; to the first and last of these I am especially indebted for many like acts of friendship through the years. My wife's critical attention, animated by an undying hostility to Byron, strengthened the book throughout. Lastly, despite the comedy of so inscribing a work on these themes, I dedicate this study to my parents.

Permission to reprint is gratefully acknowledged to the following: to the Hogarth Press, for quotations from *The Standard Edition of The Complete Psychological Works of Sigmund Freud*, and to Basic Books, Inc., in respect of *The Collected Papers of Sigmund Freud*, volume 4, Paper XI, "Contributions to the Psychology of Love: A Special Type of Choice of Object Made by Men," pp. 200–201, and Volume 2, Paper XXXII, "Further Recommendations in the Technique of Psycho-Analysis; Recollection, Repetition and Working

7

Through," pp. 369–370; edited by Ernest Jones, M.D.; authorized translation under the supervision of Joan Riviere, published by Basic Books., Publishers, New York, by arrangement with the Hogarth Press, Ltd., and the Institute of Psycho-Analysis, London; to Princeton University Press, for selections from pp. 85–87 of *The Collected Works of C. G. Jung*, ed. Herbert Read, Michael Fordham, Gerhard Adler, and William McGuire; trans. R. F. C. Hull. Bollingen Series XX. Vol. 9, Part 1, *The Archetypes and the Collective Unconscious*, © 1959, 1969 by Bollingen Foundation.

Abbreviations

BLJ	Leslie Marchand, ed. *Byron's Letters and Journals*. Vols. 1–6. London, 1973–1976.
BNYPL	*Bulletin of the New York Public Library*
CLS	*Comparative Literature Studies*
ELH	*Journal of English Literary History*
HLQ	*Huntington Library Quarterly*
JEGP	*Journal of English and Germanic Philology*
KSJ	*Keats–Shelley Journal*
KSMB	*Keats–Shelley Memorial Bulletin*
LBC	John Murray, ed. *Lord Byron's Correspondence*. 2 vols. London, 1922.
LJ	Rowland E. Prothero, ed. *The Works of Lord Byron: Letters and Journals*. 6 vols. London, 1898–1901.
Marchand	*Byron: A Biography*. 3 vols. New York, 1957.
Medwin	E. J. Lovell, ed. *Medwin's "Conversations of Lord Byron."* Princeton, 1966.
MLQ	*Modern Language Quarterly*
N&Q	*Notes and Queries*
PMLA	*Publications of the Modern Language Association of America.*
Poetry	E. H. Coleridge, ed. *The Works of Lord Byron: Poetry.* 7 vols. London, 1898–1904.
RES	*Review of English Studies*

SAQ	*South Atlantic Quarterly*
SEL	*Studies in English Literature, 1500–1900*
SiR	*Studies in Romanticism*
SP	*Studies in Philology*
Standard Edition	James Strachey, ed. *The Standard Edition of the Complete Psychological Works of Sigmund Freud.* 24 vols. London, 1957.
TLS	[London] *Times Literary Supplement*
UTQ	*University of Toronto Quarterly*
YFS	*Yale French Studies*
YR	*Yale Review*

Introduction

I by no means rank poetry or poets high in the scale of intellect—this may look like Affectation—but it is my real opinion—it is the lava of the imagination whose eruption prevents an earth-quake—they say Poets never or rarely go *mad*—Cowper & Collins are instances to the contrary—(but Cowper was no poet)—it is however to be remarked that they rarely do—but are generally so near it—that I cannot help thinking rhyme is so far useful in anticipating & preventing the disorder.

Writing to his half sister Augusta in 1805 of his relief in having exchanged "the Trammels or rather *Fetters*" of the "domestic Tyrant" his mother for the freedom of Trinity College, Cambridge, Byron commented: "I am allowed 500 a year, a Servant and Horse, so Feel as independent as a German Prince who coins his own Cash, or a Cherokee Chief who coins no Cash at all, but enjoys what is more precious, Liberty. I talk in raptures of that *Goddess* because my amiable Mama was so despotic."[1] In one respect this early, seemingly casual letter poses the central question that any psychoanalytically-influenced study of Byron must face. So pat a confession of the source of cherished public values in the child's relationship to his mother sets a trap for mechanical interpretation: one almost suspects that, with many others similarly obvious, it has been planted in Byron's letters and journals by a Freudian tempter. "All convulsions end with me in rhyme," Byron wrote Thomas Moore in 1813, "and to solace my midnights, I have scribbled another Turkish story" (*BLJ* 3: 184). And the same week he noted in his journal: "To withdraw *myself* from *myself* (oh that cursed selfishness!) has ever been my sole, my entire, my sincere motive in scribbling at all; and publishing is also the continuance of the same object, by the action it affords to the mind, which else recoils upon itself" (*BLJ* 3: 225). These passages imply close ties between poet and poem and suggest that writing is a protective distraction. The protagonists of Byron's earlier works find no similar resource against the mind's lethal tendency to turn upon itself: they confront their anxieties with stern gestures of denial and repression, and the consequences of their refusals are epitomized in Byron's image of the scorpion stinging itself to death.

Byron's statements, however, should not be interpreted so simply. To reduce to the aftereffects of a complex the very real services he later rendered by word and deed to the cause of liberty would be both meanspirited and obtuse: the political beliefs and actions must be seen in their social context. Furthermore, the letters are not unmediated expressions. As he writes about his predicament, Byron already transforms it: hyperbole and irony, literary exuberance, contribute their own energies to his plaint. We misunderstand him—and lose the wit of the letters as well as of the poems—if we fail to take into account the pleasure he found in dramatically setting forth his misery. Finally, Byron's immediate, overwhelming, and lasting success, not only in England but also on the Continent, is the best evidence that his works transcend the personal situation of their author.

Surely it is part of the appeal of Byron and of artists like him that the boundaries between unconscious impulse and deliberate choice, between neurotic re-enactment and liberating mastery, remain tantalizingly fluid. Most of Byron's compelling works are fictions of the self, in a manner sometimes more oblique, sometimes more direct. There is an increase in self-consciousness and esthetic distance between his early, avowedly cathartic Oriental tales and the final cantos of *Don Juan*, but the curve is never as smooth as the purist might wish. At the end of his career the old topics still exert their fascination on Byron (though their grip relaxes), and from the outset he shows an interest in experimenting with structure and in manipulating the responses of his readers that asks for rhetorical, and not only psychoanalytic, criticism. When private, specific meanings pale in comparison to the active interplay of author and reader it is the resonance rather than the genesis of an image which captures us. Yet if it is foolish to limit Byron's art to its genesis, it is equally mistaken to exclude what is known of Byron's first years from attempts to understand the poetry.

The marriage made in 1785 between the cavalier Captain John

Byron and the rather naive Scots heiress, Catherine Gordon, began to show strains well before Byron's birth. The Captain quickly consumed his wife's fortune, and by 1787, after previous moves to escape the bailiff, he decamped to France, leaving his pregnant and by then financially-pressed spouse to arrange her own accouchement. By the time his son was born in London on January 22, 1788 he had returned to England, but the need to evade creditors kept him hiding in the country. Byron thus began his life in a world of frequent and disrupting relocations, of squabbles, and of separations between his parents, who before his second birthday were living at opposite ends of Queen Street, Aberdeen. There Byron's only overnight stay with his father ended the next morning when the Captain declared that "he had had quite enough of his visitor," and told the nurse that she might take him home again. Already at this age Byron was displaying a "violent" and "sullenly passionate" temper and an "uncontrollable spirit." In 1790 Captain Byron left for good, nevermore to see wife or child.[2]

It is probable that from Mrs. Byron's deep though erratically manifested attachment to her only son grew the sense of worth that made Byron's creativity possible. At the same time, the characteristic fragmentation and multiplication of the self in Byron's work and its skeptical challenge to the knowability and reliability of phenomena are suggestive of the problems specific to the phase of development that D. W. Winnicott has called the "holding environment": that first stage in which the infant is wholly dependent on the mother whose "good-enough mothering" is the indispensable requisite to his trust in the stability of the self and world. Equally prominent in the plots of Byron's poems are the conflicts of autonomy versus dependence upon a nurturing female presence that are the natural problems of this period.[3]

I propose these parallels not because I wish to undertake the chimerical project of reconstructing Byron's past, but because they provide a perspective from which the poems themselves may be illuminated. Let me turn to a moment in the poetry. Readers of *Don Juan* have always found the description of the foundering of the *Trinidada* in the second canto a harrowing experience. Much of the unsettling power of the sequence arises from the spare, realistic manner of the narrative, the details of which Byron readily acknowledged to have taken from various accounts of actual maritime misfortunes, chiefly those collected and published by Sir J. G. Dalyell in 1812 under the title *Shipwrecks and Disasters at Sea*. Byron's habitual respect for factual accuracy kept him close to the sources when creating his

fiction, and many of his stanzas are scarcely more than versified quotations. Under such circumstances one would not expect to find much
that is personally distinctive; yet one aspect of Byron's choice of materials is in the highest degree representative of the major concerns of
his poetry.

Some time after he had finished the first draft of the second canto
he inserted among the leaves of the manuscript a fragment of a letter
upon which he had written a further four stanzas across the back and
in the blank spaces. Byron's afterthoughts are often rich clues to the
preoccupations that underlay his accretive mode of composition—
they include the verses on the death of Princess Charlotte in the last
canto of *Childe Harold,* the conclusion of Eve's curse in *Cain,* and
Julia's letter in the first canto of *Don Juan*—but none is so telling as this
apparently haphazard addition:

> There were two fathers in this ghastly crew,
> And with them their two sons, of whom the one
> Was more robust and hardy to the view,
> But he died early; and when he was gone,
> His nearest messmate told his sire, who threw
> One glance at him, and said, "Heaven's will be done!
> I can do nothing," and he saw him thrown
> Into the deep without a tear or groan.

> The other father had a weaklier child,
> Of a soft cheek, and aspect delicate;
> But the boy bore up long, and with a mild
> And patient spirit held aloof his fate;
> Little he said, and now and then he smiled,
> As if to win a part from off the weight
> He saw increasing on his father's heart,
> With the deep deadly thought, that they must part.

> And o'er him bent his sire, and never raised
> His eyes from off his face, but wiped the foam
> From his pale lips, and ever on him gazed,
> And when the wished-for shower at length was come,
> And the boy's eyes, which the dull film half glazed,
> Brightened, and for a moment seemed to roam,
> He squeezed from out a rag some drops of rain
> Into his dying child's mouth—but in vain.

> The boy expired—the father held the clay,
> And looked upon it long, and when at last

> Death left no doubt, and the dead burthen lay
> Stiff on his heart, and pulse and hope were past,
> He watched it wistfully, until away
> 'T was borne by the rude wave wherein 't was cast;
> Then he himself sunk down all dumb and shivering,
> And gave no sign of life, save his limbs quivering.
>
> (II, 87–90)[4]

The symmetry of this scene produces an uncanny force: the duplication of father and son gives it the aura of a paradigm pointing
beyond the particular situation toward universal experience. The
changes Byron made in his version of the anecdote suggest the
paradigm's source of power. Here is the original "Shipwreck of the
Juno, 1795":

> Mr. Wade's boy, a stout healthy lad, died early, and almost without a
> groan; while another, of the same age, but of a less promising appear-
> ance, held out much longer.... Their fathers were both in the fore-top,
> when the boys were taken ill. [Wade], hearing of his son's illness, an-
> swered, with indifference, "that he could do nothing for him," and left
> him to his fate.

The cruel lack of compassion Wade shows for his son Byron somewhat mitigates by introducing a religious acceptance of the dis-
pensations of providence. The alteration probably represents his inef-
fectual attempt to deny the element that had initially aroused his
attention: paternal hostility. The two texts form, in fact, a sort of
composite in which the original corresponds to unconscious motivation and Byron's revision to the conscious rationalizations that seek to
gloss over unacceptable desires; as such, they reveal the situation that
recurs again and again in Byron's works: a son confronted by the
enmity of his father (or father figure), which is masked as stoicism or
determinism.

Consideration of the relationship between the two pairs of fathers
and sons will expand the dimensions of the episode. The indifferent
father is linked with a "robust" and "hardy" son, but the boy's seeming strength is no defense against his harsh plight and he is the first to
succumb. The second son, "weaklier" and "delicate," surprisingly
proves the more enduring. In ascribing to this son an anxious wish
(not in the chronicle) to ease his father's grief by patiently bearing his
suffering, Byron emphasizes his filial devotion. The father is recipro-
cally dedicated to his child, but his efforts are unavailing and the boy

perishes. What is common to both these pairs is the death of the son: both fathers are also reduced to a moribund condition, but they do survive their crushed offspring. The vignette presents a single configuration in several variations: whatever the modulations in the outline (a son whose apparent fortitude is illusory, another whose appearance of fragility is deceptive, an unfeeling parent, and a loving one) the unchanging element is the death of the son in the face of the father.

Here then are two parental images as they typically occur in Byron's work. Associated with the figure of the mother are what psychoanalysis accurately if inelegantly calls two-body conflicts: dependence, separation, autonomy. The figure of the father usually belongs to the later developmental stage of the three-body conflicts subsumed under the name of the oedipus complex, and with Byron the first tensions of mother and son shade regularly into the triangular situation of hero, important woman, and dominating older man. The study that follows takes as its point of departure the endeavor to trace this constant feature of Byron's plots through its many metamorphoses, figurative as well as literal. Oedipal content of this nature resides close to the surface in Byron's work but it does not lose in significance thereby; on the contrary, careful attention to it can bring into relationship aspects of the poetry which initially seem unconnected. Even a political satire like *The Vision of Judgment* is connected by genial inversion to the threatening father who darkens Byron's poetic universe: its gentlemanly good humor rests upon the tolerance of the Almighty which permits George III to slip into heaven.

In their final place in *Don Juan* the stanzas describing the fathers and dying sons are succeeded by the depiction of a rainbow:

> Now overhead a rainbow, bursting through
> The scattering clouds, shone, spanning the dark sea,
> Resting its bright base on the quivering blue;
> And all within its arch appeared to be
> Clearer than that without, and its wide hue
> Waxed broad and waving, like a banner free,
> Then changed to a bow that's bent, and then
> Forsook the dim eyes of these shipwrecked men.
>
> (91)

Byron deprives the rainbow of its traditional meaning as a symbol of reconciliation: its appearance presages no relief for the doomed mariners. Those who in reading the sequence would lay most stress on this stanza might find Byron a cheap cynic, or, more sympathetically, a cosmic ironist. An image of Byron as the visionary poet of an irremediably fallen world can be forcefully supported by such passages.[5] The yearnings for a vanished happiness which haunted him, however, spring from the psychological materials revealed by the letter to Augusta and the episode of the dying sons. As contemporary critics were quick to charge, Byron is an extraordinarily repetitive poet, and it was his own situation—disguised, displaced, and freely heightened—that he drew upon in his writings. Byron's self-dramatizing imagination is the basis of his art, and that imagination worked on—and against—a single narrative pattern throughout his career.[6] The relationship between poet and poem nonetheless varies from the most seemingly objective to the most apparently direct, and the bridges from private to public, personal to general, are built in many different ways.

Don Juan is at once Byron's most obsessive poem and his most free. In it he learned to reveal, and to revise, himself: to return to his origins and to transform them. The endless monologue no longer denies or represses: it exemplifies and encourages self-expression. In *Don Juan* Byron found the form in which he could master the difficult skill of truly listening to himself, of letting himself talk.[7] The elaborately displaced fictions of the tales and dramas are superseded by a far slyer art, which witnesses both the unchanging core of the self and, through the multiple roles Byron assumes, the struggle of desire to dissolve and reform it.

Byron habitually saw history as he saw his own life, and precisely because his expression in *Don Juan* is unrestricted he goes beyond mere self-expression to illuminate the cultural situation in which he is placed, remaking and exploiting tradition as he remakes and exploits the self. In *Don Juan* Byron opposes the burdens of the past with the resources of drama, and combats his isolation by inviting the reader into his theater.

PART I: Titans and Exiles

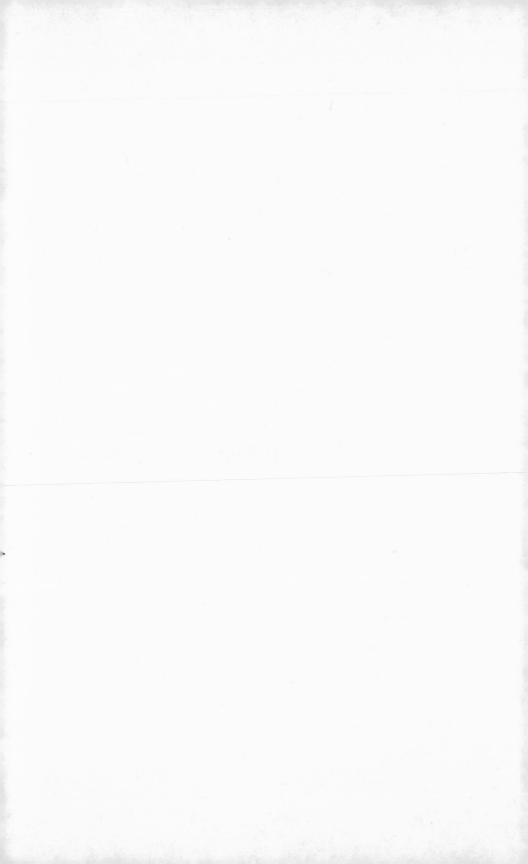

1

Perspectives on the Hero

The publication of *Childe Harold's Pilgrimage* in 1812 brought fame to Byron, but even the succeeding century and a half has not brought agreement on the nature of the poem. The diversity of opinion accurately mirrors the loose construction of a work which Byron candidly admitted made "no pretensions to regularity." But if the first two cantos serve various and often contradictory artistic purposes, they nicely adumbrate several of the major themes and modes of his poetic career. Certain situations recur again and again in *Childe Harold* and the tales: eventually Byron made artistic capital out of what at first would seem to be only a limitation.

"I by no means intend to identify myself with *Harold*," Byron wrote to R. C. Dallas before the appearance of his poem, "but to *deny* all connexion with him. If in parts I may be thought to have drawn from myself, believe me it is but in parts, and I shall not own even to that. . . . I would not be such a fellow as I have made my hero for all the world" (*BLJ* 2: 122). This famous letter testifies to Byron's unwillingness publicly to acknowledge his relationship to Harold, but tacitly concedes the self-expressive ends Harold fulfilled. A manuscript reading preserved by E. H. Coleridge records that at one stage Harold was revealingly named "Childe Burun," and even without this detail the closeness of author and character is evident. The nature of Byron's self-dramatization can be perceived by calling upon the circumstances of his life, as he always teased his readers to do.[1]

As the last sentence quoted from the letter to Dallas suggests, the need to repudiate Harold springs directly from the transparency with which Byron had employed him to set forth troubling aspects of his own personality. Byron could at once indulge and maintain his distance from disturbing parts of himself by splitting them off into ostensibly independent actors. Initially then (and only initially) the divided self-presentation that is a fundamental instinct of Byron's imagination must be apprehended as a strategy of control. The lofty attitude Byron as narrator strains to achieve and his condescension to Harold are reflexes of the unease Harold discloses. Even though Byron's literary techniques are not yet skilled enough to communicate any very convincing sense of Harold, the emotions which he represents are not factitious: the very heavy-handedness with which Byron executes the conventionally Spenserian style that is the chief distancing device obliquely reinforces the reader's sense of the urgency to him of separation from Harold.

What perspectives does Harold offer? This is the picture Byron gives of the mood in which he departed from England:

> And now Childe Harold was sore sick at heart,
> And from his fellow Bacchanals would flee;
> 'Tis said, at times the sullen tear would start,
> But Pride congealed the drop within his ee:
> Apart he stalked in joyless reverie,
> And from his native land resolved to go,
> And visit scorching climes beyond the sea;
> With pleasure drugged, he almost longed for woe,
> And e'en for change of scene would seek the shades below.
>
> (6)

The journey is no pilgrimage to a shrine but a flight from a painful state of mind, and the language betrays its futility. The "scorching climes" and "shades below" to which Harold turns for distraction seem also welcomed as punishments, as if his depression were the manifestation of a guilt that can only be suffered, not removed. In a self-perpetuating process the pride Harold invokes to combat his unhappiness increases his isolation: "Then loathed he in his native land to dwell," says a previous stanza, "Which seemed to him more lone than Eremite's sad cell" (4).

A source for the guilt underlying these lines is found in the opening of the poem. Much is made of Harold's jaded debauchery, his familiarity with "Sin's long labyrinth" (5), his exhausted "Satiety" (4). Yet the fanfare of Harold's precocious decadence sounds less plangently than the note of an unsatisfied craving for affection which his haughty posture tries to hide. Stanza 9, according to E. H. Coleridge the result of great elaboration, cries "And none did love him!" and then reiterates: "Yea! none did love him." Only the mask of Harold permitted Byron so radical a confession.

The portrait of himself as a sensitive youth determined to repress his disappointment, desperately embracing travel rather than letting it be seen, acquires further particulars in the next stanza:

> Childe Harold had a mother—not forgot,
> Though parting from that mother he did shun;
> A sister whom he loved, but saw her not
> Before his weary pilgrimage begun:
> If friends he had, he bade adieu to none.
> Yet deem not thence his breast a breast of steel:
> Ye, who have known what 'tis to dote upon
> A few dear objects, will in sadness feel
> Such partings break the heart they fondly hope to heal.
> (10)

These lines may be stilted, but they reflect the primary image of Byron's consciousness. His father, whose absences had already made him an awesome, intermittent shadow to his son, died not long after quitting his family, when Byron was three and a half. Byron was raised alone by his mother in straitened circumstances in Scotland, the object, as her only and male child, of her powerful and ambivalent feelings for her husband. Her temperamental nature, aggravated by memory of the wounds his father had given her, clashed incessantly with the desire for independence Byron naturally displayed as he grew into adolescence. He sought the feminine supportiveness he missed at home in his half sister Augusta, the fruit of his father's scandalous elopement and subsequent first marriage with Lady Carmathen. The close conjunction in his imagination of mother and sis-

ter, evident in the stanza just cited, was repeated with stronger marks
of the emotional weight invested in Augusta in a cancelled verse of
"Childe Harold's Good Night":

> My mother is a high-born dame,
> And much misliketh me;
> She saith my riot bringeth shame
> On all my ancestry.
> I had a sister once I ween,
> Whose tears perhaps will flow;
> But her fair face I have not seen
> For three long years and moe.

Byron and Augusta were separated from infancy while she lived with
various relatives in England. There is more than a little poignancy in
the way he pours out his heart in his early letters to this sister whom
he scarcely knew and hastens to assure of his eternal constancy: emotions blocked elsewhere were channeled into their occasional meetings and regular correspondence.

Throughout his formative teenage years Byron filled his epistles
to Augusta with elaborate, ironic accounts of the tirades of his "amiable" mother and of his resentment of "maternal bondage," as he felt
it, a resentment heightened after he experienced the comparative
liberty of Harrow in 1801. "For my own part I can send nothing to
amuse you," he wrote his sister from Southwell in August 1805,
"excepting, a repetition of my complaints against my tormentor
whose *diabolical* disposition (pardon me for staining my paper with so
harsh a word) seems to increase with age, and to acquire new force
with Time. The more I see of her the more my dislike augments...."
(*BLJ* 1: 75). One extended description, and it is only one of many,
concludes rhetorically:

> Such, Augusta, such is my mother; *my mother!* I disclaim her from this
> time, and although I cannot help treating her with respect, I cannot
> reverence, as I ought to do, that parent who by her outrageous conduct
> forfeits all title to filial affection. To you, Augusta, I must look up, as my
> nearest relation, to you I must confide what I cannot mention to others,
> and I am sure you will pity me....
>
> (*BLJ* 1: 66)

An outburst of Mrs. Byron's against Augusta led Byron to an explicit
declaration of his switched loyalties: "this has given the finishing

stroke to *filial*, which now gives way to *fraternal* duty. Believe me,
dearest Augusta, not ten thousand *such* mothers, or indeed any
mothers, Could induce me to give you up" (*BLJ* 1: 68).

Byron's loud proclamations of emancipation from his mother are
the other side of his highly-charged involvement with her. The frustrated wish for a stable, harmonious family life exacerbating his rage
emerges in the sketches of Harold's servants and companions in
"Childe Harold's Good Night." "Yet marvel not, Sir Childe, that
I/Am sorrowful in mind," the page tells Harold:

> For I have from my father gone,
> A mother whom I love. . . .
>
> My father blessed me fervently,
> Yet did not much complain;
> But sorely will my mother sigh
> Till I come back again. . . .

The parental solicitude of the "staunch yeoman" also points up by
contrast the deficiencies of Harold's situation:

> My spouse and boys dwell near thy hall,
> Along the bordering Lake,
> And when they on their father call,
> What answer shall she make? . . .

Harold dismisses the "unmanly moaning" (12) of his fellow travelers,
but the "lighter mood" to which he pretends is a frail shell. Another
deleted verse of "Childe Harold's Good Night" expresses a
profounder emotion:

> Methinks it would my bosom glad,
> To change my proud estate,
> And be again a laughing lad
> With one beloved playmate.

This regressive impulse often surfaces in the poem, as in the second
canto: "Ah! happy years! once more who would not be a boy!" (II,
23). Byron's nostalgia, otherwise surprising in a twenty-one-year-old
aristocrat enjoying the adventures of his expedition, derives its intensity from its idealizing quality. Lines like these look back not to any

real happiness, now lost, but to a harmony that Byron had never known and therefore regretted the more passionately: in all his work imaginative desire fills out the already potent force of memory.

There is no way to prove that the original of the "one beloved playmate" invoked by "Childe Harold's Good Night" is the type of the perfectly benevolent mother, or that the scene itself develops from the child's wish for an unruffled union with her, although its tonality at least suggests the presence of such components. In considering the roots of Byron's self-dramatization, however, the importance of the distance he felt between the actual "Mrs. Byron furiosa" (*BLJ* 1: 94) and these idyllic yearnings can scarcely be overestimated. Whether any woman placed as Mrs. Byron was could have satisfied the demands of her lame and moody son, and whether Byron's picture of his mother is objectively accurate (it is supported by those acquainted with her), are questions that may claim sympathetic interest but do not affect the main concern, which is only with her influential, ambivalent role in the formation of his psychic universe. Her decisive position is clarified by Byron's citation of Zeluco as a model for Harold: the hero of Moore's novel blames the excesses of his character upon the doting attentions of his widowed mother and by his melodramatic career hastens her death.

Associations with the central figure of the mother color many of the materials of the first two cantos of *Childe Harold*. For all Harold's purported erotic knowledgeability, the subject of sexuality, and especially female sexuality, arouses an uneasy fascination. The demeanor of Spanish women provokes in the callow Englishman a tinnily puritanical denunciation of "young-eyed Lewdness" (I, 46) and the "voluptuous ways" of Vice (I, 65). The attitudes revealed by the poem significantly complement what is learned of Byron's behavior from other sources, which are perhaps more detailed but are less intimate because less disguised. At Malta in 1809, for example, Byron became violently infatuated with the celebrated Mrs. Constance Spencer Smith, challenging a young officer to a duel over her reputation and even arranging a tryst for the following year. His letters describe the brief but intense course of "this most ambrosial amour," but the oblique account of it which appears in his poem is decidedly cool, emphasizing Harold's aloofness to the charms of "fair Florence."[2] The stanzas treat sexual attraction as if to acknowledge it were to be contaminated, and the incident is made the occasion of cynical generalizations about women and love:

Not much he kens, I ween, of Woman's breast,
Who thinks that wanton thing is won by sighs;
What careth she for hearts when once possessed?
Do proper homage to thine Idol's eyes;
But not too humbly, or she will despise
Thee and thy suit, though told in moving tropes:
Disguise ev'n tenderness, if thou art wise;
Brisk Confidence still best with woman copes:
Pique her and soothe in turn—soon Passion crowns thy hopes.

'Tis an old lesson—Time approves it true,
And those who know it best, deplore it most;
When all is won that all desire to woo,
The paltry prize is hardly worth the cost:
Youth wasted—Minds degraded—Honour lost—
These are thy fruits, successful Passion, these!
If, kindly cruel, early Hope is crost,
Still to the last it rankles, a disease,
Not to be cured when Love itself forgets to please.
(II, 34–35)

The fear of women and hostility toward them evinced by these lines, the conviction that by accepting her physical nature a woman forfeits her integrity, is one half the view of women in *Childe Harold*. The obverse is well represented by the sentimental comments on the cloistered lives of Albanian wives:

. . . apart,
And scarce permitted, guarded, veiled, to move,
She yields to one her person and her heart,
Tamed to her cage, nor feels a wish to rove:
For, not unhappy in her Master's love,
And joyful in a mother's gentlest cares,
Blest cares! all other feelings far above!
Herself more sweetly rears the babe she bears
Who never quits the breast—no meaner passion shares.
(II, 61)

The clue to the exaggerated contrast in this picture of woman as either debased harlot or saintly mother lies in the resurgence of the regressive impulse here apparent. In a major paper of 1910 extending his investigations of infantile sexuality Freud located the springs of this

rigid dichotomy in the resentment of the male child over his realization that his mother has granted the privilege of sexual intercourse to
his father instead of to him.[3] Basing his argument on the very contradiction that would seem to preclude his conclusion, Freud demonstrates that the two opposing views of women actually form part of a
single developmental history beginning in a fixation of the infantile
feelings of tenderness for the mother. The practices of Byron's Scots
nurse usually looked to as the inception of Byron's sexual attitudes
were rather the confirmation of the tendencies inherent in this primary relationship.

Certainly there are few ideas so ancient, tenaciously ingrained,
and widely spread in our culture as this quasi-magical image of woman, yet there are valid reasons for dwelling on its personal stamp in
Byron. The childhood circumstances already outlined strongly favor
the predisposition, and cultural diffusion alone cannot explain the
recurrence and force in Byron's works of this double portrait and its
corollary, the man painfully ridden by a remorse-laden adult sexuality, and a wish for return to a pure, pre-sexual innocence. Patterns of
conduct according with Freud's hypothesis run throughout Byron's
life: the disjunction, or perhaps one should say, conjunction, between
his only half-joking repugnance at seeing a woman eat any food more
substantial than lobster salad and champagne and his delighted
classification of mistresses like Marianna Segati and Margarita Cogni
as "splendid animals" is virtually a textbook illustration of ambivalence toward female physicality. This prevailing cast in Byron's
makeup exhibits structural ramifications in his subsequent poetry.

Release of the full potential of this material waited upon events
that did not occur until Byron had largely completed the first two
cantos of *Childe Harold*. At this stage its treatment is often flat, as in
the stanza just quoted, or cursory, as in Byron's equanimous presentation of the Spanish women who abandon their conventional
feminine role to join in battle against the French invaders. The brave
heroine of Saragoza is described as "all unsexed" (I, 54), but the
possibly threatening implications of the transformation are ignored,
or reconciled without strain:

> Yet are Spain's maids no race of Amazons,
> But formed for all the witching arts of love:
> Though thus in arms they emulate her sons,
> And in the horrid phalanx dare to move,

'Tis but the tender fierceness of the dove,
Pecking the hand that hovers o'er her mate:...

(I, 57)

A similar toning-down is produced by the numerous erasures in the revelatory lyric, "Childe Harold's Good Night": no doubt they proceeded from several motives, but their effect is to withdraw from view the parts of the self that Byron had begun to explore through Harold.

Fixed from the outset as a "shameless wight" (I, 2) and deprived of the authorial concentration that might have brought him to life, Harold is too stolid to hold the reader's interest. He remains an outsider—"little recked he of all that men regret" (II, 16)—but one whose latent grandeur in that role is undercut by the mocking opening stanzas. Byron originally planned to play off this sullen caricature of himself against the ironic narrator, but revisions and accretions made on his return to England gradually imparted to the narrator an increasingly Haroldian character.[4]

Byron's progress toward such "coherent self-dramatization" has been regarded as the achievement of *Childe Harold*.[5] Although the blurring of his instinct to divide his self-presentation has its price— the replacement of two consciousnesses by one restricts Byron's rhetorical effects and sacrifices the self-analysis fragmentation might have encouraged—the lessening of the drama of character illuminates the drama of thematic juxtapositions. From these Byron teaches the reader to extract a meaning not wholly enunciated in the poem itself. All four cantos of the poem constitute with increasing sureness of purpose a vast act of cultural memory, a determination to make the past available so that through it men like Harold can escape the limitations of the self. If in the first cantos Byron was unready to exploit the opportunities for inward exploration offered by his original plan, he was more successful in the complementary pursuit of exploring history and his place in it.

Stanzas 34–44 of the first canto illustrate the simplest type of Byron's narrative method. On the surface, stanzas 34–37 invoke Spain's chivalrous past in hopes of revitalizing her degraded present, but two qualifications run throughout the passage. The poem makes the reader fully conscious, as the narrator initially appears not to be, of the "gothic gore" of such legendary glories: it is only distance that lends enchantment, an awareness Byron had already gained at Lisbon. By manipulating time to bring the future into the present of his

narrative, Byron causes the battle of Albuera to appear as the consequence of the narrator's shallow invocation. The "mailed splendour"
of the wars of Christians and Paynims is recreated in stanza 40 by the
"rival scarfs" and "arms that glitter" of the French, English, and
Spanish armies. Aesthetically the effect is fine, but it is beautiful only
to those who can remain safe spectators: "for one who hath no friend,
no brother there." This kind of invocation of the past is thus revealed
as another form of the self-absorption that plagues Harold; it betrays
a lack of human sympathy. To those who are dangerously involved,
the deaths of battle serve only to "fertilise the field that each pretends to gain" (I, 41). But this reductionism is excessive, and the
narrator makes a balanced appraisal in stanza 43, the alliteration rein-
forcing the now-won sense of the inseparability of the two terms:
"Oh, Albuera, glorious field of grief!" Byron again casts his poem into
the future to the time when Albuera will be remembered and "shine
in worthless lays, the theme of transient song," just as in the present
the battles of the Moors and Knights are part of the region's
folksongs: "Teems not each ditty with the glorious tale?" The diction
is curious, but it has an edge: by having overcome his isolation and
participated in the events imaginatively the narrator can comprehend
the ways in which they are both glorious and mean. Through the
narrator the reader too learns to view himself within the full range of
meaning created by the sweep from past to future.

This method is Byron's simplest because the realization is articulated almost fully by the narrator. There are, however, many instances in which the perception of the reader must be built up beyond
the consciousness of the narrator. The narrator, for example, uses the
bullfight scene (I, 68–79) chiefly for the satiric comparison it affords of
the English and Spanish Sundays, in this offering a forecast of *Beppo*
and *Don Juan*. But within the structure of the poem the bullfight
serves also as an epitome of the aesthetically pleasing but vicious
cycle of destruction the canto has illustrated several times. Byron's
poems regularly move toward such summarizing symbols, often
dramatically presented: this, the Albanian campfire of the second
canto, the dying gladiator of the fourth, and so on. The bullfight, an
example of the meaningless cycle, is also coordinate with Harold's
second lyric, "To Inez," a statement of private misery. At the beginning of the canto Harold's gloom seemed comic, but it is made convincing by his subsequent experiences.

The second canto continues these explorations of the past and of narrative techniques. The poem opens with the narrator seated by a desolate temple, musing on the obscurity that has befallen it:

> ... nor ev'n can Fancy's eye
> Restore what Time hath laboured to deface.
> Yet these proud Pillars claim no passing sigh;
> Unmoved the Moslem sits, the light Greek carols by.
>
> (II, 10)

The abstract force of years that has overwhelmed the meaning of the temple is personified in Lord Elgin, who boasts "To rive what Goth, and Turk, and Time hath spared" (II, 12). Elgin is the paradigm of modern man—rootless, unaware of tradition, and hence destructive of it.[6] Like Harold—"little recked he of all that men regret"—he is trapped in his ignorance, which the poem exposes as the cause of selfishness and spiritual impoverishment.

A lament like the narrator's "All, all forgotten" (II, 53) is less an absolute statement than a challenge for the poet to meet by reasserting historical continuity. It is only to men like Harold and Elgin that the past is unknown or irrelevant. The elegy for Greece with which the second canto concludes belies its overt statement:

> The Sun, the soil—but not the slave, the same;—
> Unchanged in all except its foreign Lord,
> Preserves alike its bounds and boundless fame
> The Battle-field, where Persia's victim horde
> First bowed beneath the brunt of Hellas' sword,
> As on the morn to distant Glory dear,
> When Marathon became a magic word,
> Which uttered, to the hearer's eye appear
> The camp, the host, the fight, the conqueror's career,
>
> The flying Mede, his shaftless broken bow;
> The fiery Greek, his red pursuing spear;
> Mountains above—Earth's, Ocean's plain below—
> Death in the front, Destruction in the rear!
> Such was the scene—what now remaineth here?
> What sacred Trophy marks the hallowed ground,
> Recording Freedom's smile and Asia's tear?
> The rifled urn, the violated mound,
> The dust thy courser's hoof, rude stranger! spurns around.
>
> (II, 89–90)

The stanzas are an astonishing tour de force. The narrator asserts the fact of loss, but the vivid present tense shows that the glory of the past is sustained within the sympathetic poet and the receptive audience, who can read meanings into the landscape so that "all the Muse's tales seem truly told" (II, 88). "The rifled urn" and "the violated mound" are the acts of an Elgin, with whom the poem began, but will not be those of a reader of the poem, whom Byron has taught "a lesson of the young" (II, 91). "He that is lonely, hither let him roam," the narrator declares, and Greece is therapeutic because by teaching those capable of understanding to apprehend themselves as part of an ongoing history and culture it reveals the proper dimensions of personal woe. In the stanzas Byron added after the original ending at 92 the poem implicitly distinguishes between two forms of past-centered consciousness. "How selfish Sorrow ponders on the past," exclaims the narrator in stanza 96, and it is this sort of merely personal self-absorption that afflicts Harold and generates his solipsism. To this mind the past is dead, and he is its victim; the public past of history he either tramples in ignorance, like Elgin, or nostalgically glorifies in shallow paeans to vanished, illusory grandeur, like the narrator's invocation of Spanish chivalry. But the poem demonstrates that a return to the past can also provide the enlargement necessary to inspire future action. Note stanza 82:

> But, midst the throng in merry masquerade,
> Lurk there no hearts that throb with secret pain,
> Even through the closest searment half betrayed?
> To such the gentle murmurs of the main
> Seem to re-echo all they mourn in vain;
> To such the gladness of the gamesome crowd
> Is source of wayward thought and stern disdain:
> How do they loathe the laughter idly loud,
> And long to change the robe of revel for the shroud!

This despairing figure might appear to be Harold or his kind, but it is instead "the true-born son of Greece," whose consciousness of his country's shame is the prelude to its regeneration.

These examples suggest that for all its declamatory, ostensibly direct rhetoric, even the early *Childe Harold* should be read with an eye to an overall dialectic pattern. The context of the entire poem recasts the sense of particular lines; meaning emerges from consideration of the shifts and ironic juxtapositions of the total structure, and not alone from overt statement. And yet it must be confessed that the Greek patriot is an index not only of the failure of Harold, who understands neither his sketchily presented personal past nor the signs of history around him, but also of the central division in the poem. The attempt to bring together the private and public realms visible here in embryo becomes a major concern of the cantos of *Childe Harold* Byron wrote after his exile from England, but it is not until *Don Juan* that he fully succeeds in making them converge. In his later poems history is psychological biography writ large: the recovery of the past of the culture corresponds with and complements Byron's investigation of his own past in the search for self-knowledge.

Byron's skill in these early cantos is chiefly to be seen in the adroit manipulation of large narrative units, but already there are moments when his meaning is contained within an apparently offhand comparison. The best example occurs in the description of "Fair Florence" (II, 30). Initially she is handsomely complimented as "a new Calypso," but Harold's refusal to join her "lovers' whining crew" hints that the lady is really a Circe. Here the language of the poem embodies its effort to recover the past, for the allusion conveys the dangerous charm of Mrs. Spencer Smith as no realistic description could do. The double image of woman it expresses is a rudimentary foreshadowing of the way in which Byron was to fuse his psychic imperatives with literary tradition.

The single most important event of Byron's life thus far occurred when he had been back in England less than three weeks after a two-year absence: the sudden death of his mother on August 1, 1811. "I heard *one* day of her illness, the *next* of her death," he wrote a friend, borrowing another's words in trying to express the shock he was only beginning to weigh in full: "I now feel the truth of Mr. Gray's observation, 'That we can only have *one* mother' " (*BLJ* 2: 67). The loss of the person who had been the fulcrum of his existence throughout his childhood and from whose temperamental regard he had derived his precarious sense of self-esteem would have been overwhelming at any time, but Byron's own unsettled situation increased its severity. He had just learned that John Wingfield, a Harrow schoolmate whom he once referred to as the "best and dearest of my friends," had perished of fever with the army in Portugal.[7] The memorial stanzas inserted in the first canto of *Childe Harold* witness Byron's sorrow, and before his mother was buried a further disorienting blow struck: Charles Skinner Matthews, the most promising of Byron's Cambridge circle, drowned while swimming alone in the Cam. Under this renewed adversity Byron's letters grow despairing:

> My dearest Davies,—Some curse hangs over me and mine. My mother lies a corpse in this house; one of my best friends is drowned in a ditch. What can I say, or think, or do? I received a letter from him the day before yesterday. My dear Scrope, if you can spare a moment, do come down to me, I want a friend. . . .
>
> (BLJ 2: 68)

The bereavements continued. In October Byron heard of the death of John Edleston, the Cambridge chorister who had aroused the strong attachment obliquely recorded in the "Thyrza" poems, and he confessed to Hobhouse that he was "more affected than I should care to own elsewhere" (BLJ 2: 114).[8] The year 1811 also brought the death of Hargreaves Hanson, another Harrow friend and the son of the family's general business agent.

This terrible series deepened still more Byron's agonized reaction to the loss of his mother. "There is to me something so incomprehensible in death," he wrote Hobhouse, "that I can neither speak nor think on the subject.—Indeed when I looked on the Mass of Corruption, which was the being from whence I sprang, I doubted within myself whether I *was*, or She *was not*" (BLJ 2: 69). The specter of total psychic annihilation evident in this passage is not hyperbolic: the circumstances of his upbringing had made Byron's sense of his identity unusually dependent on his mother. Mrs. Byron's maid recalled Byron's exclamation of dismay as he sat by her body: "Oh, Mrs. By, I had but one friend in the world, and she is gone!" The outburst seems entirely natural, but the mores to which Byron felt he had to conform are almost too patly expressed in the reply of the servant, who "represented to him the weakness of thus giving way to grief." Accounts of Byron's behavior at the funeral reveal a significant and characteristic pattern: his struggle to repress any outward sign of the emotions that gripped him suggests that he too construed them as "weakness" unbefitting his ideal of manliness.[9] The feelings that were thus denied immediate release were transformed into the compelling motivation of his major poetry.

"If I am a poet," Byron said to Trelawny years later, ". . . the air of Greece made me one."[10] Yet if any one influence deserves recognition as paramount in what was surely an overdetermined conclusion, it is the traumatic death of Mrs. Byron at this juncture in her son's life.[11] The psychological conflicts the loss of his mother reawakened and his mode of response to them meet the readers of his poetry long before they reach the fictionalized portrait of his childhood in *Don Juan*. It was while writing the tales which made him the bestselling poet of his generation that Byron characterized poetry as the cathartic "lava of the imagination"; in them the young writer tests his strategies, confronting his own most painful anxieties with artfully developed fictions.

The Giaour, the first of the tales, manages its innovations least successfully. The story of Leila's discovered intrigue with the Giaour, her murder by Hassan, and the Giaour's avenging murder and remorse, is simple, but Byron presents it in apparently unconnected dramatic scenes that involve the reader by forcing him to supply the links. The use of multiple narrators, whose limited perspectives must be amplified and interpreted, increases the reader's participation, and the additions made in successive editions of the poem emphasize Byron's interest in thus manipulating audience response.[12] But the analysis that a divided presentation makes possible succumbs (as, more happily, does *Childe Harold*) to the temptation of a compelling voice which expresses—but here does not penetrate—the complex of impulses that Byron would seek to explore throughout his career. The collapse of the structure into the Giaour's blindly self-justifying monologue diminishes the perspectives available to the reader, and the obscurity of the narrative is too great to justify. The climactic position of the final monologue reinforces the tendency to focus upon the psychology of the protagonist.

The dramatic present tense employed in much of the tale obscures the movement of *The Giaour* towards this retrospect, but its structural relationship to other Romantic poems should be noted. The Giaour's final speech is an attempt to comprehend a moment in the past that has determined the present; like the "spots of time" that control the values of *The Prelude*, it is an act of memory, partly obsessive and partly surveying. Byron's characters turn to their private pasts as the narrator of *Childe Harold* turns to the public past of history; *The Giaour* opens with an extended lament for the decay of Greek glory now sunk in "self-abasement" that illustrates the parallel between the two searches. The Giaour gains no insight, however, but remains frozen in his guilt for Leila's death. Hassan, not he, was the murderer, but he seems to assume the guilt because had their roles been reversed he too would have killed Leila:

> She died—I dare not tell thee how;
> But look—'tis written on my brow!
> There read of Cain the curse and crime,
> In characters unworn by Time:
> Still, ere thou dost condemn me, pause;
> Not mine the act, though I the cause.
> Yet did he but what I had done
> Had she been false to more than one.
> Faithless to him, he gave the blow;
> But true to me, I laid him low:
> Howe'er deserved her doom might be,
> Her treachery was truth to me; . . .
>
> (1056–1063)

Only forgiveness could reconcile the vicious contradiction heavily accentuated by the jog-trot rhythm of "treachery" and "truth to me," and the Giaour's incapacity to have forgiven Leila appears to entail a self-consuming incapacity to forgive himself for a crime he did not commit. Years of suffering have not brought the enlightenment that would ease his plight: he remains incapable of imagining himself as acting any differently from Hassan.

These hints of a demonic parody of cooperation between the Giaour and Hassan to crush Leila and themselves have earlier been made explicit:

> Ah! fondly youthful hearts can press,
> To seize and share the dear caress:
> But Love itself could never pant
> For all that Beauty sighs to grant
> With half the fervour Hate bestows
> Upon the last embrace of foes,
> When grappling in the fight they fold
> Those arms that ne'er shall lose their hold;

> Friends meet to part; Love laughs at faith;
> True foes, once met, are joined till death!
>
> (645–654)

The Giaour does die with his foe, for his life stops with Hassan's: because he is unable to outgrow the rigidity that caused it he must forever relive the catastrophe. His self-incarceration in a monastery is the emblem of a psychic arrest as total as Hassan's actual death.

The rivals are so paired as virtually to be doubles, and their fraternity is reinforced by the allusion to the myth of Cain and Abel. Leila, ostensibly the focus of the plot, is presented more sketchily than are the twinlike foes who struggle for her, but she is not the only woman in the tale. The engrossing core that drove *The Giaour* through fourteen editions in two years may be approached through the multiplication and duplication to which both the feminine and masculine figures are subject.

One of the most effective moments produced by Byron's abrupt, irregular narrative style is the introduction of Hassan through a description of the ruin of his palace after his death. Included in the scene is a reminiscence of the former "luxurious coolness" of the courtyard fountain:

> And oft had Hassan's Childhood played
> Around the verge of that cascade;
> And oft upon his mother's breast
> The sound had harmonized his rest; . . .
>
> (308–311)

The first glimpse of Hassan surprisingly shows not the ruthless murderer of his faithless beloved but an infant enveloped in liquid maternal happiness. The significance of this detail shortly becomes apparent.

At some point following his vengeance on Leila Hassan goes forth "to woo a bride/ More true than her who left his side" (533–534). It is on this expedition that he is ambushed and killed by the Giaour, who commands a survivor to return to the palace with proof of his triumph. The Tartar is met by Hassan's anxiously expectant mother:

> He drew the token from his vest—
> Angel of Death! 'tis Hassan's cloven crest!
> "Lady, a fearful bride thy Son hath wed:

> Me, not from mercy, did they spare,
> But this empurpled pledge to bear...."
>
> (715–720)[13]

The "fearful bride" is of course Death, but in context the phrase implicates in Hassan's calamity the innocent for whom he is traveling. When taken with the attitudes the men hold toward Leila, whose infidelity is the immediate occasion of their misery, the lines complete a portrait of the alluring but fatal siren. *The Giaour* thus offers an image of woman in the two aspects already noted: the unreliable, sexually promiscuous beauty whose charms destroy, and the nurturing, enduring mother.

A salient feature of Byron's poem is the ambivalence that nonetheless fringes the portrait of the mother. This episode is structurally congruent with one frequent in myth and folklore, in which a malevolent woman demands, and receives, the head of a man who has flouted her authority. If the parallel seems farfetched, it is worth considering the climax of the curse pronounced upon the Giaour for his assassination of Hassan:

> But one that for thy crime must fall,
> The youngest, most beloved of all,
> Shall bless thee with a *father's* name—
> That word shall wrap thy heart in flame!
> Yet must thou end thy task, and mark
> Her cheek's last tinge, her eye's last spark,
> And the last glassy glance must view
> Which freezes o'er its lifeless blue;...
>
> (767–774)

The fitness of this improbable doom (the Giaour seems childless and ends in a monastery) becomes apparent only when it is understood that it exactly inverts the situation at the heart of *The Giaour*: if it is accepted that Hassan and the Giaour are two aspects of a single figure, the father is to be punished in the death of his daughter for the woe he as son caused his mother.

These interpretations rest upon assumptions drawn from the psychoanalytic literature: that situations are often represented by their opposites, that separate characters occurring in proximity may be fragments of a single figure, that in general juxtaposed elements may be regarded as related even in the absence of causal links.[14]

These principles, well established in their own discipline, can lead to a coherent account of Byron's poem. With their aid the essential nature of the central triangle of the plot is manifest: infused into the exotic and violent action of the surface is a displaced and disguised version of the conflicts between father, mother, and son.

Two interwoven but not identical struggles are evident in *The Giaour*. The first focuses on Hassan and his mother, and clustered around it are the images of safe enclosed spaces and fluid, maternally centered well-being characteristic of the oral stage of development. The good mother acquires the overtones of an ogre, however, and Hassan dies as soon as he quits her protection in favor of another, a disaster which reflects the child's fear that if he asserts his independence from the being who nourishes him he will be crushed by the wrath his attempt provokes. The second struggle is less obscured, and oedipal. Byron's depiction of the rivalry of Hassan and the Giaour for Leila is funded by the energy of the son's desire to replace his father in the affections of his mother. The Giaour's emulation of Hassan, his defense of the other's cruelty and his vying with him in hardness, is an afterimage of the son's wish to be like the powerful figure whom he is trying to overcome.

Insofar as the Giaour does briefly wrest Leila from Hassan he gains an equivocal victory in this oedipal contest, and it is the guilt any such success engenders that explains the gloomy conclusion of Byron's poem. The last sight of the Giaour, forever fixed in a hysterical confession and justification of his conduct before an "old man" whom he repeatedly calls "father," taps subterranean currents that cannot be accounted for by the melodramatic scene of half-penitent villain and monk alone. "I began a comedy and burnt it because the scene ran into *reality*," Byron confided to his journal a few months after the publication of *The Giaour*, "—a novel, for the same reason. In rhyme, I can keep more away from facts; but the thought always runs through, through... yes, yes, through" (*BLJ* 3: 209). The particular enervation sensed in *The Giaour*, despite its abundant incident, proceeds from its view of a world in which the heroes die or fail while parental figures persist.

The familial conflicts of Byron's next tale, *The Bride of Abydos*, substantiate these comments. Selim, the effeminate protagonist, is thought the natural son of Giaffir; in Canto II, however, Selim discloses himself as the child of a brother whom Giaffir has killed, and the delayed revelation makes clear that the masculine rivalry epitomized in the feud of brothers is an epiphenomenon of the struggle of son against father. The story opens as Giaffir, who dotes on his daughter Zuleika, orders her to marry an elderly suitor whom she does not know:

> Affection chained her to that heart;
> Ambition tore the links apart.
> . . . .
>
> "Enough that he who comes to woo
> Is kinsman of the Bey Oglou;
> His years need scarce a thought employ;
> I would not have thee wed a boy.
> And thou shall have a noble dower:
> And his and my united power
> Will laugh to scorn the death-firman. . . ."
>
> (191–192; 205–211)

These plans are opposed by Selim and Zuleika, who love each other and whose tenderness contrasts sharply with the harshness of the parent they ostensibly share. Selim asks Zuleika to meet him that evening, telling her ominously "Think not I am what I appear," and in Canto II he presents himself dressed in the garb of a band of fierce marauders whom he improbably claims to lead.

Selim's original effeminate manner is the first of many instances of transvestitism and pseudotransvestitism in Byron's work that questions of sexual power render of great importance: it provides the key to the underlying stresses of *The Bride of Abydos*. Selim, restricted to the harem by Giaffir, has been deprived of any opportunity to prove himself. The ploy is evidently designed to protect Giaffir from the recriminations of his "son" by prolonging his inferior status and denying him manhood. The demeanor imposed on him, however, serves Selim by effectively masking the resentments with which he seethes (109–114): it shields him from the wrath of his "father" as well as shames him.

That the resentments involve a woman and do not spring merely from a desire for revenge is suggested by Selim's frequent secret meetings with Zuleika at night, always associated with the unconscious. The prospect of her marriage clarifies the true basis of the enmity between Selim and Giaffir. Giaffir's decision to dispose of Zuleika to a man his own age, announced with a spiteful reference to mere boys, is a secondarily elaborated version of the father's absolute possession of the mother as it appears to the jealous son. It is this bond that Selim challenges, and the child's belief that life flows from the all-giving mother, though rationalized in the poem as the political power Giaffir hopes to gain, is still visible in Giaffir's expectation that the union will magically bring him immunity from "the death-firman." Zuleika's maternal nature is confirmed in the description of her chamber, the only light in a black landscape. "All that can eye or sense delight/ Are gathered in that gorgeous room" (564–565): as she leaves it for her assignation with Selim Byron informs us that she carelessly forgot "Her mother's sainted amulet,/ Whereon engraved the Koorsee text,/ Could smooth this life, and win the next" (551–553). Zuleika passes from this tranquil environment, redolent of jewels, perfume, and music, to a grotto that had formerly been an equally idyllic retreat but has suddenly become a storehouse of arms presided over by Selim. As Selim recounts the death of his father and his bitterness at having been raised "like the nephew of a Cain" his extravagance acquires plausible motivation. He rages against Giaffir, but the wish-fulfilling fantasy that chiefly motivates him shows through his plea to Zuleika to elope with him:

> Thou, my Zuleika, share and bless my bark;
> The Dove of peace and promise to mine ark!
> Or, since that hope denied in worlds of strife,
> Be thou the rainbow to the storms of life!
>
> (878–881)

The Biblical rhetoric is ironic, as almost always with Byron. The dove and the rainbow, emblems of forgiveness, are undercut by the "thousand swords" Selim knows are necessary to sustain the paradise he imagines. The continual strife he relishes precludes the peace he invokes. He explains the savagery by a savage determinism: "Yet there we follow but the bent assigned/ By fatal Nature to man's warring kind" (910–911). The taint in the appeal is exposed by its effect on Zuleika:

> Zuleika, mute and motionless,
> Stood like that Statue of Distress,

> When, her last hope for ever gone,
> The Mother hardened into stone;
> All in the maid the eye could see
> Was but a younger Niobe.

(973–978)

Byron's simile reveals the cause of Zuleika's startling disappointment. The child's first wish is for the undivided attention of his mother that would gratify all his oral needs, but if Selim desires Zuleika for himself it is no longer as a dependent infant. In the oedipal struggle he desires as well the power over the mother enjoyed by the father, evidenced in *The Bride of Abydos* by Giaffir's ability to treat Zuleika as an instrument of his will. In this double conflict autonomy requires independence from both parents, and the simile declares that Selim is to be self-sufficient: having rebelled against his father to prove his manhood, Selim will not be mother's precious baby either. The attitude towards women here embodied includes a prominent hostile component: if women are sought for their nurturance they are also shunned lest that very nurturance stifle freedom. Hence the pastoral grotto is converted to a bristling warrior hideout and Selim turns Zuleika to stone, a bride who will never wed, a Niobe who will never have children. He attains the likeness to his father he seeks, and between them the two demolish the woman both regard as "the child of gentleness." Selim, however, sadly lacks the strength to survive a direct confrontation with paternal authority: Giaffir breaks in and kills him with a single shot. The dénouement exposes the son in all his weakness, the fantasy nature of his power betrayed by the utter inability of his troops to succor him. In a final manifestation of the tangled mixture of wishes and resentments that animate the tale Selim perishes because he turns to look at Zuleika: "That pause, that fatal gaze he took,/ Hath doomed his death, or fixed his chain" (1047–1048). Giaffir is left to mourn the loss that his tyrannical opposition to the life of the next generation has brought about: as in *The Giaour*, the unrelenting antagonisms permit no real winners.

This bleak conclusion is the more striking because until the end the residues of desire in *The Bride of Abydos* give it the shape of that comic fairytale in which a despised bastard is revealed as a prince, rights the injustice done his slain father by ousting the usurper and recovering his inheritance, rescues the girl from her unwanted and senescent fiancé, and lives blissfully with her ever after. Byron works against the expectations aroused by this rhythm, and the pattern of filial frustration is typical of his works. Even in situations in which that outcome seems to have been prepared Byron does not allow the younger man to supplant his senior.

This narrative pattern originates in Byron's early life. Neglected, financially exploited, and ultimately widowed by her husband at twenty-six, Mrs. Byron naturally turned to her son. The unfortunate necessity of vicarious emotional satisfaction no doubt contributed to his mother's pride in Byron and her unshakeable confidence in his future greatness: his success would compensate for the blank spaces in her own life, and from him she might draw the sustenance her husband had denied her. The positive aspects of the many enveloping women in Byron's poems pay tribute to his mother's solicitude, but it was surely in part to escape the pressure of these demands, beyond the capacity of any child to fulfill, that Byron strove so vigorously to escape the maternal embrace. And if Byron attracted to himself much of his mother's expectations from men, there were inevitably those other moments of fury in which he became the scapegoat of her resentments against them. "When she has occasion to lecture me," Byron wrote indignantly to Augusta in 1804,

> ... she flies into a fit of phrenzy, upbraids me as if I was the most undutiful wretch in existence, rakes up the ashes of my *father*, abuses him, says I shall be a true Byrrone [sic], which is the worst epithet she can invent. Am I to call this woman mother? Because by natures law she has authority over me, am I to be trampled upon in this manner? Am I to be goaded with insult, loaded with obloquy, and suffer my feelings to be outraged on the most trivial occasions?
>
> (*BLJ* 1: 56)

The same displacement onto Byron's head of an anger whose real object was his father is apparent in another letter to Augusta the following spring:

> I assure you upon my *honour*, jesting apart, I have never been so *scurrilously* and *violently* abused by any person, as by that woman, whom I think I am to call mother, by that being who gave me birth, to whom I ought to look up with veneration and respect, but whom I am sorry I cannot love or admire. Within one little hour, I have not only [heard]

myself, but have heard my *whole family* by the fathers side, *stigmatized* in
terms that the *blackest malevolence* would [perhaps] shrink from, and that
too in words [you] would be shocked to hear.

(*BLJ* I: 66)

The pose Byron assumes in these letters is histrionic, but the
complex of feelings generated by these scenes persisted throughout
his life. Two years before his death Byron described them to Medwin
with undimmed intensity:

I was not so young when my father died, but that I perfectly remember
him.... My mother, when she was in a rage with me, (and I gave her
cause enough,) used to say, "Ah, you little dog, you are a Byron all over;
you are as bad as your father!" It was very different from Mrs. Malaprop's saying, "Ah! good dear Mr. Malaprop, I never loved him till he
was dead." ... He ran out three fortunes, and married or ran away with
three women.... He seemed born for his own ruin, and that of the other
sex.[15]

This dread image of his father, compounded of what he saw himself
and of what, in her frustration, his mother angrily related to him,
opens several broad avenues into Byron's work.[16]

Captain Byron disappeared from his son's view at a period long
recognized by psychoanalysis as a crucial one in the child's development: the onset of the oedipal phase.[17] If, because his security de-
pended on her continued love, Byron initially took his mother's side
against the man who had "ruined" her, the accounts just quoted
suggest that he must have come to regard with deep ambivalence his
father's ability to offend her without sacrificing her affection. It seems
a plausible reconstruction that Byron desired to imitate his father's
prerogatives but feared the consequences of crossing his mother, consequences vividly present in stories of his father's bad end on the
Continent. The distance between himself and a potent figure like
"Mad Jack" must have seemed insurmountable to a small boy already
wounded in self-esteem by the feelings of inadequacy attached to his
clubfoot. Linked as he was to his mother, Byron would have regarded
his father with a volatile mixture of jealousy and awed envy.

The effects in this situation of Captain Byron's premature death
are not difficult to understand. The magnified shadow he cast in his
son's eyes remained fixed, its distorted, terrible power intact, unmod-
ified by subsequent, more realistic, experience. To this weight was

added the guilt commonly suffered by young children who interpret the loss of a parent as the distressing fulfillment of covert and culpable wishes.[18] The doubts of inferiority, the emulousness, and the guilt inspired by his father grew into the enormous psychological investment Byron made in his lineage. Coming into his title only at ten, Byron found it a welcome reassurance, but his touchy consciousness of an aristocratic heritage cut both ways.[19] Throughout its history, as Marchand's biography shows, the family was as notorious for its violent eccentricity as for its accomplishments. "It is ridiculous to say that we do not inherit our passions, as well as the gout, or any other disorder," Byron insisted to Medwin, and the sense of an exalted legacy to which he had to live up but which would in the end prove fatal marks his entire life. He placed an invocation to his forebears at the very head of his first printed collection of poems; in "On Leaving Newstead Abbey" (written in 1803) he salutes the "mail-cover'd Barons" of his line and their heroic descendants, concluding ambitiously —and, in retrospect, ominously—with a third-person pledge that thus early indicates his dramatic view of himself as the perpetuator of an exacting tradition: "He vows that he ne'er will disgrace your renown:/ Like you he will live, or like you he will perish;/ When decay'd, may he mingle his dust with your own!" The lines seem less the sign of a healthy ego-ideal than the warning of a menacing super-ego ready under stress to turn against its possessor.

This family constellation—the imposing ancestors, the father who abused his wife, squandered her money, philandered with other women but never forfeited her loyalty, and the much-travailed but ever-faithful mother, resented but needed—foreshadows the characteristic patterns of Byron's life. In it are the seeds, for example, of both the recurrent types of his relationships with women and the homosexual pedophilia that allowed him to play the dominant male role without risking a sexual encounter with a mature woman. And if this constellation in itself can tell nothing of the genius that makes Byron's poetry worth reading, it nonetheless is a guide to the materials he fashioned and refashioned throughout his career. The sudden death of his mother, shattering precisely because it corresponded so closely with the implications of sentiments he had often expressed, uncovered as well the prior trauma of the loss of his father and the disturbances brought in its train. Robbed of the opportunity to resolve normally the oedipal conflicts inherent in his predicament, Byron was virtually prevented from conceiving in his works of a youth earning his manhood against the older men who stand in his path. The dilemma of *The Giaour* and *The Bride of Abydos* is the dilemma of the succeeding works.

The next tale, *The Corsair,* is the longest of this group, and the greater scope allows Byron to try several new poetic notes. The story opens without prologue as a band of pirates await the return of their ship; among the voices Byron singles out "woman's gentler anxious tone." The protagonist, Conrad, is first heard giving orders, supervising even the mundane details of warfare, rusty carbine-locks and uncomfortable sword-grips, which provide a realistic overlay to the tale. Conrad has stopped by his island only, it seems, that he may be shown quitting it: no sooner does he arrive than he informs his love, Medora, of his intention to leave on a fresh raid. The heart of the first canto is a domestic scene unfolding in her boudoir in which she pathetically attempts to entice him into staying. The carefully chosen fruits, cool water, and voluptuous sherbets that accompany her plea jar strangely with the ascetic indifference the poem insistently ascribes to Conrad: these too seem seductively catalogued chiefly so that he can display his rigorous self-sufficiency by rejecting them.

The chief intention of the scene is undoubtedly to exhibit Conrad's epical resistance to feminine temptation, but undercurrents suggest that his brusque departure veils an inner insecurity:

> From crag to crag descending, swiftly sped
> Stern Conrad down, nor once he turned his head;
> But shrunk whene'er the windings of his way
> Forced on his eye what he would not survey,
> His lone, but lovely dwelling on the steep:
> And she—the dim and melancholy Star,
> Whose ray of Beauty reached him from afar,
> On her he must not gaze, he must not think—
> There he might rest—but on Destruction's brink:
> Yet once almost he stopped—and nearly gave
> His fate to chance, his projects to the wave:
> But no—it must not be—a worthy chief
> May melt, but not betray to Woman's grief.
>
> (505–518)

The passage pictures no confident hero but a man fearfully and desperately denying a threat to his self-definition as a "worthy chief": it is not until Conrad is safely on board that he again "mans himself" and "feels of all his former self possest" (532).[20]

Conrad's precariously maintained heroic persona is paradigmatic of the instability of all Byron's images of the self. This worried view leads naturally into the numerous instances of deceptive appearance and disguise in his works, like that of Selim in *The Bride of Abydos*. When the self presented to others is not solidly grounded it becomes a facade the wearer may delight in assuming or fear to have torn off. Prior to attacking the palace of Seyd, his enemy, Conrad infiltrates it by posing as a Dervise, a choice that emphasizes his denial of his inner life. The ruse gives him an advantage in the fight not available to those committed to a "sincere" exterior, but the darker elements inherent in role playing are not long in surfacing.

Conrad sets fire to the palace, but forfeits his success by lingering to rescue the members of the harem endangered by the conflagration. The consequences make one wonder whether the creator, like the character, is uneasy about such lowerings of the guard toward women: Conrad is captured and Seyd plans his torture. As in the previous tales, the apparent antagonists are linked by their common "sternness," and "Not much could Conrad of his sentence blame,/ His foe, if vanquished, had but shared the same" (976–977). By his tender act, however, Conrad has inspired the love of Gulnare, a discontented odalisque. With a wonderful blend of insinuation and flattery she attempts to persuade Seyd to release him:

> Pacha! the day is thine; and on thy crest
> Sits Triumph—Conrad taken—fall'n the rest!
> His doom is fixed—he dies; and well his fate
> Was earned—yet much too worthless for thy hate:
> Methinks, a short release, for ransom told
> With all his treasure, not unwisely sold;
> Report speaks largely of his pirate-hoard—
> Would that of this my Pacha were the lord!
>
> (1309–1316)

The assured insincerity of these lines is appealing; with them Byron moves from mere exotic adventure to verbal game, from violence to the arts of manipulation that he was to analyze so delicately in *Don*

Juan. Yet the events of the third canto connect Gulnare's talent for feigning to sinister aspects of her character.

When her casuistry fails Gulnare purchases freedom by assassinating Seyd, over Conrad's fervent protests. He is so appalled by the deed that saves his life that he refuses to speak with her; distraught, Gulnare, like Selim, cries out, "I am not what I am." She, who first appears as a "kind lady" and "shape of air," rapidly becomes the opposite. This reversal presages the extinction of female beneficence: Conrad and Gulnare return to his island to find Medora dead. The poem ends with Conrad's mysterious flight, the sterility of the conflict recapitulated in the metaphor of shattered granite Byron applies to his heart.

The inconclusive, anticlimactic nature of this ending is misleading. The structure of *The Corsair* is based on psychological patterns, not linear plot development, and the poem is completed when they are fully disclosed. The epigraphs from Dante Byron prefixed to each canto are clues to the essential conflicts on which his tale is built: all three are taken from the famous episode of Paolo and Francesca in Canto V of the *Inferno*. Much is revealed about Byron's poem by the oblique relationship between it and Dante's story of a wife who takes as lover her husband's younger brother and their death at his outraged hands.[21]

Sinclair translates the verse at the head of the first canto as "There is no greater pain than to recall the happy time in misery." Francesca's memory in hell of her former bliss with Paolo seems puzzlingly remote from the situation of the first canto of *The Corsair,* in which there is as yet no trouble. Sense may be made of it by looking beyond the literal level to ascertain just what "the happy time" in Byron's poem suggests. The configuration of Conrad and Medora echoes that of a son determined by an immense effort of will to flee the safe but restrictive maternal embrace. Suspended in the first canto like a precipitate are the reminiscences of the infant's harmonious union with his mother which he abandoned in perilously seeking to become a man. The strife that follows this first stage forms the materials of the next canto.

The epigraph to the second canto is Dante's question to Francesca: "What occasion did love grant you to know your uncertain desires?" The word Sinclair translates as "uncertain," *dubbiosi,* contains overtones of "morally dubious," "illicit," as well, and such a rendering, though bald, would be faithful to both Dante's and Byron's spirit. The duplication of Medora in Gulnare argues that the

enmity between Conrad and Seyd represents the son's oedipal struggle with the father for the mother. Gulnare's distaste for Seyd and her
position as his bought slave reflects the son's jealous belief that his
father's possession of the mother is illegitimate. By imitating a
privileged figure—the disguise as Dervise—Conrad gains the authority to challenge paternal power, but he soon crumbles before it. As in
The Bride of Abydos, it is the protagonist's failure to be ruthlessly self-
sufficient, the moment in which he glances toward a woman, that
brings his downfall. Having exposed his weakness he collapses to the
status of a dependent child, and the role of the protective mother is
resumed by Gulnare, who visits him in his claustral cell, a shining
agent of mercy.

This admittedly schematic outline accounts for Conrad's sudden
repugnance to Gulnare. Her murder of Seyd is a fearful demonstration of the magical forces attributed to the mother, and it is also a
severe affront to his self-esteem. Throughout the poem Conrad tries
to define himself by superiority to women: it is consistent that he
should both hold himself above Medora's pleas and act as the guard-
ian of damsels in distress. For Conrad to owe his life to a woman is
equivalent to his having lost it: it is the evidence that he is not yet a
man. The troop of vassals Gulnare arbitrarily acquires publishes her
ascendancy and the corresponding decline of Conrad:

> And Conrad following, at her beck, obeyed,
> Nor cared he now if rescued or betrayed;
> Resistance were as useless as if Seyd
> Yet lived to view the doom his ire decreed.
> (1616–1619)

The loss of autonomy marks Conrad's failure of the test he courted:
he is once more his mother's satellite. This configuration is the bridge
between the tales and *Don Juan*. "As thou seest, [it] does not leave me
yet," Francesca says to Dante of her love for Paolo in the line Byron
chose for his last epigraph: the obsessions that continued to grip him
are amply visible in *The Corsair*.

In the "advertisement" to the next tale, *Lara*, Byron advised the
reader that he "may probably regard it as a sequel to the *Corsair*," a

counsel that deserves thorough consideration. The eighteenth stanza, in which Conrad/Lara is described, is the *locus classicus* of the Byronic hero:

> There was in him a vital scorn of all:
> As if the worst had fall'n which could befall,
> He stood a stranger in this breathing world,
> An erring Spirit from another hurled;
> A thing of dark imaginings, *that shaped*
> *By choice the perils he by chance escaped:*
> But 'scaped in vain, for in their memory yet
> His mind would half exult and half regret:
> With more capacity for love than Earth
> Bestows on most of mortal mould and birth,
> His early dreams of good outstripped the truth,
> And *troubled* Manhood follow'd *baffled* Youth;
> With thought of years in phantom chase *misspent*,
> And *wasted* powers for better purpose lent;
> And fiery passions that had poured their wrath
> In hurried desolation o'er his path,
> And left the better feelings *all at strife*
> In *wild* reflection o'er his stormy life;
> But haughty still and loth himself to blame,
> He call'd on Nature's self to share the shame,
> And charged all faults upon the fleshly form
> She gave to clog the soul and feast the worm;
> Till he at last confounded good and ill,
> And half mistook for fate the acts of will.
> Too high for common selfishness, he could
> At times resign his own for others' good,
> But not in pity—not because he ought,
> But in some strange *perversity* of thought,
> That sway'd him onward with a secret *pride*
> To do what few or none would do beside;
> And this same impulse would, in tempting time,
> Mislead his spirit equally to crime;
> So much he soared beyond, or sunk beneath,
> The men with whom he felt condemned to breathe,
> And longed by good or ill to separate
> Himself from all who shared his mortal state; . . .
>
>   (313–348; italics added)

There have been excellent studies of the ancestry of this figure in the Gothic tradition,[22] but conventional as much of the passage is, it should not be referred entirely to convention: the contempt for the "fleshly form" that "clog[s] the soul," for example, has particular resonance when coming from a writer conscious that his beauty was marred by a clubfoot. The echo at the outset invites comparison with Satan, but the lines sound a note of frustration rather than of absolute metaphysical evil. Lara appears forever at odds with himself; ignorant of his true desires, he dissipates his energies in pursuits that bring no satisfaction. "Dark imaginings," not clear motives, govern Lara's choices, and the portrait that emerges is of a powerful neurotic compulsion beyond the direction of the conscious mind. Two lines sum up his character's predicament: "Till he at last confounded good and ill/ And half mistook for fate the acts of will." Because Lara is blind to the causes of his actions he sees his life as ruled by an incomprehensible fate: what is unrecognized in the self returns as a fantasy of external forces. The "freedom" the Byronic hero vaunts is a maze matching the chaotic inner life of which he is the prisoner.

Stanza 18 is too static to analyze the pattern it describes. It is a late addition to the text not in the original manuscript, another instance of dramatic structure yielding to the weight of a single character. The insight into the origins of Lara's character that it lacks, however, is provided by stanza 2:

> The Chief of Lara is returned again:
> And why had Lara crossed the bounding main?
> Left by his sire, too young such loss to know,
> Lord of himself,—that heritage of woe,
> That fearful empire which the human breast
> But holds to rob the heart within of rest!—
> With none to check and few to point in time
> The thousand paths that slope the way to crime;
> Then, when he most required commandment, then
> Had Lara's daring boyhood governed men.
>
> (11–20)

In this stanza the link between the Titanic protagonists through whom Byron expressed himself and the early death of his father is explicit. Deprived of a model in the world of men, Lara reacts to his painful bewilderment by prematurely inventing a self that claims omnipotence. This fantasy of perfect self-sufficiency cannot admit the turmoil that called it into being without confessing the failure to resolve it, and so is forever liable to disruption by the internal division of the self. Only by incessant triumphs over other men can Lara reassure himself of his worth, but the fates of the Giaour, of Selim, and of Conrad have already shown that such triumphs are hollow.

Lara adds to the actual workings-out of familial conflicts depicted by its predecessors a substantial portrait of the psychological state of the son caught in Byron's particular situation. Less narrowly bound in its plot to the oral and oedipal struggles already discussed, *Lara* is nonetheless clearly related to them: it is not fortuitous that Byron based the death of Lara on the story of a son murdered after leaving his mother and while making a "visit of pleasure" to a woman.[23] *Lara* is more steadily self-contemplative and analytic than Byron's previous work, although the connotations of "analytic" are perhaps too detached to be appropriate. The pressures behind *Lara* (and the invocation of fatalism and stoic pride to defend against repressed emotions) are audible in Byron's own voice almost two years later, after they had erupted in his marriage:

> . . . my circumstances have been and are in a state of great confusion— my health has been a good deal disordered, and my mind ill at ease for a considerable period. Such are the causes (I do not name them as excuses) which have frequently driven me into excess, and disqualified my temper for comfort. Something also may be attributed to the strange and desultory habits which, becoming my own master at an early age, and scrambling about, over and through the world, may have induced. I still, however, think that, if I had a fair chance, by being placed in even a tolerable situation, I might have gone on fairly. But that seems hopeless,—and there is nothing more to be said. . . . I believe I may have said this before to you, but I risk repeating it. It is nothing to bear the *privations* of adversity, or, more properly, ill fortune; but my pride recoils from its *indignities*. However, I have no quarrel with that same pride, which will, I think, buckler me through every thing. If my heart could have been broken, it would have been so years ago, and by events more afflicting than these.
>
> (*BLJ* 5: 44–45)

Lara is as much a symptom as an evaluation of the traumatic events hinted in Byron's last sentence, but it points some of the directions Byron took to transform his personal tensions into poems of broader interest.

Lara begins with the significant return of its protagonist to his native land. His unexplained reappearance after many years perplexes his countrymen, but whether or not the self-awareness should be ascribed to Conrad/Lara, the pattern is clear: after the collapse of his independence the failed adult naturally seeks to recover the peaceful existence of childhood associated with home. Lara reclaims his fiefdom, gaining by inheritance (like his creator) the authority lost in his encounter with Seyd. His position is a reminder that if one axis of this inquiry is psychological, another must be political. The theater of the tales is often the uneasy boundary between the Titanic figure and the society he execrates. Even on the island Conrad/Lara does not live in solitude: he nominally participates in a community depicted as an alternative to the corrupt civilization on which it nonetheless parasitically preys for sustenance. The description of Lara in stanza 18 recalls a commonplace of Aristotle's *Politics*, the character of the man cut off from the *polis*:

> And he who by nature and not by mere accident is without a state, is either a bad man or above humanity; he is like the "tribeless, lawless, heartless one" whom Homer denounces—the natural outcast is forthwith a lover of war; he may be compared to an isolated piece at draughts . . . But he who is unable to live in society, or who has no need because he is sufficient for himself, must be either a beast or a god; he is no part of a state.[24]

Byron presents the Byronic hero as both personally self-destructive and socially pernicious, and though it is detrimental to linear exposition each of these interrelated aspects must be considered.

The poem is scarcely underway when Lara meets a ghost who frightens him into unconsciousness. The episode would seem no more than Gothic claptrap were it not symmetrically paired with the crisis in the plot. At a feast given by a neighbor, Otho, Lara is challenged by a guest as mysterious as himself. Lara's "heedlessness of all around/ Bespoke remembrance only too profound" (488–489) of the crimes hinted against him, but Byron offers no details of the accusations that precipitate a challenge. The two incidents taken together explain the mystification. The specific deeds are unimportant because they represent all Lara's uncomprehended past: the actions he committed but never fully understood return in the guise of a double. Ezzelin's accusations are self-reproaches externalized: his questions reveal intimate knowledge, and he appears to Lara as a "stranger" precisely because he is the self Lara's conscious mind has repressed. The essence of Lara's "stern" self-control is the denial of just those psychic stresses Ezzelin symbolically manifests, and their continued force is proved by the previous swoon. What follows reflects the dynamics of the unconscious. Ezzelin misses the appointed day, as one would expect of so shadowy a creature, and Lara angrily demands that Otho redeem the pledge he gave for his guest. Lara's fury at a secondary object further illustrates the misdirection that results from his lack of self-knowledge; in the ensuing fight Otho is seriously wounded, and the code of honor he shares with Lara causes them to sink the country into pointless war.

Byron draws attention to the context that enlarges a private grievance into mass bloodshed. The action is carefully placed at a moment when individual power is competing with a nascent central authority:

> Throughout that clime the feudal Chiefs had gained
> Such sway, their infant monarch hardly reigned;
> Now was the hour for Faction's rebel growth,
> The Serfs contemned the one, and hated both:
> They waited but a leader, and they found
> One to their cause inseparably bound;
> By circumstance compelled to plunge again,
> In self-defence, amidst the strife of men.
>   (871–878)

Here, as in *Marino Faliero*, where Byron was to develop the situation, the Titanic figure allies himself with the oppressed people against the aristocracy. Lara frees the serfs, but Byron exposes the revolutionary act as self-aggrandizing. The narrator mordantly observes: "And cared he for the freedom of the crowd?/ He raised the humble but to bend the proud" (897–898). From such motives comes only a sterile cycle of "alternate victors":

> What boots the oft-repeated tale of strife,
> The feast of vultures, and the waste of life?
> . . . .
> It was too late to check the wasting brand,
> And Desolation reaped the famished land;
> The torch was lighted, and the flame was spread,
> And Carnage smiled upon her daily dead.
>   (909–910; 923–926)

The parody of the Lord's prayer is a characteristic emphasis that furnishes the proper comment on Lara's spurning of a crucifix at his death: the self-repression and consequent hollow pride destroy life.

Lara's defeat is accompanied by the revelation that his faithful page Kaled is a woman in disguise. The unmasking is connected to the delayed account of Ezzelin's fate in an ambiguous "peasant's tale": "And charity upon the hope would dwell/ It was not Lara's hand by which he fell" (1241–1242). The conjunction of the two revelations suggests that once again Gulnare/Kaled has resorted to assassination in order to preserve her beloved, but the obfuscation is appropriate. Since the murder re-enacts what Lara does internally it might fittingly be imputed to both of them: Gulnare/Kaled's futile protectiveness parallels Lara's attempt to repress the conflicts in himself. Her intervention, moreover, again discloses the fundamental link between them. The master-page relationship is a wishful inversion of the true situation, for Lara, far from dominating Kaled, is wholly dependent on her. As each act of rescue is a fresh insult she is inevitably unable to keep him alive: he is killed, and the last glimpse of her is in a revealing image:

> Her eye shot forth with all the living fire
> That haunts the tigress in her whelpless ire;
> But left to waste her weary moments there,
> She talked all idly unto shapes of air, . . .
>
> (1251–1254)

Lara's death is the final exposure of his pretensions to adult competence, and at the level of the psychological turmoil that animates these tales the corollary to his failure to establish himself as a man by defeating Otho is the failure to win the mother. Not yet a man himself, he cannot give her the child she desires, and Kaled's frustration is another sign of the demands that Byron's protagonists unhappily discover they are too weak to satisfy.

The desires and fears reflected in these works appear practically without disguise in *The Siege of Corinth*. Anonymous accusations of treason but mainly the refusal of Minotti, the "inexorable sire" of Lanciotto's love, Francesca, to permit their marriage, have driven Lanciotto from Venice. Blocked at home, he transforms himself into Alp, a beturbaned Moslem, and rises to command the army besieging the city which Minotti, accompanied by his daughter, has been sent to govern. The opposition of father and suitor is an only barely displaced representation of the oedipal contest, and Alp's rebellion against the land of his sires is this primary antagonism writ large.

The central episode of *The Siege of Corinth* is a miraculous midnight apparition of Francesca as Alp walks regretfully amidst the slaughter of the previous days of battle. When she declares her enduring love Byron arouses expectations of a blissful reunion, but they are startlingly reversed. Francesca harshly allows Alp the time of one cloud's passage before the moon to renounce his new faith or suffer eternal damnation:

> But pause one moment more, and take
> The curse of Him thou didst forsake;
> And look once more to Heaven, and see
> Its love for ever shut from thee.
>
> (639–642)

This ultimatum provokes a reciprocal display of "deep interminable pride" from Alp, who justifies his intransigence by a familiar determinism: "What Venice made me, I must be." Francesca then vanishes as suddenly as she appeared.

Francesca's comings and goings, witnessed as they are by Alp alone, strongly urge that this interview be regarded not as an actual occurrence but as a projection of his doubts and hopes. The foundation of fact on which Byron insisted and his customary reprinting of sources is deceptive, for the consistency of his stories owes little to their historical bases. Alp's violent rejection of the demands he imagines Francesca as making betrays how deeply he is afraid of losing the independent identity he has achieved as a Moslem. Because he could not maintain himself in Venice Alp equates Francesca's not unreasonable requests with utter capitulation, and so the woman he loves appears to him as a threatening figure. In contriving to be rejected by her he reveals himself as the son who does not expect to wrest his woman from parental authority, and the plot bears out his impotence.

The description of Minotti in battle explicitly renders his role as a menacing father. An "old man" with white hair, he is a redoubtable enemy to his juniors: "Though aged, he was so iron of limb,/ Few of our youth could cope with him" (792–793). His severity is attributed in part to the loss of his only son, but that cause only brings into relief his fury against those of the next generation who dare to cross him: "Of all he might have been the sire/ Who fell that day beneath his ire"

(801–802). Alp meets him as the Turks gain the advantage and in vain offers him quarter "For thine own, thy daughter's sake":

> "Never, Renegado, never!
> Though the life of the gift would last for ever."
>
> "Francesca!—Oh, my promised bride!
> Must she too perish by thy pride!"
>
> "She is safe."—"Where? where?"—"In Heaven;
> From whence thy traitor soul is driven—
> Far from thee, and undefiled."
> Grimly then Minotti smiled,
> As he saw Alp staggering bow
> Before his words, as with a blow.
>
> "Oh God! when died she?"—"Yesternight—
> Nor weep I for her spirit's flight:
> None of my pure race shall be
> Slaves to Mahomet and thee—..."
>
> (851–863)

The reply destroys Alp's motives for fighting, and Byron invokes a stray bullet to give a realistic explanation of the death the speech has already caused. Minotti's answer lends further credence to the interpretation that Alp's interview with Francesca is an inner dialogue externalized.

Minotti announces Francesca's decease almost as if it were the consequence of his will, and if his stern satisfaction is the final evidence of the terrible, unbending father, it is also on another level a sign of the association of the Christians in this tale with an unforgiving rigidity. Byron completes this identification by having Minotti make his last stand in a church filled with the dead above and tombs below. Perverted from an institution of grace, the church "throughout the siege, had been/ The Christians' chiefest magazine" (981–982). With a fine irony Byron places Minotti under a sweetly smiling Madonna, and as the Turks advance he sighingly crosses himself and fires the powder. In the holocaust bodies are so mutilated that "Not the matrons that them bore/ Could discern their offspring more" (1048–1049). "Christian or Moslem, which be they?" the narrator rhetorically inquires, and the question epitomizes the technique of the poem. The tale makes its meaning by manipulating conventional symbols, and forecasts the brilliant exploiter of stock properties Byron was to become. *The Siege of Corinth* initially appears to flatter the English reader by its comfortable opposition of devout Christian and infidel Turk, but Byron rejects these prejudices and subverts his story. Alp is no barbarian, but a gentle youth victimized by the fanatic Venetians. Beneath the surface contrast of martyr and heathen the enemies are kin, and their essential indistinguishability is stressed again in the oxymoronic final line "Thus was Corinth lost and won!"

Yet in the end the private situation depicted in the poem outweighs the political: the mourning mothers occur at its conclusion. Here as elsewhere Byron's additions are the clues to his preoccupations: all of the following but the first couplet was inserted after the fair copy:

> Christians or Moslem, which be they?
> Let their mothers see and say!
> When in cradled rest they lay,
> And each nursing mother smiled
> On the sweet sleep of her child,
> Little deemed she such a day
> Would rend those tender limbs away.
>
> (1041–1047)

The yearning for the shattered harmony of mother and son remains the base of Byron's fictional world.

These themes receive their clearest expression in *Parisina,* the last and most compact of the narratives written in the four turbulent years between the triumph of *Childe Harold* and Byron's scandal-ridden departure from England in April 1816. The tale is founded on a passage in Gibbon which Byron gives in his "advertisement":

Under the reign of Nicholas III. [A.D. 1425] Ferrara was polluted with a domestic tragedy. By the testimony of a maid, and his own observation, the Marquis of Este discovered the incestuous loves of his wife Parisina, and Hugo his bastard son, a beautiful and valiant youth. They were beheaded in the castle by the sentence of a father and husband, who published his shame, and survived their execution. He was unfortunate, if they were guilty: if they were innocent, he was still more unfortunate; nor is there any possible situation in which I can sincerely approve the last act of the justice of a parent.

This episode, with Gibbon's verdict upon it, already reads like one of Byron's fictions: his development of it sharpens the conflict.

The name of the father, Nicholas, Byron changes to Azo. The metrical grounds he adduces in explanation, however, ignore one effect of the change: to reinforce the closeness of the father and his illegitimate son. Secondly, Byron adds to the adultery a highly suggestive complication unknown in either Gibbon or more detailed Italian accounts of the incident: in Byron's version Parisina, Azo's wife, was originally intended for Hugo. Equally absent from the original source is any discussion of Hugo's mother, and Byron's most revealing invention is to raise her into prominence by making Hugo resentfully conscious of the stigma he feels attached to her abandonment by Azo years before.

When the affair with his young stepmother is discovered Hugo thus presents himself as doubly wronged, having lost both his mother, Bianca, and his bride to his father's turpitude:

> Nor are my mother's wrongs forgot,
> Her slighted love and ruined name,
> Her offspring's heritage of shame;
> But she is in the grave, where he,
> Her son—thy rival—soon shall be.
> . . . .
> 'Tis true that I have done thee wrong—
>   But wrong for wrong:—this,—deemed thy bride,
>   The other victim of thy pride,—
> Thou know'st for me was destined long;
> Thou saw'st, and coveted'st her charms;
>   And with thy very crime—my birth,—
>   Thou taunted'st me—as little worth; . . .
>   (243–247; 252–258)

Hugo's outburst establishes the psychological unity of the mother figure whom the narrative divides and duplicates as Bianca and Parisina. Byron could hardly have made it more explicit than he does by the phrase "her son—thy rival" that the incest acts out the son's desire to dislodge the father from his mother's affections. Hugo's reference to Parisina as merely "deemed" Azo's bride, as if she were not actually so, illustrates the intensity of his wishes.

Joined with his resentment of his father, however, is Hugo's poignant need to prove himself before him. His frustrated affection and emulation gleam through his acceptance of the death sentence Azo passes on him:

See what thy guilty love hath done!
Repaid thee with too like a son!
I am no bastard in my soul,
For that, like thine, abhorred control;
....

For though thou work'dst my mother's ill,
And made thy own my destined bride,
    I feel thou art my father still:
And harsh as sounds thy hard decree,
'Tis not unjust, although from thee.
Begot in sin, to die in shame,
My life begun and ends the same:
As erred the sire, so erred the son,
And thou must punish both in one.
(294–297; 307–315)

The sensation of guilt so thoroughly outweighs in Hugo's mind the
justice of his claim to Parisina that he unsays his grievances. With this
pathetic acknowledgment of paternal authority he reverts to the
status of a child, and acquiesces in the subordinate position to which
all Byron's protagonists are reduced.

The submission will seem less surprising if the childhood conflicts invested in this scene are considered in full. Insofar as Parisina
does return his love Hugo succeeds in defeating Azo, and the exposure of the affair confirms his victory. The adultery is fitting retribution for Azo's crimes, and Hugo flaunts the knowledge that Azo
cannot punish the adulterers without suffering himself. For the child
to overcome his father in the oedipal struggle, however, is to disrupt
the stable environment in which he feels safe and to lose the father's
love he desperately prizes. For his own security part of the child
prefers to lose, and the consequence of this ambivalence is Hugo's
identification with his father and acceptance of his decree, which
destroys his own integrity but reaffirms the order of his world. Since
triumph would leave the son as lacking in a model for adult masculine
behavior as if the father had not been present at all, an undefeated
Hugo, who prides himself on having ridden in battle by his father's
side, would be very nearly in the same predicament as the fatherless
Conrad/Lara. In different ways each character betrays the same failure
to resolve normally the oedipal tensions.

The dilemma could be ameliorated only by forgiveness from Azo,
which he is too wounded to conceive. Like all Byron's stunted

"heroes," he denies his pain beneath a "stern" demeanor and takes refuge in determinism, telling Parisina: "Not I, but thou his blood does shed" (220). Byron reminds the reader of the possibility of charity by the judicious use of capitals: ". . . the crowd in a speechless circle gather/ To see the Son fall by the doom of the Father!" (405–406). This sterile negation of the Christian ritual of atonement, echoed in *The Two Foscari*, suggests that Byron himself could not believe in any intermission of the oedipal strife. Hugo's execution tears from Parisina a scream like "a mother's o'er her child/ Done to death by sudden blow" (490–491), and Byron's simile, not literally true, points straight to the psychological center of the tale. In the sources Parisina too was beheaded: Byron has her rather go mad, a change indicative of the increased inwardness of his treatment. Azo lives on in an affectless existence "past all mirth and woe," denying his responsibility and trying to console himself "With all the consciousness that he/ Had only passed a just decree;/ That they had wrought their doom of ill;/ Yet Azo's age was wretched still" (576—579). The misery Byron imagines for him, like that of the other surviving parent figures already met, is the faint, distorted image of a son's wish to matter in his father's eyes.

A composite portrait of the Byronic hero may now be sketched: a thwarted figure, ignorant of his essential self, who represses his inner dismay under a shell of sternness. The historical background against which he is set or through which he moves amplifies his predicament and offers a contextual source of self-knowledge, but with only partial success. He is unable to win the woman he loves from his rivals, who are generally father figures, and though her picture contains ominous shadows, he is incapable of maintaining a healthful existence apart from her. The recurrence and strength of this configuration, parallel to the vision of a child still dependent on his mother and jealous and fearful of the omnipotent father, is massive testimony of its hegemony in Byron's imagination. The furor surrounding Byron's incest with his sister and the breakup of his short-lived marriage with Annabella Milbanke has obscured the older and deeper pattern of which those events were a consequence, a pattern which provides an insight into the works of Byron's early artistic maturity.

2

The Sublime Self and the Single Voice

*T*he ease with which we fall into speaking of his "exile" from England in 1816 marks Byron's power to impose his myth on us; in reality he chose to quit a situation made intolerable by the strain marriage brought to his ingrained conflicts. He announces in the epigraph affixed to Canto III of *Childe Harold* that the motive of the poem is distraction from his troubles: "Afin que cette application vous forcât á penser à autre chose: il n'y a en vérité de remède que celui-là et le temps." "Long-absent Harold reappears at last" in order that his creator may "fling/ Forgetfulness" about himself:

> He, who grown agéd in this world of woe,
> In deeds, not years, piercing the depths of life,
> So that no wonder waits him—nor below
> Can Love or Sorrow, Fame, Ambition, Strife,
> Cut to his heart again with the keen knife

> Of silent, sharp endurance—he can tell
> Why Thought seeks refuge in lone caves, yet rife
> With airy images, and shapes which dwell
> Still unimpaired, though old, in the Soul's haunted cell.
>
> 'Tis to create, and in creating live
> A being more intense that we endow
> With form our fancy, gaining as we give
> The life we image, even as I do now—
> What am I? Nothing: but not so art thou,
> Soul of my thought! with whom I traverse earth,
> Invisible but gazing, as I glow
> Mixed with thy spirit, blended with thy birth,
> And feeling still with thee in my crushed feelings' dearth.
>
> (5–6)

It may seem curious that Byron should have sought relief by reassuming a persona initially intended to express the melancholy aspects of his nature. The language of stanza 5 suggests that Byron now more purposefully intends Harold to embody the "lone caves" and "haunted cells" of the soul, and to make them available for scrutiny by externalizing them, but the program is again unimplemented. The links between Harold and Byron are superficially indicated in the next ten stanzas and then Harold largely vanishes.

The reasons for his disappearance should be considered. Readers have long noted the irony of Byron's having grown into his protagonist, but Harold's redundance is also the sign of a reorientation: he becomes redundant because Byron endeavors to repudiate those aspects of the self which he symbolizes. The drive towards exposure baldly stated in Matthew Arnold's remark that Byron dragged the pageant of his bleeding heart across Europe is deceptive: it forms part of the dominant drive toward "forgetfulness" in the poem.[1] As stanza 6 suggests, Harold (and, more inclusively, the writing of Canto III) enables Byron to overcome personal disaster by restoring his response to the outside world, but he is not a means of probing the self. Harold is truly an *alter* ego: the bearer of rejected parts of the self. Like the heroes of his tales, Byron turns from introspection to a stoic denial of grief: "Yet am I changed; though still enough the same/ In strength to bear what Time cannot abate,/ And feed on bitter fruits without accusing Fate" (7). Declaring to Augusta his confidence in the work, Byron explained: "I am certain in my mind that this Canto is the *best* which I have ever written; there is depth of thought in it throughout and a strength of repressed passion which you must feel before you find" (*BLJ* 5: 159).

Canto III of *Childe Harold* displays a wholly natural impulse of recoil from the strivings obliquely recorded in the tales: to evade further bruises by retirement to a less assertive posture. The poem tests the possibility of attitudes not unlike maternal dependence, and these fantasies, if regressive in content, are reparative in function: through them Byron regenerates the values threatened by the bitterness of his separation. Alternately, he seeks to keep his urgent private griefs at a distance by adopting the voice of grave and exalted meditation on grandly public themes. These strategies engender conflicting crosscurrents, and the shape of the canto is determined by Byron's repeated oscillations between them. When either fails he turns to the other, and when it proves unsatisfactory he returns anew to the first. The very essence of the poem is an effort to rehabilitate the self: to read the poem is to watch the process.

The great set piece on Waterloo is symptomatic of Byron's wish to appraise the stresses of his character while yet remaining safely above them. His habitual identification with Napoleon provided a perspective on himself that the device of Harold no longer furnished. Extreme in all things, capable of governing an empire but not his own passions, Napoleon is a paradigm of Byron's Titanic figures:

> But Quiet to quick bosoms is a Hell,
> And *there* hath been thy bane; there is a fire
> And motion of the Soul which will not dwell
> In its own narrow being, but aspire
> Beyond the fitting medium of desire;
> And, but once kindled, quenchless evermore,
> Preys upon high adventure, nor can tire
> Of aught but rest; a fever at the core,
> Fatal to him who bears, to all who ever bore.
>
> (42)

This tyrannical will can issue only in self-destruction. Within three stanzas Byron replaces the metaphors of fire and warmth with those of cold and sterility:

> He who ascends to mountain-tops, shall find
> The loftiest peaks most wrapt in clouds and snow;

> He who surpasses or subdues mankind,
> Must look down on the hate of those below.
> Though high *above* the Sun of Glory glow,
> And far beneath the Earth and Ocean spread,
> *Round* him are icy rocks, and loudly blow
> Contending tempests on his naked head,
> And thus reward the toils to which those summits led.
>
> (45)

The imaginative poverty of these lines is directly related to the attitude they strike. In them the narrator reaches for "the grandeur of generality," presenting himself as the sage moralist contemplating the eternal truths of the human condition. This oratorical voice is the Byron who thrilled a generation, and it is also Byron as he would have liked to see himself, the master of an ideal, impersonal stance. Byron writes about Napoleon because he feels an affinity with him, but in the poem the connection is not acknowledged. None of the self-consuming passion imputed to Napoleon is permitted to disturb the measured tones of the speaker.

The narrator forcefully repudiates the Titans whom Napoleon exemplifies, but the abruptness of the rejection hints at the sympathies being exorcised by the deliberate act of will: "Away with these! true Wisdom's world will be / Within its own creation, or in thine,/ Maternal Nature!" (46). The configuration of these stanzas is identical with that of the tales: from the world of destructive masculine aggressiveness Byron turns to a sheltering environment characterized by its womanly overtones. For Byron inquiry into the self and inquiry into history are parallel, and just as Canto III shies away from investigating the turbulent inner life it illustrates, so it seeks to counteract the lessons of history which are the amplified image of that turbulence with an ahistorical, benevolent, feminine nature. "Shelley, when I was in Switzerland," Byron later told Medwin in an apposite phrase, "used to dose me with Wordsworth physic even to nausea,"[2] and Byron briefly tried to heal his wounds according to the prescription:

> Where rose the mountains, there to him were friends,
> Where rolled the ocean, thereon was his home;
> Where a blue sky, and glowing clime, extends,
> He had the passion and the power to roam;
> The desert, forest, cavern, breaker's foam,

Were unto him companionship; they spake
A mutual language, clearer than the tome
Of his land's tongue, which he would oft forsake,
For Nature's pages glassed by sunbeams on the lake.
(13)

The distinctively maternal qualities of the nature appealed to in the
third canto are evident in the associations it evokes. In the midst of
beautiful landscape Harold achieves a mood in which his heart can
"leap kindly back to kindness, though Disgust/ Hath weaned it from
all worldlings" (53). The tranquility of nature leads to one specific
image: "There was soft Remembrance, and sweet Trust/ In one fond
breast," continues stanza 53, "And in its tenderer hour on that his
bosom dwelt." The literal reference is to Augusta, but the scene
half-disclosed by "weaned" points to an earlier memory which is
developed in the following stanza:

And he had learned to love,—I know not why,
For this in such as him seems strange of mood,—
The helpless looks of blooming Infancy,
Even in its earliest nurture; . . .
(54)

In his "Epistle to Augusta" Byron connects his response to nature still
more explicitly than he does here with memories of his childhood and
of his sister.[3] His nature borrows its power from the intense nostalgic
yearnings invested in it, and if the third canto is Wordsworthian it is
perhaps because Byron sensed that the descriptive language of the
older poet had been made to serve a similar function.[4] The picture
Byron gives of Lake Leman implicitly identifies the gratification he
hopes to recover by withdrawing into nature with the situation of
infant and mother:

Is it not better, then, to be alone,
And love Earth only for its earthly sake?
By the blue rushing of the arrowy Rhone,
Or the pure bosom of its nursing Lake,
Which feeds it as a mother who doth make
A fair but froward infant her own care,
Kissing its cries away as these awake; . . .
(71)

The interrogative, wishful note of this and succeeding stanzas betrays the contradictions which beset this solution. The unspoiled harmony Byron seeks is repeatedly disrupted by the correlative intrusions of history and his own preoccupations. Wherever he looks, the landscape reveals battlefields and the ruins of past civilizations: it is the book not of God or of womanly fostering but of man's depredations. Like Wordsworth's, the nature he sees is "half-created" by the perceiving mind, but it can therefore never be free of his projected anxieties and ambitions. As the merely analogical use of natural imagery to describe Napoleon suggests, nature for Byron supplies emblems of his already existent condition and not independent, lasting, spiritual solace. The assertive and aspiring elements of his character are exemplified by the fervent (if nominally disciplined) response to Napoleon and the glowing praise of Morat and Marathon, "true Glory's stainless victories" (64). His passionate determination that he must, and would, excel in the world of men calls forth the magnificent description of Waterloo and the elegiac stanzas on Waterloo, but it also strengthens the instinct to place a "silent seal" (8) on any emotions which might make him appear weak. Much as he longed for its contentment, Byron's own heroic temper blocked any final acquiescence in the passive, trusting role of the mother-infant relationship.

This dilemma erupts in oscillations which become more violent as the canto proceeds. It is resolved at last and unstably in the mediating figure of Rousseau, but only after a gradual evolution in his depiction shows with great precision the values involved. The persecuted, outcast author is a model of the control of private suffering in art:

> Here the self-torturing sophist, wild Rousseau,
> The apostle of Affliction, he who threw
> Enchantment over Passion, and from Woe
> Wrung overwhelming eloquence, first drew
> The breath which made him wretched; . . .
>
> (77)

Byron at this point refrains from embracing Rousseau because his political writings associate him too nearly with the *philosophes* and the destructive consequences of the domineering masculine will. The ambivalence is the same as that already noted in his attitude to Napoleon:

> But good with ill they also overthrew,
> Leaving but ruins, wherewith to rebuild
> Upon the same foundation, and renew
> Dungeons and thrones, which the same hour refilled,
> As heretofore, because Ambition was self-willed.
> (82)

From this dead end Byron retreats as before to the fantasized peace of nature. The familiar vocabulary of a second apostrophe to Lake Leman, before characterized in maternal terms, enforces the opposition of masculine and feminine and illustrates as well the fusion of sister and mother in Byron's imaginative universe: "thy soft murmuring/ Sounds sweet as if a Sister's voice reproved,/ That I with *stern* delights should e'er have been so moved" (85; italics added). The calm, complete with a chirping grasshopper "who makes/ His life an infancy" (87), is shattered by a nightstorm which corresponds to the resurgence of Byron's inner tensions. As they reassert their power the landscape is transformed into a mirror of the particular griefs of the poet separated from those he loves. The sky becomes ominously lovely "as is the light/ Of a dark eye in Woman" (92), and the "arrowy Rhone" of the previous description (71) becomes a malign masculine force confirming the severance of Byron's happiness:

> Now, where the swift Rhone cleaves his way between
> Heights which appear as lovers who have parted
> In hate, whose mining depths so intervene,
> That they can meet no more, though broken-hearted: . . .
> (94)

The layers of conflict laid bare by the failure of Byron's marriage and his self-exile from England vividly appear in the conflation of mother, sister, and lover in this scene.

Baffled in his attempt to escape into nature, Byron rises almost to frenzy:

> Sky—Mountains—River—Winds—Lake—Lightnings! ye!
> With night, and clouds, and thunder—and a Soul
> To make these felt and feeling, well may be
> Things that have made me watchful; the far roll
> Of your departing voices, is the knoll
> Of what in me is sleepless,—if I rest.

> But where of ye, O Tempests! is the goal?
> Are ye like those within the human breast?
> Or do ye find, at length, like eagles, some high nest?
>
> Could I embody and unbosom now
> That which is most within me,—could I wreak
> My thoughts upon expression, and thus throw
> Soul—heart—mind—passions—feelings—strong or weak—
> All that I would have sought, and all I seek,
> Bear, know, feel—and yet breathe—into *one* word,
> And that one word were Lightning, I would speak;
> But as it is, I live and die unheard,
> With a most voiceless thought, sheathing it as a sword.
>
> (96–97)

The frantic accumulation and halting syntax imitate a breakdown of which the cause is evident. Byron's feverish longing for "one word" to contain the complexity of his emotions is itself a barrier to his comprehending them: a rough paraphrase of this passage might read: "Since I lack the magic talisman that would open all the locks, why try speaking of myself at all?" The psychological subtext is the reverse of what is stated: the admission of defeat avoids the painful necessity of working through the pressures catalogued in the preceding stanzas. The all-or-nothing terms subconsciously justify to Byron merely reiterating in verse a despairing avowal of silence. This common gambit to reduce stress, however, prolongs and increases its severity, and an art based on such a posture offers no more satisfactory resolution of inner discord than a withdrawal into "maternal nature." The progression of imagery from the ideal maternal/sibling harmony through "lovers who have parted in hate" to the impotence symbolized by the sheathed sword is a miniature of the failure of Byron's resources.

An abrupt shift from the nightstorm in which repressed agonies have surfaced to the "dewy Morn" marks the beginning of resolution (98). It is at this point that Rousseau re-enters the poem, now shorn of his compromising engagement with the world of men. A visit to Clarens, the setting of *La Nouvelle Héloïse,* prepares the new introduction (99). Byron transforms Rousseau into a benign power within the landscape his creations "people," and the strength of his imagination counteracts the reminders of strife which have hitherto dominated Byron's vision. Most important, the novel's celebration of the trials and love of Julie and Saint Preux contrasts with the misery of Byron's separation. In this surrogate who performs what eludes Byron *in propria persona* we can see the outline of an artist figure who incorporates the values of compassion and natural energies previously associated exclusively with women. The agency of Rousseau brings Byron to a tentative utterance of faith:

> I have not loved the World, nor the World me,—
> But let us part fair foes; I do believe,
> Though I have found them not, that there may be
> Words which are things,—hopes which will not deceive,
> And Virtues which are merciful, nor weave
> Snares for the failing; I would also deem
> O'er others' griefs that some sincerely grieve—
> That two, or one, are almost what they seem,—
> That Goodness is no name—and Happiness no dream.
>
>   (114)

The fragile assertion is cut across by the experience it records so proudly and resentfully: surrounding echoes of *Coriolanus* characterize Byron's stance more accurately than the moderation here grudgingly conceded.[5] The stanza avows a trust and faith in the possibilities of expression which are desired rather than achieved.

The declaration is followed immediately by Byron's apostrophe to his daughter: "My daughter! with thy name this song begun!/ My daughter! with thy name thus much shall end!—/ I see thee not—I hear thee not—but none/ Can be so wrapt in thee; Thou art the Friend/ To whom the shadows of far years extend" (115). Readers generally have judged this conclusion arbitrary, but its suddenness indicates the profound appeal the image of the innocent child holds for Byron. As he muses on the delights which he has been denied of tending Ada's growth the reversal of their positions becomes apparent. It is not the prospect of supervising her ascent to maturity which seizes his imagination, but the hope that she might redeem him: "Fain would I waft such blessing upon thee,/ As—with a sigh—I deem thou might'st have been to me!" (118). As in Wordsworth's address to Dorothy at the close of "Tintern Abbey," this shift reveals beneath the overt affirmation a regressive wish. The possibilities brought by a daughter are that she paradoxically regenerates the desired situation in which he is restored by the mother figure in whom he needs to believe: "I know that thou wilt love me ... I know that thou wilt love me . . . Still thou would'st love me . . ." (117). The configuration of the father nourished by the daughter-mother shall be encountered more dramatically in Canto IV, and its revelation of a mind still obsessed by the past suggests why the forward-looking optimism on which Byron attempts to end could be for him only a vulnerable and impermanent *modus vivendi*. A poem of failure, however, is not a failed poem: *Childe Harold* III vividly dramatizes the desperate questionings of its author.

Manfred teaches more about the relationship in Byron's work of this period between "forgetfulness," with its two components of stern self-repression and desire to return to an earlier, untroubled stage of existence, and the role of women, or, to give the subject the broad context its complex development deserves, between Titanic aspiration and idealized harmony. The drama has profited less from the revaluation accorded Byron than one might have hoped. The formulation of E. H. Coleridge that "the motif of *Manfred* is remorse—eternal suffering for inexpiable crime" now appears too simple, but other categories limit apprehension of the play even as its stock rises.[6] For E. E. Bostetter and others the play depicts an existential dilemma and proffers a correspondingly existential resolution.[7] In his largely dismissive attitude Andrew Rutherford appears to stand at the opposite pole, but, in this like the favorable criticism, Rutherford assumes that *Manfred* is Byron's "supreme attempt to claim significance and value for the Byronic hero."[8] Rather, *Manfred* is the fullest manifestation of the psychological patterns already traced. Readings that seek to dignify Manfred into an existential hero misconstrue the drama, minimizing the turmoil that constitutes its affective power. Studies of the structure of the play apart from Byron's implication in it fail to convey that sense of uncontrollable pressures which is what engages the reader.[9] "My pang shall find a voice," Manfred exclaims (II, ii, 50), and that impulse to express the inner tensions of "alienation from within"[10] is the surest point of departure.

Yet the drama undeniably invites the grandiose terms applied to it. On the surface its pattern is that of the hero's quest. Defying the spirits he has evoked, Manfred in the very first scene arrogates to himself Promethean status:

Slaves, scoff not at my will!
The Mind—the Spirit—the Promethean spark,
The lightning of my being, is as bright,
Pervading, and far darting as your own,
And shall not yield to yours, though cooped in clay!
                                                        (I, i, 153–157)

Arcane researches and a darkly hinted violation of taboo, conversation with spirits and a descent into the underworld, combine to sound mythic resonances. Manfred's triumph over the infernal powers who demand his submission in the last scene seems to declare the absolute omnipotence of the human will. When Murray omitted Manfred's last line from the first edition Byron protested that he had "destroyed the whole effect & moral of the poem" (*BLJ* 5: 257). The line—"Old man! 'tis not so difficult to die"—is Manfred's assertion that he dies unconquered by any force, natural or supernatural. Like Prometheus, he contrives to surmount his oppressive situation.[11]

The play nonetheless exposes Manfred's boast. He is no Prometheus seeking a boon for mankind, but a ceaseless self-tormentor whose most insistent desire is absolution from the painful self-consciousness which is the Promethean heritage: "Forgetfulness—... Oblivion—self-oblivion!" (I, i, 135–144). Manfred's sorrows are private, not the paradigm of an unjust human condition. Byron called Manfred's speech to the sun "one of the best in the thing" (*BLJ* 5: 249), and the apostrophe depicts a benevolent nature:

Most glorious Orb! that wert a worship, ere
The mystery of thy making was revealed!
Thou earliest minister of the Almighty,
Which gladdened, on their mountain tops, the hearts
Of the Chaldean shepherds, till they poured
Themselves in orisons!
                                                        (III, ii, 9–14)

Though Manfred again and again bemoans the inability of nature to assuage his suffering, the fault is in him and not in nature.[12] Persistently counterpoised against the gloomily alienated figure who dominates the play are the innocence of the shepherds and the "humble virtues" of the Chamois Hunter (II, i, 63–73). Manfred beholds "pure vales" where "the patriarchal days are not/ A pastoral fable" (I, ii, 49–50). Society does not need redemption; Manfred alone, like Milton's Satan, is cut off from joy.

Byron's treatment of the Chamois Hunter who saves Manfred's life reveals the distortions inherent in existential interpretations of the drama. Manfred condescends to his rescuer, but the peasant stoutly refuses to be overawed:

> *Man.*   Preach [patience] to mortals of a dust like thine,—
>   I am not of thine order.
> *C. Hun.*   Thanks to Heaven!
>   I would not be of thine for the free fame
>   Of William Tell; but whatso'er thine ill,
>   It must be borne, and these wild starts are useless.
>   (II, i, 37-41)

The symbolic topography of the play supports the hunter. He comments that "My way of life leads me but rarely down" to the level of Manfred's castle, and that he habitually occupies higher reaches of the Alps than does Manfred is significant (II, i, 11). The mountains are emblems of Manfred's isolation, but because he dwells peacefully within their majesty they ennoble the hunter. He easily prevents Manfred's purposed suicide; in contrast to him Manfred is "all feebleness" and he tamely accepts the hunter as his guide (I, ii, 114–125).

It is important thus to emphasize the positive elements before which Byron stations Manfred because a proper understanding of the central conflict of the play depends upon recognition of the essential nature of the objects which he approaches with such wistfulness and defiance. The secondary characters do not create dramatic tension, but they are more than foils for the protagonist's self-revelation: they precisely define his dilemma.

Byron's pattern of setting Manfred in relief against other male figures culminates in the soliloquy which opens the last scene of the play. Manfred recalls a night he "stood within the Coliseum's wall,/ 'Midst the chief relics of almighty Rome":

> And thou didst shine, thou rolling Moon, upon
> All this, and cast a wide and tender light,
> Which softened down the hoar austerity
> Of rugged desolation, and filled up,
> As 'twere anew, the gaps of centuries;
> Leaving that beautiful which still was so,
> And making that which was not—till the place
> Became religion, and the heart ran o'er
> With silent worship of the Great of old,—

The dead, but sceptred, Sovereigns, who still rule
Our spirits from their urns.

(III, iv, 31–41)

This passage is usually dismissed as conventionally picturesque, but it merits longer attention.[13] The vision is a memory, and it is about memory; moreover, it is the only remembrance in the play which does not blast Manfred with remorse. He who sought only "forget-fulness" encounters Rome, the potent symbol of history, and bows before it. In the face of achievements that have survived the ages, assimilated to the natural forces which appear to erode them, he who proclaimed the omnipotence of his will acknowledges the sway of 'The dead, but sceptred, Sovereigns, who still rule/ Our spirits from their urns." In recognizing the supremacy of the "Great of old" Man-fred obliquely passes judgment on his own solipsism, and his death immediately thereafter confirms the bankruptcy of his Titanic preten-sions.

The new peace in Manfred's voice is purchased by this submis-sion. The legendary Caesars, mentioned three times in the first thirty lines of the soliloquy, are the inclusive symbol of the masculine au-thority to which he now bows. It may seem strange to suggest that one current of the action is Manfred's struggle to earn a place in the world of men, for the contest is indirect, and spectral; most impor-tant, Manfred is in effect defeated before the play begins. To phrase the issue in this way, however, emphasizes the ubiquitous and deci-sive presence of fathers, father figures, and ancestors in the drama. In Act III the servant Manuel contrasts Manfred unfavorably with his father, "whom he nought resembles":

> *Manuel.*   I speak not
> Of features or of form, but mind and habits;
> Count Sigismund was proud, but gay and free,—
> A warrior and a reveller; he dwelt not
> With books and solitude, nor made the night
> A gloomy vigil, but a festal time,
> Merrier than day; . . .
>
> (III, iii, 15–23)

Next to the vivid recollection of the "jocund times" of the former count Manfred seems shrunken, and the "patriarchal days" as-sociated with the Chamois Hunter hark back to the same richness of existence from which Manfred sadly feels himself to have declined. His scorn of the hunter springs from resentment at having had to be rescued: as with Gulnare's rescue of Conrad, the act reminds him of his inadequacy, and underscores his failure to achieve independence.

The Chamois Hunter is one of two older men who in the course of the action judge Manfred: the other is the Abbot. His analysis in Act III has the ring of authorial pronouncement; condemnation of Manfred is so absorbed in admiration and pity that Byron seems to be delicately placing the best possible construction on the characterological strains reflected in the play, describing himself to himself and making his apologia to the world:

> This should have been a noble creature: he
> Hath all the energy which would have made
> A goodly frame of glorious elements,
> Had they been wisely mingled; as it is,
> It is an awful chaos—Light and Darkness—
> And mind and dust—and passions and pure thoughts,
> Mixed, and contending without end or order,—
> All dormant or destructive.
>
> > (III, i, 160–167)

The inner frustration and outer torpor repeat a malady familiar from the tales and *Childe Harold* III, and the reader's interest in the accurate diagnosis is increased by Byron's choice of speaker: the Byronic hero is once more confronted by an older male figure of solid personal authority.

The solicitous Abbot by his very strengths exacerbates the self-doubt Manfred tries to conceal under a show of bravado. In a scene which in configuration and tone virtually duplicates the final confession of the Giaour to a monk, Manfred acknowledges to the Abbot the failure of his hope to have been the benefactor of mankind:

> Aye—father! I have had those early visions,
> And noble aspirations in my youth,
> To make my own the mind of other men,
> The enlightener of nations; . . .
>
> > (III, i, 104–107)

Manfred rationalizes his disappointment by a prickly integrity—"I could not tame my nature down; for he/ Must serve who fain would sway" (III, i, 116–117)—but the grandiloquent manner does not disguise the lack of accomplishment; indeed, the excess of the contempt toward worldly achievement suggests rather its continuing appeal. The Abbot presses Manfred until he is forced to admit the utter sterility of his arrogance:

> *Abbot.*   And why not live and act with other men?
> *Man.*   Because my nature was averse from life;
>   And yet not cruel; for I would not make,
>   But find a desolation. Like the Wind,
>   The red-hot breath of the most lone Simoom,
>   Which dwells but in the desert, and sweeps o'er
>   The barren sands which bear no shrubs to blast,
>   And revels o'er their wild and arid waves,
>   And seeketh not, so that it is not sought,
>   But being met is deadly,—such hath been
>   The course of my existence; . . .
>   (III, i, 116–134)

The simile equates ocean and desert as emblems of a psychological wasteland.[14] Since in the great address which completes *Childe Harold* Byron hails the ocean as the primal, vital "Image of Eternity" (IV, 183), the equivalence is at first surprising, but in both works the image of ocean is coordinate with the presence or absence of nurturing womanly energies: here therefore it can connote only infertility. In his initial speech Manfred declares: "Good—or evil—life—/ Powers, passions—all I see in other beings,/ Have been to me as rain unto the sands,/ Since that all-nameless hour" (I, i, 21–24). Though his predicament is unchanging from the start of the play, it is the paternal Abbot who reduces Manfred to this bitterly reductive account of himself, the fullest confession that his vaunts of self-sufficiency are hollow. Manfred perfectly comprehends his situation, but without Astarte he does not possess the resources to change it, and the prideful rhetoric cannot eclipse the greater substance of the Abbot.

A brief consideration of the compositional history of *Manfred* refines insight into his role. In the third act as Byron originally wrote it he is a narrow and grasping figure who threatens Manfred with damnation unless he donates his lands to the church. Manfred responds to this attempted extortion by having the Abbot carried off to a mountain peak by one of the devils in his command, who disappears with him while singing anticlerical doggerel. This crude business is "certainly d——d bad" (*BLJ* 5: 211), as Byron was ready enough to agree when it was criticized by his publisher, but the conception is significant. The caricature of the Abbot suggests that Byron, frustrations aggravated by the soul-wearying distractions of a Venetian Carnival and an ensuing fever, found violent debasement the sole recourse in answering the reproaches the Abbot embodies, while his removal by the devil seems a patently wish-fulfilling victory over a force too imposing for Byron to contemplate without fantasy. From the frenzy of the repudiation the magnitude of the imagined threat is inferred. In the revisions made some weeks later the Abbot "is become a good man," as Byron told Murray (*BLJ* 5: 219), but even in his final shape the traces of the dominant father before whom Manfred must prove himself can be discerned.[15]

Deeper than the anxieties reflected by the male figures in *Manfred* are those revolving around Astarte. It is obvious that she is the source of Manfred's despair, but to advance beyond the obvious asks careful discrimination. In an understandable effort to circumvent the scandalmongering that befuddled earlier interpretations, criticism has tended lately to minimize the importance of incest in the drama.[16] In so doing it has underemphasized the role of Astarte, for she stands at the heart of the drama, although in terms different from those which shocked Byron's contemporaries. Guilt for the commission of sin is not what eats at Manfred, however; incest is mentioned only twice in the play (II, i, 27; III, iii, 44–47), and it occupies a much less prominent place than Manfred's remorse for the death of Astarte, for which he bears the guilt but was not responsible (II, ii, 117–121). It is this paradox which should be investigated.

The vague introduction of Astarte in the first scene, indicating neither her name nor her relationship to Manfred, illustrates that she has symbolic value beyond biographical reference. Manfred asks the "most powerful" of the spirits he has summoned to assume "such aspect/ As unto him may seem most fitting," and the Seventh Spirit then appears as "a beautiful female figure." This spirit has before described himself as Manfred's personal fate:

> The Star which rules thy destiny
> Was ruled, ere earth began, by me:
> It was a World as fresh and fair
> As e'er revolved round Sun in air;
> Its course was free and regular,

Space bosomed not a lovelier star.
The Hour arrived—and it became
A wandering mass of shapeless flame,
A pathless Comet, and a curse,
The menace of the Universe;
Still rolling on with innate force,
Without a sphere, without a course,
A bright deformity on high,
The monster of the upper sky!

(I, i, 110–123)

The imagery of this speech has gone largely unnoticed. The first sentence associates the conventional language of cosmic harmony with feminine, generative, energies: "fresh," "fair," "bosomed," "lovelier." After the unspecified disaster the "free and regular" star is transformed into a monstrous "pathless Comet" "rolling on with innate force" which recalls the self-consuming will of Napoleon and Byron's Titans generally. The speech looks back nostalgically from the sterile masculine world of the present to a peacefully fostering feminine world.

In requesting "forgetfulness" from the spirits Manfred expresses a desire to reverse the progression outlined by the Seventh Spirit, in effect to undo the being he has become. Ironically, the spirits offer instead total recall: "We are immortal, and do not forget;/ We are eternal, and to us the past/ Is, as the future, present" (I, i, 149–151). Memory recalls to Manfred the happy state which he passionately wants to re-enter, but because the return is impossible the memory tortures him. His vision of the beautiful female figure for whom he yearns confirms that he longs for death only to end this cruel frustration; his true desire is for her: "Oh God! if it be thus, and *thou*/ Art not a madness and a mockery,/ I yet might be most happy" (I, i, 188–190). When she vanishes, he faints, and the swoon literalizes his predicament: deprived of her life-giving power, he is inert. The incantation which follows condemns Manfred to suffer the pains of his own hypocrisy and guile, but since these charges are not borne out by any subsequent evidence they must be understood as an externalization of Manfred's self-accusations.[17] By the end of the scene, then, the two chief components of Manfred's character have been presented: his desire for the woman affiliated with the past on whom he depends for healthful life, and the "cold breast" and "shut soul" for which he currently reproaches himself.

Manfred's interview with the Witch of the Alps, whom he calls up after having quit the Chamois Hunter, elaborates the connection between his icy control and his regressive wishes. Their meeting is set beneath a rainbow, the symbol of the covenant between man and God, and Manfred invokes the "Beautiful Spirit" in images that combine purity and fecundity:

> . . .the hues of youth—
> *Carnationed like a sleeping Infant's cheek,*
> *Rocked by the beating of her mother's heart,*
> Or the rose tints, which Summer's twilight leaves
> Upon the lofty Glacier's virgin snow,
> The blush of earth embracing with her Heaven,—
> Tinge thy celestial aspect, and make tame
> The beauties of the Sunbow which bends o'er thee.
> (II, ii, 17–24; italics added)

The simile unfolds the tableau whose myriad afterimages are seen throughout Byron's work, affecting testimony that the core of Manfred's grief is a re-enactment of the child's loss of the all-protective mother. The witch, like Astarte whom she duplicates, is a projection of Manfred's desire for the vanished security of the maternal embrace. Her serene maternal presence enables Manfred to unburden himself, and elicits from him the first history of his plight:

> From my youth upwards
> My spirit walked not with the souls of men,
> Nor looked upon the earth with human eyes;
> The thirst of their ambition was not mine,
> The aim of their existence was not mine,
> My joys—my griefs—my passions—and my powers,
> Made me a stranger; though I wore the form,
> I had no sympathy with breathing flesh,
> Nor midst the Creatures of Clay that girded me
> Was there but One who—but of her anon.
> (II, ii, 50–59)

So far from being the cause of Manfred's isolation, Astarte represents his one link with humanity; as Manuel tells Herman, she was 'The sole companion of his wanderings/ And watchings—her, whom of all earthly things/ That lived, the only thing he seemed to love . . ." (III, iii, 43–45). This extraordinary intimacy parallels the situation of the child who sees the world through the mediation of his mother; the ''Blest Babe'' passage in Book II of *The Prelude* is a helpful analogue to clarify the nature of the communion Manfred remembers. In his earliest days the infant does not distinguish between "self" and "other," so it is not surprising that in memory Astarte should appear to Manfred as an idealized extension of himself:

> She was like me in lineaments—her eyes—
> Her hair—her features—all, to the very tone
> Even of her voice, they said were like to mine;
> But softened all, and tempered into beauty:
> She had the same lone thoughts and wanderings,
> The quest of hidden knowledge, and a mind
> To comprehend the Universe: nor these
> Alone, but with them gentler powers than mine,
> Pity and smiles, and tears—which I had not;
> And tenderness—but that I had for her;
> Humility—and that I never had.
>
> (II, ii, 105–115)

Basing their interpretations on this portrait, critics have always treated Astarte as a wholly ideal figure, but it is necessary to separate her intrinsic qualities from her function in Manfred's life. The conclusion of his dialogue with the Witch reveals the threatening implications of the mother figure. The witch replies to Manfred's narrative of his miseries by offering assistance:

> *Witch.*   It may be
> That I can aid thee.
> *Man.*   To do this thy power
> Must wake the dead, or lay me low with them
> Do so—in any shape—in any hour
> With any torture—so it be the last.
> *Witch.* That is not in my province; but if thou
> Wilt swear obedience to my will, and do
> My bidding, it may help thee to thy wishes.
> *Man.* I will not swear—Obey! and whom? the Spirits
> Whose presence I command, and be the slave
> Of those who served me—Never!
>
> (II, ii, 150–159)

Manfred remains adamant despite her hope of a "gentler answer," and his refusal discloses the psychological impasse in which he is trapped. Two related strands of motivation converge in Manfred's vehement denial. Bereft of maternal support, Manfred feels himself too impoverished to be able to give, and because he cannot give, he reacts to any emotional demand made on him by another as if he were in danger of being swallowed up. The witch's sudden insistence on a vow of obedience suggests that the episode is the vehicle of its creator's fears of losing autonomy if he succumbs to the bliss he most desires: when the seductive witch offers him the chance of happiness, Manfred perceives it as the negation of his manhood. He is caught in the dilemma adumbrated in the tales: like the child, he wishes to remain with the mother, but his adult status is predicated precisely on his ability to leave her and establish his independence. To move into the world of men he must reject her, and in so doing he appears to himself to acquire the "cold breast" and "shut soul" for which Manfred feels guilty.

The scorning of the witch shows Manfred's pride to be the outer manifestation of his backward-facing longings. After such a cul-de-sac he can only descend to the underworld and parley with the dead, and in the final scene of Act II Manfred directly encounters the Phantom of Astarte. His six-times-reiterated plea, "Speak to me," affirms that his original request for "oblivion" was only a desperate substitute for his true desire, forgiveness:

> *Man.* Yet one word more—am I forgiven?
> *Phan.* Farewell!
> *Man.*   Say, shall we meet again?
> *Phan.*   Farewell!
> *Man.* One word for mercy! Say thou lovest me.
> *Phan.* Manfred! [*The spirit of Astarte disappears.*]
>   (II, iv, 152–154)

Astarte announces Manfred's impending death, but does not pardon him. What Manfred wants to be forgiven for is the masculine adult behavior which he values so ambivalently: proud of his authority, yet conscious that his will cannot restore the harmony he prizes and that each exercise of it takes him further from the oneness he knew with Astarte. It is a commonplace of the psychological literature already cited that children often interpret the death of a parent as retribution for some imagined sin of their own, and so it is that Manfred assumes the responsibility for Astarte's death as if his growing away from her were an act of murder. Because he is determined to persist in his independence his growth to manhood is an action for which he cannot imagine forgiveness. It is harshly apposite that Nemesis be the agent to resurrect Astarte, since by continually rejecting the maternal embrace Manfred nullifies the redemptive power of the virtues he attributes to her, while enshrining them as the painful reminders of a wilfully abandoned paradise.

Manfred welcomes the annunciation of his death as "grace" (II, iv, 166) and the anticipated release from his frustrations produces at the opening of Act III a note of resignation unheard before: "Inexplicable stillness! which till now/ Did not belong to what I knew of life" (III, i, 7–8). Astarte's tacit withdrawal from him is the obverse of his arrogant refusal of the Witch of the Alps, and this definitive rejection of the mother is followed by the submission to the masculine forces Manfred acknowledges in his memory of Rome. Michael Cooke has written that "Manfred becomes a hero less for what he can do than for what he can do without," but in the last act he seems to me more exhausted than heroic.[18] Manfred's rejections mark the rhythm of the play: of the Spirits, of the Chamois Hunter, of the Witch of the Alps, of the Destinies, and of the Abbot. Each repudiation prepares the next more fundamental one, and each reduces Manfred more severely than its precursor. He defines his position with ever-increasing sharpness, but the process simultaneously guarantees that the stasis which threatens him will become total.

From his first speech Manfred's consciousness is entirely retrospective: "I have essayed . . . I have done men good . . . I have had my foes. . . ." His quest for oblivion is in part a quest for absolution from the past necessary if he is to move forward: "The future, till the past be gulfed in darkness,/ It is not of my search" (I, ii, 6–7). By proposing the quest in terms of "forgetfulness," however, Manfred entails upon himself the worst alienation, the alienation from his own history. He is spared this consequence by confessing that it is rather forgiveness he seeks, but his assertiveness prevents the second formulation from being any more fruitful for him than the first.

Torn by remorse for the very qualities of daring which distinguish him, Manfred is paralyzed. He knows that in his radically subjective world the flow of time and the sense of life are measured by human action:

> Think'st thou existence doth depend on time?
> It doth; but actions are our epochs: mine
> Have made my days and nights imperishable,

> Endless, and all alike, as sands on the shore,
> Innumerable atoms; and one desert,
> Barren and cold, on which the wild waves break,
> But nothing rests, save carcasses and wrecks,
> Rocks, and the salt-surf weeds of bitterness.
>
> (II, i, 51–58)

Only fresh actions can liberate Manfred, but actions require motives and imply objects or others, and these Manfred's fixation on the irrecoverable harmony of infancy systematically eliminates. One way Manfred destroys the past, the other way he precludes a future. The present remains, but the present has been inevitably degraded into an eternity of lifelessness. The two faces of his desire, aspiration and memory, combine to diminish the value of the here-and-now: as he declares, "In life there is no present" (II, ii, 172). Hence the distortion in Manfred's sense of time: great urgency joined to the loss of all sense of time as a medium for living.[19] The Hamlet whom Manfred echoes and who provides the epigraph to the play is finally a hero not only because he perceives and reflects, but also because he cleanses Denmark of the corruption which infects it.[20] Manfred, cut off from valid action, loses even the physical glamor of Byron's earlier protagonists. W. P. Elledge is right to conclude that "in the vacuum of Manfred's selfhood our traditional interpretations of 'triumph' and 'defeat' are altogether meaningless,"[21] but it is one of the achievements of the play to set forth the psychological grounds of that appalling vacuum.

Unlike the heroes of the tales, Manfred does not compete against a man for a woman: that the struggles of the play are largely two-body rather than triangular marks the depth of their roots. The crisis at the center of *Manfred* reaches back to the crisis of separation and individuation.[22] Manfred does not so much seek for Astarte as a separate, independent being as he searches for a state prior to identity, the state in which mother and child form one organic unit. Astarte is an ideal, mirror image, a reflection in which the self can discover and ground itself, or, in this instance more accurately, a vision of wholeness imagined by a being in discord.[23] It is clear, however, that in these terms Manfred's quest for Astarte can only be, literally, self-defeating: the symbiotic reunion with Astarte Manfred desires so intensely would be the annulment of his individuality, the death of the self. To end the pain of separate identity is his goal: to fuse with another, or to die, are but different avenues to the same

destination. Manfred exists only in this tension between two funda-
mentally identical alternatives: within this static, closed system no
development is possible. His dilemma proceeds from the shattering
of an independent identity that his yearning for Astarte reveals, a
dilemma whose consequences Byron works out with rigorous com-
pleteness. The "character" to which Manfred clings is the substitute
for this lack, the grandeur of one who, incapable of advance, can only
choose to die in his own way.[24]

One objection to the argument that the bottommost stratum of
Manfred reveals mother-centered conflicts of dependence and autonomy, and beneath that of separation and individuation, may here
be anticipated. Manfred implies that Astarte shared in his "crime":

> Thou lovedst me
> Too much, as I loved thee: we were not made
> To torture thus each other—though it were
> The deadliest sin to love as we have loved.
> Say that thou loath'st me not—that I do bear
> This punishment for both—...
>
> (II, iv, 120–125)

The passage seems inapplicable to the mother-son relationship, and
firmly supports the traditional reading that in Manfred's love for Astarte Byron offers a disguised account of his love for Augusta. A
probable affair with Augusta is indeed the immediate cause of *Manfred*, but throughout his time in England Byron sought in his half
sister the warmth and stable affection of which he felt deprived by his
mother. From the first Augusta was for Byron a substitute object who
might compensate for the terrible pressures Mrs. Byron placed on
him, and sibling incest in the drama contains unmistakable evidences
of prior conflicts. The representation of Astarte as having died and
her silence in reply to Manfred's appeals for forgiveness argue that
interwoven in the drama is the remorse Byron experienced at the
death of his mother. Manfred's unremitting sense of guilt for a death
he had no part in reflects Byron's guilt for a death he too had no part
in, except in wishful fantasies. These exacted their price in the unconscious when they were unexpectedly realized.

The nature of the conflict itself is the fundamental evidence of the
traces of the mother in *Manfred*, but the secondary testimony of biography corroborates the interpretation. The maternal character which
tinges Byron's sexual attachments throughout his life is pronounced

in the period between his mother's death and the composition of *Manfred*. The predilection of Lady Caroline Lamb for page's livery has never gone unnoticed in discussions of her tumultuous affair with Byron in 1812, but that detail is less important to a consideration of her appeal for Byron than the hysterical strain generally permeating her conduct. Byron tired of her instability, but it was not without gratification: her lack of self-control assured him of his greater competence and reliability. He painted himself as he wished to be in the brilliant correspondence describing the affair to Caroline's mother-in-law, Lady Melbourne: the reasonable, patient man superior to the shrill entreaties of a ridiculous woman. In Lady Melbourne, already past sixty, Byron found the wise and indulgent older woman in whom he could confide intimately without risk of entanglement. His sense of loss lent its force to their friendship, as it did to the liaison with the forty-year-old Lady Oxford which succeeded that with Caroline. " 'I never felt a stronger passion,' " Byron later said to Medwin of Lady Oxford, " 'which she returned with equal ardour. I was as fond of, indeed more attached than I ought to have been, to one who had bestowed her favours on many. . . . Strange as it may seem, she gained (as all women do) an influence over me so strong, that I had great difficulty in breaking with her, even when I knew she had been inconstant to me; and once was on the point of going abroad with her,—and narrowly escaped this folly.' "[25]

Lady Oxford sailed from England without Byron at the end of June 1813, before a planned farewell meeting of the lovers could take place. It was at this moment of renewed loneliness that Augusta re-entered Byron's life. For almost a decade she had been the object of his warmest feelings, but he had not seen her since going abroad in 1809. Married for six years already to Colonel George Leigh, Augusta now came up to London to escape in the company of her celebrated half brother the worries heaped high by three unwell children and the improvidence of her husband. For the first time Augusta and Byron had the pleasure of extended contact, their natural delight in rediscovered affinities intensified by circumstances. They saw each other daily for three weeks; when Augusta returned to her home at Six Mile Bottom Byron soon paid her two visits of several days each. After the second of these he brought her back to London with him; by August 5 he was talking again of going abroad—his intended companion, Augusta (*BLJ* 3: 85). Before the end of the month he was hinting to Lady Melbourne and others that the relationship had developed into incest. On the vexed question of whether it had actually done so, acrimoniously debated for a hundred and fifty years, the judicious comment of Leslie Marchand must be taken as the final word: "All that can be said is that the circumstantial evidence in Byron's letters can not be ignored, and that certain aspects of his life and correspondence can not be explained sensibly in any other terms."[26] Of the historical actuality there may yet be some doubters, but of the overwhelming psychological reality of Byron's involvement with his half sister, conditioned as it was by his whole life thus far, there can be no denial.

It was partly to extricate himself from the anxieties of this everdeepening affair with Augusta that Byron turned his thoughts to marriage: "She wished me much to marry," he wrote Lady Melbourne, "because it was the only chance of redemption for *two* persons" (*BLJ* 4: 191). No solution could have been more taxing upon the fragile defenses Byron had erected against his fears of maternal suffocation. The particular choice of Annabella Milbanke increased the burden hundredfold, and the fateful quality of the choice marks the strength of the psychic patterns which influenced it. The complacent self-righteousness which Byron mercilessly satirized after the separation constituted much of Annabella's original attraction. A woman so ostentatiously virtuous could scarcely pose a threat, especially not one who virtually signalled her indifference by refusing an offer of marriage, as Annabella did in rejecting Byron's initial proposal in 1812.

When, to his surprise, a second, tentative exploration was treated as a definite proposal and accepted in September 1814, Byron displayed the misgivings which the fears of engulfment reflected in his poems might lead us to expect. Delaying with pretext upon pretext, reluctant to divide himself from Augusta and hesitant to be thus committed, Byron stalled the wedding. He lingered in London until December 24 before setting out for Seaham, his fiancée's home. Hobhouse, who made the journey with him, recorded his friend's unloverlike lack of impatience and "almost aversion." On the day of the ceremony, January 2, 1815, Byron awakened "with the most melancholy reflections, on seeing his wedding-suit spread out before him."[27]

Once wed, Byron was driven to a course of behavior which seems to us, and seemed to him, as laid out in advance as his wedding-suit. Tenderness toward Annabella was followed by icy withdrawal or deliberate insult, as if only by that means could he be sure of his mastery. He ceaselessly baited his unfortunately humorless bride with Augusta, flaunting their closeness; the motive seems less outward, the infliction of pain on Annabella, than inward, the assertion of unbroken fidelity to the mother figure represented by Augusta. All Byron's conflicts of dependence and autonomy inevitably converged on Annabella, and the compulsion to re-enact the model of his parents' marriage inflamed the situation still further. The drama proceeded to its agonizing conclusion: in January 1816 Annabella left London with her infant daughter, Augusta Ada. Byron had sadly conspired against himself to produce the abandonment he suffered; in April he sought relief on the Continent, as his father had done. As Byron candidly confessed in a poem to his sister after the accumulating storms had broken at last: "I have been cunning in mine overthrow,/ The careful pilot of my proper woe" ("Epistle to Augusta," 23–24).

From this complex of originally mother-centered tensions, reactivated by Augusta and Annabella, *Manfred* grows. In the last scene of the play Manfred earns his death by conquering the spirits who claim him. The climactic negation is more flamboyant but less substantial than another element of the scene: the respect symbolized by the handclasp between Manfred and the Abbot who shares his final moments. The fragile parity established by that gesture marks an acceptance by the world of men which is Manfred's true, if brief, victory. With the world of women Manfred can reach no similar accommodation. Sundered from Astarte, on whom he utterly depends, it is indeed "not difficult" for Manfred to die: it is really all he can do. While he too sought to bury his past in "oblivion" Byron was equally paralyzed.

The stagnation which envelops and ultimately chokes the exercise of the hero's will is apparent also in two poems contemporary with *Manfred*. Bonnivard, the protagonist of *The Prisoner of Chillon*, explains at the outset of the tale the cause of his imprisonment:

> But this was for my father's faith
> I suffered chains and courted death;
> That father perished at the stake
> For tenets he would not forsake;
> And for the same his lineal race
> In darkness found a dwelling place; . . .

> (11–16)

The substitution of the singular "father's" in the common generic expression "fathers' faith," like Francesca's rebuke of Alp in *The Siege of Corinth* for having renounced his "father's creed" (576), emphasizes a muted familial configuration which connects this story to its forerunners: the suffering son crushed by the father he emulates.

Bonnivard is one of seven brothers, but the paternal legacy has already claimed four of the boys, "dying as their father died," before the tale begins. Two others succumb during its course; first the familiar hunter-warrior figure "formed to combat with his kind"; then the youngest:

> ... the favourite and the flower,
> Most cherished since his natal hour,
> His mother's image in fair face,
> The infant love of all his race,
> His martyred father's dearest thought,
> My latest care, for whom I sought
> To hoard my life, that his might be
> Less wretched now, and one day free; ...
>
> (164–171)

To the perishing boy Bonnivard stands *in loco parentis*, and his inability to preserve his life adds to his woes as son the frustrations of a father whose line is extinguished.

The mood of debility is a worsening of the weakness of the heroes in the tales: Bonnivard's incarceration embodies in severer form the same psychological materials as Conrad in Seyd's prison and the Giaour in the monastery. The imaginative heart of the poem is not the ideal of Liberty celebrated as the "Eternal Spirit of the chainless Mind!" in the prefatory sonnet, but Byron's depiction of Bonnivard's increasing apathy. He greets the arbitrary release he is finally accorded with pathetic reluctance:

> At last men came to set me free;
>   I asked not why, and recked not where;
> It was at length the same to me,
> Fettered or fetterless to be.
>   I learned to love despair.
> And thus when they appeared at last,
> And all my bonds aside were cast,
> These heavy walls to me had grown

> A hermitage—and all my own!
> And half I felt as they were come
> To tear me from a second home:...
>
> (372–380)

"My very chains and I grew friends," Bonnivard confesses, in words that belie the affirmation of the sonnet. The cell that encloses him "below the surface of the lake" has become an appealing retreat from the world of men—a womb, though a forbidding one. Bonnivard's dungeon and Manfred's tower, enforced imprisonment and voluntary isolation, stoic endurance and Titanic assertiveness, are revealed as two faces of the same sterile arrest. Bonnivard is separated from the energies of nature by a barred window, an emblem of the isolated self-consciousness starker even than the parallel representations in *Childe Harold* III and *Manfred*. The self-control Bonnivard achieves is, like Manfred's, a minimal triumph, but it enables him to relate his misfortunes as none of Byron's earlier protagonists can. The moving restraint of his narrative counteracts in the reader's estimation his immobility and tacit admission of defeat. His successful self-presentation draws value out of personal disaster, a transformation that is like Byron's desperate appeal to art for the power to reshape his limited self and circumstances into a more desirable image.

The intimate relationship existing in Byron's mind between artistic endeavor and the role of women is suggested by *The Lament of Tasso*. Like Bonnivard, Tasso is imprisoned, and Byron follows the legends in attributing his confinement to his love for Leonora d'Este. As his phrase for her suggests, the "Sister of my Sovereign" (106) to whom Byron imagines Tasso's fervent devotion is a figure blending sororal and maternal features. The history Tasso gives places the source of his idealization of Leonora in the solitary reveries he enjoyed as "a truant boy" (160):

> And with my years my soul began to pant
> With feelings of strange tumult and soft pain;
> And the whole heart exhaled into One Want,
> But undefined and wandering, till the day
> I found the thing I sought—and that was thee;
> And then I lost my being, all to be
> Absorbed in thine;—the world was past away;—
> *Thou* didst annihilate the earth to me!
>
> (166–173)

Tasso's self-liquidating absorption in Leonora parallels Manfred's dependence on Astarte, and other links are evident too. "A Princess was no love-mate for a bard" (124), Tasso laments, and the next line reveals that in the thoughts animating Byron's verse *lèse-majesté* is infused with oedipal prohibitions. "I told it not—I breathed it not," continues Tasso, and editors since E. H. Coleridge have caught the echo of the "Stanzas for Music" in which Byron expressed his remorseful love for Augusta: "I speak not, I trace not, I breathe not thy name . . . ."

Byron portrays Tasso occupying the time of his imprisonment with *Jerusalem Delivered,* finding in composition "wings wherewith to overfly/ The narrow circus of my dungeon wall" (22–23). The epic becomes for him a compensation for unrequited love, and he refers to it as a "long-sustaining Friend" in words which mark a second occurrence of the motif of the redemptive daughter. The poem serves for him as Ada serves for Byron in *Childe Harold* III: "But thou, my young creation! my Soul's child!/ Which ever playing round me came and smiled,/ And wooed me from myself with thy sweet sight . . ." (37–39). However, Tasso has completed the poem, and, prevented for many years from seeing Leonora, he confesses a "taint" of "infection" from "a den like this,/ Where the mind rots congenial with the abyss" (234–235). The sense of claustrophobic restriction and loss and the therapeutic poetic activity Byron ascribes to Tasso reflect his own condition and stratagems. Whether narrated in Byron's voice or put in the mouths of dramatic characters, the common denominator of all these poems is the painful feeling of incompletion experienced by men cut off from women. A potential remedy emerges in art, for Byron an approximation of the energies he associates with women and a means of dealing with the anxieties they cause in him.

Byron begins Canto IV of *Childe Harold* by announcing Harold's demise: "With regard to the conduct of the last canto, there will be found less of the pilgrim than in any of the preceding, and that little slightly, if at all, separated from the author speaking in his own person. The fact is, that I had become weary of drawing a line which everyone seemed determined not to perceive. . . ." He continues:

> It was in vain that I asserted, and imagined that I had drawn, a distinction between the author and the pilgrim; and the very anxiety to

preserve this difference, and disappointment at finding it unavailing, so far crushed my efforts in the composition, that I determined to abandon it altogether—and have done so.

The intensity of the language shows that Byron's "anxiety to preserve" the distinction between author and pilgrim had been a psychological necessity as well as a formal device. In rejecting the strategy and conceding its failure Byron gains a simpler structure, but a less dramatic one; moreover, by sacrificing the shelter of his fictional alter ego he more deeply implicates himself. The loss of distance increases the temptation to construct a pleasing picture of his situation, an account of himself attractive in his eyes and in those of the censorious world—in short, to convert the man Byron, in some degree culpable for the scandals which surround him, into the myth of Byron the noble, unjustly wronged outcast, more sinned against than sinning.[28] The spectacular success of the later cantos of *Childe Harold* and their hold on the European mind for the remainder of the century are genuine testimony to the magisterial authority of Byron's invented self. At the same time, the public stance of intimacy intensifies the urgency of the feelings of hurt which generated the poem, and hence the oscillations between hope and despair grow more violent.

Byron seizes on Rome as the replacement of the England he lost, greeting the city as the goal of his pilgrimage:

> Oh, Rome, my Country! City of the Soul!
> The *orphans* of the heart must turn to thee,
> Lone *Mother* of dead Empires! and control
> In their shut breasts their petty misery.
> (78; italics added)

Even more than in the praise of Venice as the queen of cities with which Byron opens the canto, one feels in this apostrophe the force his private yearnings add to the customary feminine personification. The appeal the image of the child reunited with its mother held for Byron speaks out through the conventional language. Yet, as it was in *Manfred*, Rome is also an emblem of the world of men. The city, where one cannot move without "stumbling o'er recollections" (81), is the epitome of history—that is, of man's strife. Only if Byron can enclose the masculine aspects the city presents to his imagination within a purely benevolent framework can it prove nurturing.

Meditating on Napoleon and the collapse of the French Revolution into a perpetuation of the evils it sought to end, Byron is led to a bitter generalization upon mankind "rotting from sire to son":

> Bequeathing their hereditary rage
> To the new race of inborn slaves, who wage
> War for their chains, and rather than be free,
> Bleed gladiator-like, and still engage
> Within the same Arena where they see
> Their fellows fall before, like leaves of the same tree.
>
> (94)

Gladiatorial combat is the paradigm of Byron's view of history as an infinite series of "second falls" caused by "vile Ambition" (97), and the motives of self-regarding pride and hyperassertive will he discerns in history are congruent with his own oedipal resentments. His erratic progress from this nadir toward resolution is extraordinarily revelatory of his anxieties and desires.

Byron devotes five stanzas to the tomb of Cecilia Metella, whom he conjectures as "surviving all,/ Charms—kindred—children" (103), and the vision of her serene old age calms him by recalling his own happier past. Nonetheless, this surmise of maternal peace is disrupted by another bleak prospect of the *"one* page" on which the conflicts of history repeat themselves (108). These mutually exclusive alternatives are briefly reconciled in the legend of Egeria, for the nymph's love of the consul Numa illustrates the penetration of the saving feminine powers into the merciless world of men (115–118).

The example of fulfilled love contrasts too strongly for Byron with the misery of his marriage and calls forth a categorical denial of the possibility of love. The mood reverses once more:

> Alas! our young affections run to waste,
> Or water but the desert! whence arise
> But weeds of dark luxuriance, tares of haste,
> Rank at the core, though tempting to the eyes,
> Flowers whose wild odours breathe but agonies,
> And trees whose gums are poison; such the plants
> Which spring beneath her steps as Passion flies
> O'er the World's wilderness, and vainly pants
> For some celestial fruit forbidden to our wants.
>
> (120)

The rebound from the hysterical disappointment vented in this and succeeding stanzas strengthens Byron's idealization of the period anterior to adult sexuality. The heavy emphasis on "young affections" and the conceptions of "boyhood" which shape our lives, rising to the climactic outburst of "we wither from our youth" (124), expresses a regressive wish that is no mere commonplace of maturity.

The complex interweaving of the objects of Byron's resentments is suggested by a pregnant allusion in the passage beginning at stanza 132. He invokes Nemesis to punish his victimizers:

> And Thou, who never yet of human wrong
> Left the unbalanced scale, great Nemesis!
> Here, where the ancient paid thee homage long—
> Thou, who didst call the Furies from the abyss,
> And round Orestes bade them howl and hiss
> For that unnatural retribution—just,
> Had it but been from hands less near—in this
> Thy former realm, I call thee from the dust!
> Dost thou not hear my heart?—Awake! thou shalt, and must.
>
> (132)

Byron regularly called Lady Byron "a moral Clytemnestra," after the separation, and it is the apprehension of himself as a treacherously confounded Agamemnon that evokes the figure of the avenging Orestes. The link the allusion forges between Byron's anger at his spouse and matricide manifests the underlying conflation in his mind of wife with mother.

Two stanzas later Byron threatens to "pile on human heads the mountain of my curse," but the anticipated anathema issues in unexpected form: "That curse shall be Forgiveness" (135). A deleted stanza makes clear the vindictive impulses surviving beneath the proclamation of charity: "If to forgive be 'heaping coals of fire'/ As God hath spoken—on the heads of foes/ Mine should be a volcano— ...." The invocation of Nemesis thus enables Byron to mask his resentments: by transferring them to an impersonal "dread Power" he can assume the morally impeccable pose of having personally renounced vengeance. The magical verbal conjuring discharges anger while pretending to maintain his superiority to spite.

The speciousness of this familiar psychological ruse and its essential identity with the cyclical recriminations Byron denounces in history are betrayed by the immediate recurrence of the gladiator. Byron

imagines him as listening to "the inhuman shout" of the Roman
crowd at his death:

> He heard it, but he heeded not—his eyes
> Were with his heart—and that was far away;
> He recked not of the life he lost nor prize,
> But where his rude hut on the Danube lay—
> *There* were his young barbarians all at play,
> *There* was their Dacian mother—he, their sire,
> Butchered to make a Roman holiday —
> All this rushed with his blood—Shall he expire
> And unavenged?—Arise! ye Goths, and glut your ire!
>
> But here, where Murder breathed her bloody stream;—
> And here, where buzzing nations choked the ways,
> And roared or murmured like a mountain stream
> Dashing or winding as its torrent strays;
> Here, where the Roman million's blame or praise
> Was Death or Life—the playthings of a crowd—
> My voice sounds much—and fall the stars' faint rays
> On the arena void—seats crushed—walls bowed—
> And galleries, where my steps seem echoes strangely loud.
>
> (141–142)

This passage scarcely needs more comment than it has already received, but it should be noted how the vision of mother and child
Byron associates with the suffering warrior repeats his own obsession. Furthermore, the call to revenge for the Goth, which in history
produced the fall of Rome and the desolation he views around him,
parallels the appeal Byron has just covertly expressed for himself. The
revelation of the futility of vengeance in history hints equally at its
futility for the self.

Release from the destructive round on the levels both of history
and of the self comes a few stanzas later. The agent is the story of the
Roman daughter who feeds from her breast the father with whom she
is imprisoned, a story much enriched with the energy of Byron's
fantasies. "I see them full and plain," he declares, and the emphasis
on evoking and presenting is typical of the effort Byron makes in the
canto to give wish the physical substance of reality. "I see them full
and plain—/ An old man, and a female young and fair,/ Fresh as a
nursing mother" (148):

> ... Youth offers to Old Age the food,
> The milk of his own gift: it is her Sire
> To whom she renders back the debt of blood
> Born with her birth:—No—he shall not expire
> While in those warm and lovely veins the fire
> Of health and holy feeling can provide
> Great Nature's Nile, whose deep stream rises higher
> Than Egypt's river:—from that gentle side
> Drink—drink, and live—Old Man! Heaven's realm
> holds no such tide.
>
> (150)

This episode of a daughter-mother preserving an imprisoned man epitomizes the fundamental concerns of Byron's imagination.[29] Byron at last, if only momentarily, converts the aggressive masculine patterns of history, his bleak vision of mankind "rotting from sire to son," into a tableau of salvation through woman. The scene is the most explicit instance of the motif of the redemptive daughter, who reverses time and restores the father to the safe status of the child within the mother's embrace. The Roman father enjoys what Byron in his own person could only aspire towards in Canto III; he possesses the bliss denied to Byron himself, to Conrad, Manfred, Bonnivard, and Tasso: his prison has become the nurturing womb. The "Caritas Romana" is luminous testimony to the compelling desires of retreat that dominated Byron at this period.

From this resolution Byron turns to the cathedral of St. Peter's, following eighteenth-century theorists of the sublime to suggest that art expands the soul in a fashion analogous to the moral exemplum of the Roman daughter. The increasingly positive tone culminates in the praise of the Apollo Belvedere:

> But in his delicate form—a dream of Love,
> Shaped by some solitary Nymph, whose breast
> Longed for a deathless lover from above,
> And maddened in that vision—are exprest
> All that ideal Beauty ever blessed
> The mind with in its most unearthly mood,
> When each Conception was a heavenly Guest—
> A ray of immortality—and stood,
> Starlike, around, until they gathered to a God!

> And if it be Prometheus stole from Heaven
> The fire which we endure—it was repaid
> By him to whom the energy was given
> Which this poetic marble hath arrayed
> With an eternal Glory. . . .
>
> (162–163)

The passage recalls the love of Egeria and Numa which provoked Byron's earlier despair, and by showing the delusions of love transformed into art, Promethean aspiration become Apollonian control, Byron might have made of the statue a final harmonizing of the conflicts of the poem. The statue, like the prominence generally of art in the canto, suggests a development in Byron's attitude toward the self, a fuller exploration of the possibilities of treating the self as a deliberately wrought artifact. Even before he inserted the stanzas on the death of Princess Charlotte in childbirth (167–172), however, a reconciliation accomplished only through the mediation of a famous piece of classical sculpture would have seemed facile. The addition, telling as Byron's additions often are, reveals his persisting anxieties.[30] His vision of the dead mother and her boy, "pale but lovely," as "with maternal grief—/ She clasps a babe, to whom her breast yields no relief" (167), undercuts the affirmation of the "Caritas Romana." In this instance the elegiac convention that the death of a loved one is more painful for the survivors touches a particularly sensitive spot in Byron, and the new material is a distillation of the sense of having been cast out from womanly protection that darkens the entire canto.

Byron strives to conclude *Childe Harold* IV with a peroration of definitive and comprehensive closure. His grandly rhetorical address to the Ocean nonetheless gradually modulates into nostalgic childhood memories. The disparity with his mood of resignation at the moment of writing is so striking that one asks how much of the central tension of the poem remains unresolved below its statements of calm:

> And I have loved thee, Ocean! and my joy
> Of youthful sports was on thy breast to be
> Borne, like thy bubbles, onward: from a boy
> I wantoned with thy breakers—they to me
> Were a delight; and if the freshening sea
> Made them a terror—'t was a pleasing fear,
> For I was as it were a *Child of thee,*

> And trusted to thy billows far and near,
> And laid my hand upon thy mane—as I do here.
>
> My task is done—my song hath ceased—my theme
> Has died into an echo; it is fit
> The spell should break of this protracted dream.
> The torch shall be extinguished which hath lit
> My midnight lamp—and what is writ, is writ,—
> Would it were worthier! but I am not now
> That which I have been—and my visions flit
> Less palpably before me—and the glow
> Which in my Spirit dwelt is fluttering, faint, and low.
>   (184–185; italics added)

At the outset of Canto III Byron described himself "as a weed,/ Flung from the rock, on Ocean's foam" (2), and the composure he has earned in the meanwhile may be measured by the change in this image. Yet the characterization of the Ocean is significantly bisexual: it begins in stanza 179 as an epitome of masculine power, going forth "dread, fathomless, alone," and it metamorphoses into a docilely feminine creature supporting the young Byron. The last verses Byron included in the poem illustrate the struggle between the mature integration he seeks to affirm of himself and the feelings of irreparable loss that drive him toward withdrawal: "Oh! that the Desert were my dwelling-place,/ With one fair Spirit for my minister,/ That I might all forget the human race,/ And, hating no one, love but only her!" (177).

For Byron inquiry into history is an extension of inquiry into the self, and the atypically external use he makes of the past in much of *Childe Harold* IV is a further clue to the external nature of his self-presentation in the poem. Hobhouse proudly avouched that its steadily increasing length was largely owing to him:

> When I rejoined Lord Byron at La Mira . . . I found him employed upon the Fourth Canto of *Childe Harold,* and, later in the autumn, he showed me the first sketch of the poem. It was much shorter than it afterwards became, and it did not remark on several objects which appeared to me peculiarly worthy of notice. I made a list of these objects, and in conversation with him gave him reasons for the selection. The result was the poem as it now appears. . . .[31]

Approached in so gratuitously antiquarian a fashion history is not an aid to understanding the self but an evasion of it; the fresh topics provided by the "indefatigable researches" of his friend diverted

Byron from the psychological materials that are the deepest layer of
the poem. Rome teaches Byron that in contrast to her centuries of
alteration his sorrows are trivial, but she cannot help him to work
through them towards self-awareness when his paramount interest
in her history is distraction from his own. Again and again he sounds
a note of repression rather than enlightenment: "The orphans of the
heart must . . . control/ In their shut breasts their petty misery" (78);
"Upon such a shrine/ What are our petty griefs?—Let me not number
mine" (106). As the panorama of guidebook and gallery unrolls, the
sense of a corresponding inner life in the narrator diminishes.

The lack should not be confused with insincerity, for the enterprise of constructing a suitably noble image of himself was a task to
which Byron was desperately committed. The discrepancy arises because *Childe Harold* III and IV are blatantly "personal" poems in which
Byron demands that his suffering be observed, and yet when it is
asked how he came to be so miserable the answer is found *outside* the
poems themselves, in what we are assumed to know of his scandalous incest with Augusta and separation from Annabella. The poems
are personal, yet they exclude much of what we need to know to
comprehend them; in place of analysis and explanation, or even circumstantial detail, Byron offers only a rather disingenuously stoic
"silence." If his readers often fall back on biography in discussing the
poems of this period it is in part because Byron's theatrics here point
to a mystery rather than incorporate it in a self-sustaining artistic
whole. He surmounts this difficulty in *Don Juan* by a strategy of seeming intimacy, perpetually and purposefully teasing us to look beyond
his fiction, so that if we know enough to recognize in Dona Inez, for
example, a compound of Byron's wife and mother, we feel comfortable in sharing the author's private joke and not, as in *Childe Harold*,
embarrassed at hearing his stage whispers.

The fourth canto is a substantial achievement, even though Byron
sidesteps some of the problems of the self that torment him and erupt
in the poem. This canto, as well as the third, can be compared with
The Prelude. Wordsworth's poem springs from his attempt after a
period of crisis to reach equilibrium by defining himself as The Poet.
Childe Harold is analogous in its attempt to construct an omnicompe-
tent self, glossing over the stresses it reveals. In this final canto the
pains of Byron's inner situation are subsumed within the artifice of an
elevated voice rather than engaged. The mode adumbrates the possibility of a future Byron not unlike the Wordsworth of the
"philosophic mind," and as Byron's conviction of premature age in-

tensified, his distaste for Wordsworth must have been sharpened by an unacknowledged recognition of a threatening similarity. If to complete this brief comparison of the two poets the "drowsy, frowsy" *Excursion*, as Byron labelled it (*DJ*, III, 93), is matched with *Don Juan*, the juxtaposition suggests that Byron escaped the senescence that he felt had overtaken his elder contemporary because he continued to risk encounters with the unresolved trauma of his childhood, as he had not in *Childe Harold* IV.

The techniques Byron was to assemble in *Don Juan* are visible separately in the last two tales of this group.[32] The germ of *Beppo* is an anecdote Byron heard of the transformation of a Venetian into a wealthy Turk and his surprising return to his wife long after she had presumed him dead and become the mistress of another man.[33] The slight bit of gossip contains in potential the lethal combats of Byron's tales, and it especially appealed to him because instead of the self-destructive conclusions of his fictions the parties concerned devised an amicable and mutually satisfactory accommodation. As Byron tells the story he effortlessly distances its latent violence, and the happy resolution of his fears that constitutes its attraction for him becomes the artful manipulation of the reader's responses. The epigraph manifests Byron's stance: he directs himself against the English prejudice that Venice is the seat of all dissoluteness, and tantalizes his audience with the hopes of a shocking *récit*. The faithful heroines of the tales are succeeded by Laura, the supreme lady of the world who in the absence of her husband naturally takes a dilettante Count as a *cavalier servente*. Beppo's career—shipwrecked "about where Troy stood once," enslaved, turned pirate and renegade—resumes the fabric of Byron's earlier works, but he now safely relegates it to the background. With it, nonetheless, he raises expectations of a murderous encounter on Beppo's appearance, and makes that dénouement seem more likely by offhand allusions to Desdemona and Othello. But the grand scene so carefully prepared is not allowed to materialize, and Byron brilliantly dissolves any anticipations of melodrama when his characters perform their unexpected flourish of civilized behavior. Laura drowns Beppo in a flood of small talk, and he and the Count become good friends. In a cheerfully comic variation of the kinship of rivals that runs throughout the tales Beppo even puts on the Count's clothes. Beneath the worldly manner of the polished raconteur emerges a fairytale vision of the evaporation of the possessive and domineering sexual impulses that have tortured Byron.

Although what is fatuousness in her is skill in him, Laura's method of staving off crisis by verbal fluency is a counterpart of the poet's own. The narrator's seeming inability to relate his story without the interruption of random commentary is a sophisticated instance of Romantic spontaneity, but the digressions also serve a profound psychological function. The cosmopolitan comparisons of English and Italian customs, the beauty of Italy and Italian women, the merits of Titian and Giorgione, the fall of Napoleon, and the innumerable other items of conversation that pass through the narrator's mind as he attempts to convey his simple anecdote at once enlarge its slender significance and remove its ominous implications from the center of consciousness. At the conclusion of the poem Byron divorces himself entirely from the tension-filled triangle at its center: he announces that "I don't believe the half of" the stories Beppo gives out (98), and of the enduring *ménage-à-trois* says noncommittally: "Though Laura sometimes put him in a rage,/ *I've heard* the Count and he were always friends" (99, italics added). These stratagems of dissociation—the digressions, and the anticlimactic ending—enable Byron to confront his obsessions while allaying the anxieties they cause. The witty inventiveness with which he manages his own deepest concerns in *Beppo* simultaneously delights the reader and maneuvers him into a liberating awareness of his own moral assumptions and preconceptions.

The difference between *Don Juan* and *Beppo* is that the latter still lies outside Byron's personal life. The poem was published anonymously, and the speaker identifies himself only as "a nameless sort of person,/ (A broken Dandy lately on my travels)" (52). Deception could hardly have been the aim of so transparent a mask, however; rather its slight protection was guard enough to facilitate Byron's self-expression. Though Byron nonchalantly locates the anecdote "some years ago,/ It may be thirty, forty, more or less" (21), he steps openly into view in the digressions, especially the extended contrast of Turkish women and English bluestockings who dabble in mathematics (70–78). The overwhelming of the story by the observations it inspires shows Byron nearing the moment when he would take his intimate feelings as subject without the defensive postures of *Childe Harold* IV, which he was finishing as he wrote *Beppo*. The framework of *Mazeppa*, his penultimate tale, displays the manner in which Byron was most fruitfully to approach his own life.

Byron re-establishes the bleak Titanic universe in the first verse paragraph of *Mazeppa* by comparing the defeat of Charles XII by Peter the Great to the disastrous invasion of Russia by Napoleon. The crushed Swedish monarch is introduced after the decisive battle of Pultowa as a type of "Ambition in his humbled hour" (21). The fortitude with which he bears his grief is immediately recognizable as the stern self-repression of his predecessors in Byron's works; he

> ... made, in this extreme of ill,
> His pangs the vassals of his will:
> All silent and subdued were they,
> As once the nations round about him lay.
>
> (41–44)

To soothe him to sleep Charles requests a story from his companion, Mazeppa, a Cossack who switched allegiance when his pride was affronted by the czar.[34] His self-portrait describes the turbulent inner life that consumes Byron's heroes whether they speciously control it like Charles or not:

> But all men are not born to reign,
> Or o'er their passions, or as you,
> Thus o'er themselves and nations too.
> I am—or rather *was*—a prince,
> A chief of thousands, and could lead
> Them on where each would foremost bleed;
> But could not o'er myself evince
> The like control.
>
> (287–294)

Mazeppa recounts an affair of his past that illustrates once more the fascination held for Byron by oedipal stories in which a boy becomes the lover of the much younger wife of an old man, is discovered by the husband, and punished. Mazeppa tells of having been sent forth to die by the Count he cuckolded, strapped to a savage horse; the resultant half-man, half-beast is an apt emblem of his headlong desires. The alternate similes he selects to characterize the animal suggest the reverberations of the incident which led Byron to choose it:

> Untired, untamed, and worse than wild—
> All furious as a favoured child

Balked of its wish; or—fiercer still—
A woman piqued—who has her will!

(517–520)

The first image recapitulates the action, but that Mazeppa should
seize upon the frustrations of a child as the most powerful illustration
of passion betrays the strata touched on by the story. The second,
which contrives to hint that a woman is to blame for the situation, is
not supported by the plot, but its extraneousness on that level is
countered on a deeper one when it is seen as an extension of the first.
Together the images show Byron projecting into this historical material the son's unconscious resentment against the mother.

The wild ride terminates when the horse plunges his rider into a
stream and expires shortly after emerging on the other side. There are
ample indications that the journey is to be read as a parable of death
and rebirth in conventional religious terms. Mazeppa's plight is a
ghastly literalization of the Pauline cry, "Who shall deliver me from
the body of this death?", which is answered by crossing the waters in
which he declares: "My stiffened limbs were rebaptized" (589). The
nature of his salvation, however, is not Christian but maternal.
Mazeppa has resigned himself to fate and already lost consciousness
when he is rescued by the miraculous intervention of a Cossack maid.
The archetypal romance shape is fulfilled when Mazeppa says that
one day while nursing him the maid "came with mother and with
sire" (840). The outcast son is reunited with his parents and recovers
his inheritance: Mazeppa rises to lead the people who have adopted
him, and eventually exacts revenge on the Count "with twice five
thousand horse" (411).

The happy ending of the tale is thus in contrast to previous works
like *The Bride of Abydos* and *Parisina*, but beneath the changed resolution the same impulses can be discerned, now unblocked. From the
woman whose sexual charms almost destroy him Mazeppa reverts to
her benevolent double, the mother who restores him to strength. The
paired heroines repeat with a variation the pattern of *The Corsair*, but
Byron here imagines a consummated three-stage sequence of defeat
in the world of men, withdrawal to a feminine shelter, and a triumphant return to the world of men. This idyllic sequence is the expression of Byron's profoundest wish, but, like *Beppo* in another fashion,
it is a fantasy that he could more easily develop in characters removed
from him than sustain in his own person. The hostilities Conrad feels
toward Gulnare in the earlier tale reflect an ambivalence towards the

withdrawal he desired that does not intrude in *Mazeppa*. Its continuance, however, is evident in Cantos I and II of *Don Juan*, written at the same time and exhibiting the same configuration. Juan's affair with Julia, shipwreck, and resurrection on Haidée's island exactly parallel Mazeppa's experience, and demonstrate again Byron's desire to retreat from the conflicts of adult sexuality to the maternal embrace. Juan, because he is much closer to Byron than is Mazeppa, releases complexities of emotion not provoked by the tale.

The grim circumstances of the tale successfully ballast its fantasy structure, and Mazeppa's finely controlled narration further heightens its credibility. Mazeppa's love has lost none of its force with the passage of time:

> I loved her then—I love her still;
> And such as I am love indeed
> In fierce extremes—in good and ill.
> But still we love even in our rage,
> And haunted to our very age
> With the vain shadow of the past,
> As is Mazeppa to the last.
>
> (225–231)

This enduring memory of lost bliss is especially reminiscent of the Giaour, but without the obsessional frenzy that marked the earlier figure. The use of the third person underlines Mazeppa's ability to distance himself from the passion he still feels and maintain perspective upon it. The sensationalism of the episode is counterbalanced by his detachment, which extends to ironic commentary on his own emotions: "Even I for once produced some verses,/ And sign'd my odes 'Despairing Thyrsis'" (153–154). Mazeppa seems genuinely to have earned the self-possession to survive adversity; though in retreat, he has not been overcome. In the midst of disaster he takes gentle care of his horse "and joyed to see how well he fed" (62); the small touch reinforces the impression that Mazeppa's calm is not merely an icy denial of emotion. That Charles should fall asleep before the story is concluded is Byron's joke on literature that bases its appeal on exoticism, as his own had done, and also his affirmation that painful experience can be assimilated by the imagination and thus tranquilized.

The tales and *Childe Harold* III and IV warn that to remain prey to one's passions is self-destructive, but that to repress them under a stern or noble façade produces a stagnation that is equally life-defeating. Mazeppa is the first of Byron's heroes to contain both energy and control, but examination shows that his fullness is intimately related to the strata of time in the poem: the energies are largely remembered from the past, the control is a quality of the present. He appears as a representative Romantic poet, conquering time by keeping alive within himself the intense feelings of youth, an unlikely cousin of Wordsworth and Coleridge. Yet the lines quoted above suggest that this continuity has less positive overtones, for as the third person indicates, it implies a double-consciousness based on a disjunction between past and present rather than a unified self-consciousness. By his own account his yearnings still haunt Mazeppa, and "the vain shadow of the past" stands between him and true integration. There has nonetheless been a momentous advance: whereas the protagonists of the early tales are victims of the doubles they do not recognize as themselves, Mazeppa comes face to face with Mazeppa and knows that the shadow is "vain." He has acquired the maturity to acknowledge his unresolved tensions and thus prevent their undiminished vigor from spurring him to irrational and self-consuming behavior. Through irony he converts the distancing that betrays his divisions into a means of controlling them. The psychic stratagem is that of his creator, who in *Don Juan* finally turns the same detached vision on his own childhood fears and their residue and makes the double-consciousness that afflicts him the structure of a masterpiece.

PART II: The Hero in Family and Society

3

Young Sons and Old Men

Drama lay at the center of the imagination for an author who self-consciously elevated his public image to mythic proportions, whose poetry derives its energy from the tensions between dispersed, multiple aspects of the self, and who was fascinated with the enhancing (as well as the hypocritical) possibilities of role playing.[1] It is thus somewhat paradoxical that Byron's experiments in formal drama must be connected with his efforts to discipline his self-expression. In 1814 his enthusiasm for the acting of Edmund Kean roused him to declare: "I wish that I had a talent for the drama; I would write a tragedy *now*."[2] No sooner had he confided the ambition to his journal, however, than he delineated the obstacle to its realization:

> To write so as to bring home to the heart, the heart must have been tried,—but, perhaps, ceased to be so. While you are under the influence of the passions, you only feel, but cannot describe them,—any more than, when in action, you could turn round and tell the story to your next

neighbour! When all is over,—all, all, and irrevocable,—trust to memory—she is then but too faithful.

(*BLJ* 3: 245)

The tales are the evidence that in dealing with his own experience Byron did not yet possess the controlled division of sympathies that he knew a playwright required, and the structure of *Manfred* too gives way to the compelling despair of its protagonist. "I never heard that my friend Moore was set down for a fire-worshipper on account of his Guebre," Byron pleaded amusingly in reply to an article in *Blackwood's Magazine* (1820), "whereas I have had some difficulty extricating me even from *Manfred* ..." (*LJ* 4: 475). The refusal of the public to distinguish between creator and character was intuitively correct, and points to Byron's dilemma. For some time he had been discontented with his poetry. When Moore challenged the opinion he expressed to Murray in September 1817 that "he and *all* of us— Scott—Southey—Wordsworth—Moore—Campbell—I—are all in the wrong—one as much as another—that we are upon a wrong revolutionary poetical system—or systems—not worth a damn in itself" (*BLJ* 5: 265), Byron reiterated it with an explanation:

> I called Crabbe and Sam [Rogers] the fathers of present Poesy; and said, that I thought—except them—*all* of "us youth" were on a wrong tack. But I never said that we did not sail well. Our fame will be hurt by *admiration* and *imitation*. When I say *our*, I mean *all* (Lakers included) except the postscript of the Augustans. The next generation (from the quantity and facility of imitation) will tumble and break their necks off our Pegasus, who runs away with us; but we keep the *saddle*, because we broke the rascal and can ride. But though easy to mount, he is the devil to guide; and the next fellows must go back to the riding-school and the manège, and learn to ride the "great horse."
>
> (*BLJ* 6: 10)

However valuable these remarks are as literary criticism their vehemence is surprising. The picture contained in Byron's Pegasus simile of a rider who has lost control of the impulsive steed on which he can barely maintain his seat—compare Mazeppa helplessly subject to his savage horse—offers a clue.[3] The works of these years are the battle-grounds on which Byron confronted his disturbances, and the simile is a reminder that even when transformed into art such engagements are immensely unsettling. It is little wonder that Byron should have repudiated a kind of poetry that by releasing anxieties endangered his stability.

Byron sought the distance he needed in plots taken from history and in the restraining principles of neoclassicism.[4] In February 1817, after having fruitlessly "searched all" the Venetian chronicles, he asked Murray to send "an account of the *Doge Valiere* (it ought to be Falieri) and his conspiracy—or the motives of it": "I mean to write a tragedy upon the subject, which appears to me very dramatic—an old man—jealous—and conspiring against the state of which he was the actually reigning Chief" (*BLJ* 5: 174). When the extracts had not arrived by June Byron laid the project aside; he was already occupied with Canto IV of *Childe Harold,* a parallel attempt to mediate personal conflicts through history, and then with *Don Juan.*

The Doge had nonetheless captured Byron's imagination, and in April 1820 he began the tragedy. Progress was fitful; while composing the third act he lamented to Moore: "I have, at this present, too many passions of my own on hand to do justice to those of the dead" (*LJ* 5: 42). The complicated separation from her husband of his mistress Teresa Guiccioli and his participation in the attempt by the Carbonari to free northern Italy from Austrian domination precluded the detachment Byron desired.[5] These two distractions from "pure" literary concentration suggest the avenues by which the play is best approached; first, through the configuration of hero and heroine already observed in the tales, and secondly, through the political matrix the configuration here assumes. While insisting to Murray that *Marino Faliero* was not a veiled allegory of current events Byron freely admitted to his friends that the drama was "full of republicanism, so will find no favour in Albermarle Street" [Murray's establishment] (*LBC* 2: 156). "All I have done," he told his nervous publisher, "is meant to be purely Venetian, even to the prophecy of the present state" (*LJ* 5: 85), but the "present state" of Italy was one he described as "upon the eve of evolutions and revolutions" (*LJ* 5: 57). Across Europe the reactionary post-Napoleonic governments were being challenged by the rising demands of the disenfranchised. J. L. Talmon has assembled two quotations that neatly characterize the explosive decade in which Byron's play appeared:

> "There is only one serious matter in Europe in 1832," Metternich wrote, "and that is revolution"—by which he meant not palace or political revolution but "social revolution [which] attacks the foundations of society."

In the same year, the British Ambassador in Vienna, Sir Frederick Lamb, expressed the opinion that "the principle of movement and that of repose are at war openly or underhand throughout Europe, and people are much more liberal or the reverse than they are Frenchmen, or Germans, or Italians."[6]

Despite his statements of sympathy, however, Byron provides little evidence in *Marino Faliero* from which it can be decided whether the revolution Faliero embarks upon is justified.[7] The curious ambiguity of the formal and political structure asks that primary attention be paid to the inward states of the characters. The power of the drama despite its cumbersome length resides in the almost transparent clarity of the psychological conflicts invested in the political framework.

Marino Faliero opens as the Doge awaits the verdict of Venice's ruling council on Michel Steno, the young aristocrat who has accused him of being a cuckold; it should be noted that in the sexual conflict between age and youth Byron has focused upon the authoritarian older figure. The insult Steno scrawled on his chair—"Marin Faliero dalla bella moglie: altri la gode, ed egli la mantien"—is never actually spoken in the play, but the effect of the omission runs counter to the decorum that enforced it: by making the tensions that are obsessively referred to seem dark and undiscussable it heightens the oppressive atmosphere. Faliero responds to the news that Steno has been sentenced merely to a month's house arrest by renouncing his allegiance to Venice and trampling on the ducal bonnet. He rationalizes this extravagance by claiming that the patricians have degraded the sanctity of office by condoning an act of *lèse-majesté*. The justification, however, is rejected by his nephew, Bertuccio, who insists that "this fury doth exceed the provocation,/ Or any provocation" (I, ii, 136–137) and pleads with him "to suppress such gusts of passion" (I, ii, 225). The Doge's discourse on the essence of sovereignty while he has plainly forgotten "all prudence" and is no longer "sovereign of himself" is one of the ironies of the second scene (I, ii, 240–242).

The relationship between Faliero and his young wife Angiolina shown in the second act underscores the excessiveness of his rage and suggests its source. Steno's canard has blackened Angiolina as well, but she remains unruffled. To her confidante's assumption that "Some sacrifice is due to slandered virtue," she replies that virtue is above revenge: "Why, what is virtue if it needs a victim/ Or if it must depend upon men's words?" (II, i, 57–58). Faliero cannot convince her that his resentment is impersonal and she reproves him for indulging "the most fierce of fatal passions" (II, i, 401). The refusal of those closest to him to share his anger argues that its origins are deeper than his rhetoric admits. When asked whether she loves a husband many years her senior Angiolina responds with a speech revealing Byron's characteristic father-daughter pattern:

> I love all noble qualities which merit
> Love, and I loved my father, who first taught me
> To single out what we should love in others,
> And to subdue all tendency to lend
> The best and purest feelings of our nature
> To baser passions. He bestowed my hand
> Upon Faliero: he had known him noble,
> Brave, generous; rich in all the qualities
> Of soldier, citizen, and friend; in all
> Such have I found him as my father said.
>   (II, i, 93–102)

Her third person reference to herself as "Loredano's daughter" in the last act marks her essential self-definition (V, i, 140). The Doge confirms the prominence of the patriarchal figure. As he recounts to Angiolina the circumstances of their marriage the verse is studded with references to him: it was he who "willed our union," and though Faliero abandoned "all claim" granted by a "father's last injunction," she "urged in answer/ [Her] father's choice" (II, i, 291–324). Addressing Angiolina as "child" and calmly anticipating that after his death, endowed with his "Prince's name and riches," she will marry a young man, Faliero has evidently assumed the paternal role and continued the configuration of benevolent tyrant and dutiful daughter.

The disinterestedness begins to be suspect when Faliero unnecessarily declares that it was not "the false edge of agéd appetite" that led him to comply with his friend's wish, and insists that "in my fieriest youth/ I swayed such passions; nor was this my age/ Infected with that leprosy of lust/ Which taints the hoariest years of vicious men . . ." (II, i, 311–316). The sexual defensiveness recalls Othello, but the tone Byron echoes receives its particular timbre. Unlike Othello, Faliero knows that his wife is chaste, and so his subsequent tirade on the horrors of infidelity is off the mark. Its gratuitousness, however, indicates its strength of feeling, and that strength is comprehensible when taken in conjunction with the father-daughter pattern: the daughter's innocence bears the sacred import of its inverse and equivalent, the mother's purity.[8]

Since everything told of Faliero by the play emphasizes the impulsiveness of his character, his fastidiousness about his affections seems an uneasily sustained check on desires that he will not acknowledge. "For love, romantic love," he proclaims,

> which in my youth
> I knew to be illusion, and ne'er saw
> Lasting, but often fatal, it had been
> No lure for me, in my most passionate days,
> And could not be so now, did such exist.
>
> (II, i, 349–353)

The suggestions of temptation and destruction jar against the overt statement of the lines and suggest that Faliero has retreated into the role of father to protect himself from sexual desires unacceptable to him. Steno's innuendo affirms the power of sexuality and thereby despite its falsity reaches his repressed emotions, but he cannot admit to himself the true hurt without confessing that the indifference by which he guards himself is hollow. Cold pride is his weapon against this inner turmoil; he disguises his anxiety from himself by channeling it into resentment of "The violated majesty of Venice/ At once insulted in her Lord and laws" (II, i, 407–408). The feminine gender in which the city is always invoked makes still clearer the irrational forces that drive him to a conspiracy against the government. Without entirely understanding why he does so, Angiolina rightly perceives that Faliero confuses the outward form of honor—"A duty to a certain sign" (II, i, 109)—with genuine integrity.

The fathers of Faliero are even more central to the drama than is Angiolina's father. Faliero agrees to join the chief of the conspirators, Israel Bertuccio, at midnight by the church where his family is interred. The interview before the embodiment of his patrimony brings out the Doge's ambivalence toward the rebellion, and to highlight it Byron happily departed from historical accuracy and the unities he touted; he told Murray that "all that is said of his *Ancestral Doges*, as buried at St. John's and Paul's, is altered from the fact, *they being in St. Mark's*."[9] In front of the church stands an equestrian statue that Byron says in the preface he made into a Faliero. The Doge is so conscious of being "observed" by this representative of his ancestors that he alarms Israel into drawing his sword before the other comprehends that he is only speaking figuratively. For Faliero to rebel is to break an illustrious tradition of service that in the past he endeavored to fulfill. Hence he must justify the rebellion to himself by the standards of his forebears, and in soliloquy he argues that he acts because "their mighty name was dishonoured all *in* me/ Not *by* me." The price of his need to feel aligned with his heritage is the loss of free will, for the casuistry necessary to his self-respect translates the willful choice into a "task . . . forced upon me, I have sought it not." The equivocation, however, enables him to see himself as the dedicated savior of a corrupt city and therefore a faithful perpetuator of the tradition from which he cannot bear to be divorced: "Spirits! smile down upon me! for my cause/ Is yours . . . ." (III, i, 1–47). This maneuver entails upon Faliero the severe consequence that in his eyes the legitimacy of the rebellion depends entirely on its outcome: if it triumphs, he is vindicated, if it fails, he is a turncoat. Faliero comes to inhabit a world devoid of innate values where, as he declares in the last line of Act I, "the true touchstone of desert" is "Success."

The pivotal issues of the drama are not couched in the moral terms of right and wrong, but in the psychological ones of acceptance and rejection. Faliero delineates the situation, without understanding that his inability to cut loose and evaluate the rebellion on its own merits has generated it:

> If this
> Attempt succeeds, and Venice, rendered free
> And flourishing, when we are in our graves,
> Conducts her generations to our tombs,
> And makes her children with their little hands
> Strew flowers o'er her deliverers' ashes, then
> The consequence will sanctify the deed,
> And we shall be like the two Bruti in
> The annals of hereafter; but if not,
> If we should fail, employing bloody means
> And secret plot, although to a good end,
> Still we are traitors, honest Israel;—thou
> No less than he who was thy Sovereign
> Six hours ago, and now thy brother rebel.
>
> (III, i, 67–80)

The language illustrates the displacement of sexual energies discussed above and testifies again to the mirroring of political and family conflicts. The conspirators are in the position of brothers banding together against the father for possession of the mother in order to become procreators themselves. Israel assures Faliero that the insurgents are reliable: he tells him that in compensation for his son who "died in arms . . . for this faithless state . . . Not one of all those strangers whom thou doubtest,/ But will regard thee with a filial feeling,/ So that thou keep'st a father's faith with them" (I, ii, 556–563). The Doge's misgivings are outweighed by the unconscious appeal of the opportunity to excel the sires who awe him and achieve the status of father himself.

The reader who finds this emphasis exaggerated should consider the significance of the biography Byron invents for Bertram, the Bergamask who reveals the cabal to the authorities. Even before the betrayal his "hesitating softness" and capacity to "weep like an infant o'er the misery/ Of others, heedless of his own, though greater" (II, ii, 68–71) cause his fellow rebel Calendaro to distrust him:

> I apprehend less treachery than weakness;
> *Yet as he has no mistress, and no wife*
> To work upon his milkiness of spirit,
> He may go through the ordeal; it is well
> *He is an orphan, friendless save in us*:
> A woman or a child had made him less
> Than either in resolve.
>   (II, ii, 78–84; italics added)

Calendaro misinterprets the absence of ties on which he counts: Bertram's mild freedom from the resentments that animate the other conspirators and lack of lover and offspring are the signs of a failure to establish an independent manhood. Further examination of Byron's interweaving of psychology and politics illuminates the portrait of Bertram.

When his companions advocate the blanket extirpation of the patricians Bertram urges compassion until Israel silences him: "Dost thou not see, that if we single out/ Some for escape, they live but to avenge/ The fallen? and how distinguish now the innocent/ From out the guilty?" (III, ii, 282–285). The refusal to discriminate dehumanizes Israel and raises the paradox of all revolutionary idealisms that resort to violence to bring about humanitarian goals. Byron shows that beneath their lofty purposes the conspirators are as cruel as those they charge with oppression, and no more trustworthy. The reader is repeatedly reminded that they have lied to their supporters about the nature of their plans; as in the tales, the enemies are identical. The Doge assents to Israel's proposition, but the very outburst in which he dooms those he loves most reveals the yearning for a lost harmony that impels him to bloodshed:

> All these men were my friends; I loved them, they
> Requited honourably my regards;
> We served and fought; we smiled and wept in concert;
> We revelled or we sorrowed side by side;
> We made alliances of blood and marriage;
> We grew in years and honours fairly,—till
> Their own desire, not my ambition, made
> Them choose me for their Prince, and then farewell!
> Farewell all social memory! all thoughts
> In common! and sweet bonds which link old friendships
> . . . .
>
> Farewell the past! I died to all that had been,
> Or rather they to me: no friends, no kindness,
> No privacy of life—all were cut off:
> They came not near me—such approach gave umbrage;
> They could not love me—such was not the law;
> They thwarted me—'twas the state's policy;
> They baffled me—'twas a patrician's duty;
> They wronged me, for such was to right the state;
> They could not right me—that would give suspicion; . . .
>   (III, ii, 319–328; 347–355)

The new echo of *Othello* is striking. Othello bids farewell to his occupation because he mistakenly believes that the woman who is the foundation of his universe has betrayed him. Faliero reverses the sequence of martial and sexual impotence: in this speech the insufficiently punished slander of Angiolina appears as the culmination, not the inception, of his helplessness. A phrase Byron had used years earlier to articulate his sense of Annabella's treachery blends with Shakespeare's words at the close of Faliero's speech: "I had only one fount of quiet left,/ And *that* they poisoned! my pure household gods/ Were shivered on the hearth. . . ."[10] The merely oblique appropriateness these allusions hold to Angiolina's known rectitude is the key to the nature of the feelings with which Byron has endowed the crisis. Faliero looks back to a period before he was singled out for his present eminence which he idealizes as a time of noncompetitive mutuality, and his yearning for that lost happiness is parallel with his yearning for the pure woman untouched by even the slightest gossip of carnality. In this outline may be discerned a powerful wish to return to the safe world of the mother which the child experienced prior to the upheavals of sexuality and the rivalries of manhood, the areas in which Faliero feels himself suffering defeat. It is this regressive fantasy that distorts and fuels his response to actual circumstance. Like Manfred, he desires withdrawal, and like Manfred he copes with grief by a deliberate hardening that ensures his misery. He treats the men with the same impersonality he has bewailed in their treatment of him—"these men have no private life"—and thus places himself on the same level as his opponents (III, ii, 382). Finally he consecrates himself to:

> the absorbing, sweeping, whole revenge,
> Which, like the sheeted fire from Heaven, must blast
> Without distinction, as it fell of yore,
> Where the Dead Sea hath quenched two Cities' ashes.
> (III, ii, 420–423)

The simile exposes Faliero, for God did not indiscriminately destroy Sodom and Gomorrah. At Abraham's reminder that it "be far from thee to do after this manner, to slay the righteous with the wicked: and that the righteous should be as the wicked, that be far from thee," God agrees to spare the city if ten righteous men can be found within it. Though in the end God vents his anger, he first saves Lot and his family; Faliero, by refusing to entertain the concept of mercy, unleashes the forces of death, and their first victims are his own emotions. His revulsion from the slaughter he is about to instigate is moving, but Faliero sacrifices his inner life to the image of himself as Jehovah, the omnipotent father infinitely superior to all tormenting anxieties. He tells his nephew that he favors striking immediately "that/ I might not yield again" to the "weak false remorse/ Which yearn'd about my heart" (IV, ii, 44–48).

Bertram is the symmetrical opposite of Faliero. In Act IV he betrays the conspiracy rather than permit harm to the patrician Lioni, "the only son/ Of him who was a friend unto my father" (IV, i, 249–250). Their relationship epitomizes Byron's fusion of psychology and politics. It is the fruit of a patron-client relationship between the families that has endured through several generations, and illustrates the kind of community that Faliero asserts no longer exists. The feudal structure on which the intimacy is built explains the discrepancy. Bertram switches sides not because he becomes convinced of the injustice of the rebellion, but because of a psychological situation that the language of the play renders perfectly explicit: he renounces his brother conspirators lest he forfeit the love of his official father. At the moment of decision Bertram defines himself as the obedient son and accepts his subordinate status, in clear contrast to Faliero, whose first action is to abrogate his oath of allegiance and proclaim his independence. Faliero is in the tragic predicament of precluding the harmony he desires by his own hypertrophied masculine will.

Faliero too employs a feudal vocabulary, and his attitudes towards the urban institutions against which he contends ask that an aspect of Byron's fundamental analogy between personal and historical past less apparent in his earlier works be explored. For Faliero authority is earned by personal valor, not conferred by state office, and he harks back repeatedly to his exploits at the battle of Zara. His loyalty to the traditions of his house precedes his zeal for Venice, and his world is the extended family of the medieval hierarchy. He speaks in terms of "fiefs," "serfs," and "retainers," and wishes to be joined in the uprising by his own "vassals":

> These city slaves have all their private bias,
> Their prejudice *against* or *for* this noble,
> Which may induce them to o'erdo or spare
> Where mercy may be madness; the fierce peasants,
> Serfs of my country of Val di Marino,
> Would do the bidding of their lord without
> Distinguishing for love or hate his foes;
> Alike to them Marcello or Cornaro,
> A Gradenigo or a Foscari;
> They are not used to start at those vain names,
> Nor bow the knee before a civic Senate;
> A chief in armour is their suzerain,
> And not a thing in robes.
> (IV, ii, 15–29)

The days when a chief in armor was the source of legitimacy were over in 1820, and those whom Faliero scorns as city slaves were loudly defending their rights to private judgment. The rule by oligarchy and the patron-client relationship made their last stand in the

aristocratic society of eighteenth-century England before slowly giving way to the rising power of the industrial middle classes. Faliero's
resentful description of the nobles who "wrong" him because they
conceive it their duty to "right the state" exemplifies a major development of Byron's era, the continued shift of power from the
monarchy to Parliament and the painful transition from a theory of
government with an assumed identity of class interests to a full-
fledged counterpoint of checks and balances between opposed
classes. Faliero's dilemma is to demand the kind of respect and freedom enjoyed by the protagonists of the tales in a world organized
along the impersonal and rationalized lines of modern adminis-
trations. Before Faliero, the Titanic hero is either stateless or merely
nominally stated, like Lara. In the drama Byron places the hero fully
within the state, only to watch him—god or beast—turn on it and
break away, driven by the need to prove his autonomy into a self-
consuming isolation. *Childe Harold* holds out the hope that the imagination can recapture the glories of the past, but *Marino Faliero*
suggests that the present no longer offers the ample fields of action in
which merit may test itself. The Byronic hero "ceased to have meaning," Jacques Barzun writes, "only when the triumph of political
democracy made group action possible and necessary, thereby dwarf-
ing the value of individual acts and rendering 'the hero' ridiculous."[11]
Hence for Byron the historical past becomes as burdensome as personal memory: the latter reminds him of a lost security, and knowledge of his culture teaches him how limited the opportunities of
redemption through heroism have become.

Faliero's refusal to discriminate the innocent from the guilty rebounds against him when the rebellion is crushed. He confronts the
victors without faltering:

> Failing, I know the penalty of failure
> Is present infamy and death—the future
> Will judge, when Venice is no more, or free;
> Till then, the truth is in abeyance. Pause not;
> I would have shown no mercy, and I seek none;
> My life was staked upon a mighty hazard,
> And being lost, take what I would have taken!
> I would have stood alone amidst your tombs:
> Now you may flock round mine, and trample on it,
> As you have done upon my heart while living.
>   (V, i, 255–264)

The last lines bare the hurt that feeds Faliero's expressed political convictions; the stark vision of solitary revenge corresponds more faithfully to his motives than the rhetoric of founding a republic in which he had previously made them acceptable to himself. The incredulous question of Benintende, the presiding judge, exactly characterizes the impulses that direct Faliero:

> And can it be, that the great Doge of Venice,
> With three parts of a century of years
> And honours on his head, could thus allow
> His fury, *like an angry boy's,* to master
> All Feeling, Wisdom, Faith and Fear, on such
> A provocation as a young man's petulance?
>> (V, i, 239–244; italics added)

An earlier speech of Benintende's prominently displays the saturation in oedipal content that fascinated Byron in this story:

> Our fathers had not fixed the punishment
> Of such a crime, as on the old Roman tables
> The sentence against parricide was left
> In pure forgetfulness; they could not render
> That penal, which had neither name nor thought
> In their great bosoms; who would have foreseen
> That nature could be filed to such a crime
> As sons 'gainst sires, and princes gainst their realms?
>> (V, i, 186–193)

The council responds like a threatened father determined at any cost to defend his authority against an insurgent son and scarcely inquires into the grounds of the rebellion before ordering instant mass executions. When Angiolina pleads for clemency for her husband she is rebuffed with the same fallacious argument he used against the patricians: that mercy is incompatible with justice. Neither Faliero nor Benintende will risk the charity Angiolina nobly implores for fear of seeming weak; in the world of men as Byron harshly imagines it "the truth is in abeyance" not because it is unknowable but because all the parties are more concerned with maintaining their sternness than with right and wrong.

Unlike Shakespearean tragedy, which ends with the restoration of order (however diminished in contrast with the struggles of the protagonist), *Marino Faliero* ends in a stalemate. Faliero continues to deny the legitimacy of the tribunal and recognizes only that he has failed. In his confession of defeat an ancient image is charged with personal significance: "Fortune is female: from my youth her favours/ Were not withheld, the fault was mine to hope/ Her former smiles again at this late hour" (V, i, 267–269). His ordeal brings Faliero no self-awareness, and despite the exhortations of Angiolina he remains incapable of pardon. The sensitivity that initially ennobles him is eroded by the pressure of his psychic imperatives until he, like Macbeth, for whom Byron's affinity is displayed by frequent, almost reflexive, echoes in the drama and throughout his writings, can only "bear-like, fight the course."[12] Just before dying Faliero recalls a prophecy foretelling his destruction that externalizes the rigidity of a character whose sombre grandeur irradiates the final terrible curse he pronounces on Venice. The murmurings of the citizens after his decapitation support the grievances of the rebels, and the ex post facto testimony thickens the air of frustration that hangs over the action. The only clear pattern is the defeat of each man who defies the authority senior to him. Though Steno has the advantage of youth and natural sexuality he fades into nothingness beside the imposing figure of the Doge. In the last moments Angiolina refuses even to acknowledge his apology, condemns him to his own self-contempt, and in a phrase which, through its suggestion of castration, joins the themes of sexual and political impotence, accuses him of having "Dis-crowned a Prince, cut off his crownless head,/ And forged new fetters for a groaning people!" (V, i, 407–465). Faliero succumbs to Benintende, and Bertram, whose inability to separate himself from Lioni produces the Doge's downfall, is as destroyed by acquiescence as the Doge is by revolt. He begs forgiveness of his brother conspirators knowing that he "never can/ Retrieve my own forgiveness" (V, i, 132–133), and says of the betrayal that "I did not seek this task; 'twas forced upon me" exactly as the Doge declared of the rebellion, "the task is forced upon me, I have sought it not" (III, i, 10). The complete stultification entailed by either course tellingly demonstrates Byron's characteristic refusal to portray a successful resolution of the oedipal conflict.

    Marino Faliero was mounted at Drury Lane in 1821 without Byron's permission, and the reviews indicate the rich vein of contemporary political dissent he had struck in this episode of quashed revolution. The *Morning Chronicle* (April 26) declared that "the times . . . prepare the minds of men for the bold and daring sentiments with

which it abounds," and the *European Magazine and London Review*
(LXXIX [January–June, 1821], 453) observed disapprovingly that:

> the audience . . .—excepting the Boxes,—seemed to reserve all their
> vivacity and applause entirely for those passages that upheld the pro-
> jectors of crime, and that named these ancient conspirators against social
> order, who could bear allusion to the worthy personages of our own day,
> who profess the same commendable tenets. The anti-patriotic sentiments
> scattered throughout the play seemed to constitute its strongest, and
> almost only, hold upon public opinion.

Several elements contributed to the failure of the production, among
them a mediocre actor in the title role, and it closed after seven per-
formances.[13] Commenting to Medwin some while later on the actors
of the day, Byron made a revealing association: "I can conceive nothing equal to Kemble's Coriolanus; and he looked the Roman so well,
that even 'Cato,' cold and *stiltish* as it is, had a run. That shews that
an actor can do for a play! If he had acted 'Marino Faliero,' its fate
would have been very different."[14] *Marino Faliero* does resemble
Coriolanus, and the relationship between the two plays obtains beyond the level of deliberate imitation. Byron habitually envisioned
himself and the events around him in Shakespearean terms; the
memories of *Othello* and *Macbeth* incorporated in the texture of *Marino
Faliero* are symptomatic of the web woven in casual letters and journals. In this network Coriolanus occupies an especially prominent
position. The echoes have already been heard at the close of *Childe
Harold* III, and Byron often focused his sense of himself at moments of
crisis by borrowing the words of the truculent aristocrat who grandly
retorts upon his exilers "I banish you!"[15] This profound identification
is further evidence of the fear of maternal dominance shaping Byron's
heroes. Behind Coriolanus stands the gigantic presence of Volumnia,
and in his final capitulation to her Byron saw the specter he dreaded:

> O mother, mother!
> What have you done! Behold, the heavens do ope,
> The gods look down, and this unnatural scene
> They laugh at. O my mother, mother! O!
> You have won a happy victory to Rome;
> But for your son—believe it, O believe it!—
> Most dangerously you have with him prevailed,
> If not most mortal to him.
> (V, iii, 182–189)

The anxieties powerfully exemplified for Byron in the destruction of Coriolanus left their legacy in Faliero's stubborn resistance to Angiolina.

Early in January 1821 Byron set forth to Murray his determination to produce "regular tragedies, like the *Greeks,*" for which he had "tried a Sketch in *Marino Faliero.*" He continued: "as I think that *love* is not the principal passion for tragedy (and yet most of ours turn upon it), you will not find me a popular writer. Unless it is Love, *furious, criminal,* and *hapless,* it ought not to make a tragic subject: when it is melting and maudlin, it *does,* but it ought not to do; it is then for the Gallery and second price boxes" (*LJ* 5: 217–218). A month later he reiterated his strictures: "I have also attempted to make a play without love. And there are neither rings, nor mistakes, nor starts, nor outrageous ranting villains, nor melodrame in it" (*LJ* 5: 243–244). Byron's resolve to combat the fustian that ruled the English stage is easily comprehensible, but the strategies of a literary campaign alone do not account for the aversion to love. He admits that passionate, unfortunate love is proper material for tragedy, but excludes it from consideration nonetheless. The peculiar solecism in the reasoning prompts a question as to why after having conceded their suitability Byron should have rejected stories based on *"furious, criminal,* and *hapless"* attachments.

Much light is shed on this prohibition by the reply Byron made in 1817 to Murray's observation that his projected drama risked comparison with *Venice Preserved*: "I am aware of what you say of Otway—and am a very great admirer of his—all except of that maudlin bitch of chaste lewdness and blubbering curiosity Belvidera—whom I utterly despise, abhor, & detest" (*BLJ* 5: 203). Byron's contempt for Belvidera points toward the "more unadulterated heroic temper"[16] of *Marino Faliero* which clearly differentiates it from its precursor; his violence suggests the impulses beneath the transformation. Jaffeir, the protagonist of *Venice Preserved,* consistently apprehends his divided political allegiances from the perspective of a paramount love for his wife. He joins the conspiracy against the Senate because the father-in-law who persecutes him happens to be a senator, and he betrays it and his best friend when one of the plotters makes lewd advances to Belvidera. Jaffeir thus sacrifices both friendship and conviction for the sake of a woman (who has in effect pre-ferred her father to him) and becomes, like Coriolanus, a prototype of the fate Byron most feared. Hence the excessive dislike of Belvidera and the role in *Marino Faliero* allotted Angiolina, whose charity exemplifies the escape from the destructive round and who must yet be rejected. Byron's taboo on love is an attempt to protect himself from conclusions similar to Jaffeir's.

Byron's next drama, *Sardanapalus*, bears out these remarks. On January 13, 1821 Byron "read over a passage... in Mitford's *Greece*, where he rather vindicates the memory of this last of the Assyrians," and later that evening he discussed the new work with Teresa: "She quarreled with me, because I said that love was *not the loftiest* theme for true tragedy; and, having the advantage of her native language, and natural female eloquence, she overcame my fewer arguments. I believe she was right. I must put more love into *Sardanapalus* than I intended" (*LJ* 5: 172–173). The journal entry gives a tantalizing glimpse of Byron's original intentions, conscious or otherwise. Mit-ford suggests—and Byron transferred the text into a note to his finished composition—that the notorious motto "Eat, drink, play; all other human joys are not worth a fillip" should perhaps be inter-preted as inviting "to civil order a people disposed to turbulence" rather than recommending "immoderate luxury." Mitford's specula-tion serves Byron's desire to minimize the threat of love, and the result is a highly revealing portrait of Byron's wishes: he converts the very type of the evils of man's subjection to sensuality into an ironic, aloof, enlightened humanitarian.

When Teresa recorded her version of the argument she proudly declared that "the sublime love of Myrrha was conceived that night," but examination of the drama reveals that in yielding to her persua-sions Byron did not alter his fundamental patterns.[17] The invention of Myrrha gives Byron's drama the macrostructure of a popular seventeenth-century dramatic genre, the tragedy of the conflict be-tween love and honor which glorifies the protagonist who abandons his duty for love. Antony and Cleopatra are the most famous exem-plars of this motif, and the many correspondences between *Sar-danapalus* and Dryden's *All for Love* have been noted by Michael Cooke.[18] Byron invariably achieves his happiest voice by rewriting

history and playing against the expectations generated by convention, and he expands his artistic range by assuming and revising the
ethos and form of heroic drama. There is a significant distinction
between his play and Dryden's: Cleopatra tempts Antony from
Roman virtue, whereas Myrrha seeks to waken Sardanapalus from
indolence to fulfill the responsibilities of a monarch. He uses love for
her as an excuse for dereliction, but hedonism offends her Greek
ideals and she stoutly opposes the pretext. The reversal of tradition is
consonant with Byron's wariness of domination by women: lest Sardanapalus seem as submissive as Jaffeir, even his most rhapsodic
exaltations of Myrrha must appear the product of his will rather than
her charms.

The opening soliloquy of Salemenes states the levels of conflict in
Sardanapalus:

> He hath wronged his queen, but still he is her lord;
> He hath wronged my sister—still he is my brother;
> He hath wronged his people—still he is their sovereign—
> And I must be his friend as well as subject:
> He must not perish thus. I will not see
> The blood of Nimrod and Semiramis
> Sink in the earth, and thirteen hundred years
> Of Empire ending like a shepherd's tale;
> He must be roused. In his effeminate heart
> There is a careless courage which Corruption
> Has not all quenched, and latent energies,
> Repressed by circumstance, but not destroyed—
> Steeped, but not drowned, in deep voluptuousness.
>
> (I, i, 1–13)

The failure of the king's marriage is thus the first statement of the
drama, and its primacy is explained at Zarina's appearance in Act IV.
The importance of the fraternity between Salemenes and Sardanapalus is affirmed by its second place in the speech; although
related merely by marriage only they constantly refer to each other as
"brother," and since during most of the play they represent opposed
courses of action they figure as the good and bad brother in affectionate sibling rivalry. Third in order is the issue of legitimate government, and the contemporary political ramifications of Byron's fresh
story of revolution are loaned a fortuitous emphasis by the resem-
blances between the decadent Assyrian and the profligate George

IV.[19] Over all these loom the king's terrifying ancestors, Nimrod and Semiramis, and the fierce "man-queen" dominates the drama.[20] In their first interview Salemenes attempts to shame Sardanapalus into action by reminding him that "Semiramis—a woman only—led/ These our Assyrians to the solar shores/ Of Ganges" (I, ii, 126–128), and the king's effeminacy is best understood through its connection with her belligerency. Legend recounts that Semiramis murdered her husband and was in turn slain by her son for having committed incest; with her the *mater edax* sighted briefly throughout Byron reaches archetypal proportions.

Sardanapalus justifies his withdrawal by invoking against the martial code of his brother a philosophical benevolence beyond the scope of heroic drama:

> *Sar.* I leave such things to conquerors; enough
> For me, if I can make my subjects feel
> The weight of human misery less, and glide
> Ungroaning to the tomb: I take no license
> Which I deny to them. We all are men.
> *Sal.* Thy Sires have been revered as Gods—
> *Sar.*   In dust
> And death, where they are neither Gods nor men.
> Talk not of such to me! The worms are Gods;
> At least they banqueted upon your Gods,
> And died for lack of farther nutriment.
> These Gods were merely men; look to their issue—
> I feel a thousand mortal things about me,
> But nothing godlike,—unless it may be
> The thing which you condemn, a disposition
> To love and be merciful, to pardon
> The follies of my species, and (that's human)
> To be indulgent to my own.
>   (I, ii, 261–278)

Sardanapalus appears to have forsaken the hostile world of men for the nurturing role of woman, but so favorable an interpretation of his conduct is complicated by the concluding slide into self-indulgence. In every speech the king modulates from a praiseworthy care for the people into a willful assertion of utter indifference to anything outside himself: "I have, by Baal! done all I could to soothe them:/ I made no

wars, I added no new imposts,/ I interfered not with their civic loves,/
I let them pass their days as best might suit them,/ Passing my own as
suited me" (I, ii, 356–360). When Salemenes warns of an intrigue
against the throne Sardanapalus exculpates himself of all responsibility by positing man's innate depravity:

> If then they hate me, 'tis because I hate not:
> If they rebel, 'tis because I oppress not.
> Oh, men! ye must be ruled with scythes, not sceptres,
> And mowed down like grass, else all we reap
> Is rank abundance, and a rotten harvest
> Of discontents infecting the fair soil,
> Making a desert of fertility.
>
> (I, ii, 407–418)

The king declares his revulsion from cruelty but he also misses no
occasion to dramatize himself as the misunderstood good man.
Myrrha seconds the appeal to preserve the empire and receives an
equally self-centered response: "At least I will enjoy it" (I, ii, 551). His
repudiation of glory is not selflessness but the mask of a Titanic will;
the wit defends against violent propensities the conscious mind
wishes to repress. Irony replaces the pride by which previous Byronic
heroes protected themselves from their inner stresses, but the love
Sardanapalus proclaims is identical in origin with Manfred's contempt. The impulse behind his withdrawal is shown by the feminine
manner he adopts: by forgoing the customary exercises of manhood
he hopes to recover the untroubled security of the child. One might
invoke the concept of identification: Sardanapalus seeks to become,
in his manner and philosophical benevolence, the nurturing mother
Byron always covertly and ambivalently desires. The familiar Byronic
configuration is clinched by the conception of Myrrha as an ad-
monisher to duty with none of the disturbing sexual power of a
Cleopatra. Like Manfred, however, Sardanapalus precludes the success of his regression by his continued assertiveness. He has merely
retreated from the larger world where he risks appearing diminished
in comparison with his forebears to reign tyrannically within the ac-
commodating sphere of the pleasure pavilion.

The conflicts Sardanapalus wishes to avoid invade his sanctuary
when the priest Beleses and the soldier Arbaces confederate and revolt. In the soliloquy that opens the second act Beleses prays to his
god, the sun, for an omen, but his auguries are baffled. The uncer-

tainty Beleses confesses is the salient aspect of the speech; in Shakespearean drama prophecies are invariably accomplished and those who disrupt the cosmic order are swept away in the bloodshed they have begun. In Byron's drama the natural order returns only dubious quotidian symbols that neither support nor condemn human actions. The play ends with the triumph of the rebels imminent but not yet established or clearly justified, and the open-endedness of the political structure requires that we again look inwards for the motives that determine the fates Byron assigns to characters. The sexual emphasis is developed in the portrait of Arbaces. He scorns the astrological science of his companion, insisting that his "star is in this scabbard" (II, i, 67), and the phrases Sardanapalus employs to describe him mark the nature of the aggressive energy which finds an outlet in the warrior code; the king stigmatizes him as "a mere tool, a kind/ Of human sword in a friend's hand..." (V, i, 460–461). For Arbaces battle is a means of discharging libido, as his own words confirm:

> And yet it almost shames me, we shall have
> So little to effect. This woman's warfare
> Degrades the very conqueror. To have plucked
> A bold and bloody despot from his throne,
> And grappled with him, clashing steel with steel,
> That were heroic to win or fall;
> But to upraise my sword against this silkworm,
> And hear him whine, it may be—...
>
> (II, i, 81–88)

The observation in the tales of the intimate bond between enemies is extended to its analytic conclusion in these lines; Byron now hints that warfare gratifies the desires more healthfully expressed in sexual mutuality. The imagery reads in the reverse direction as well, however, and hints an equation of sexual passion with destructiveness that is the key to the drama.

Sardanapalus tries to dissociate himself from the aggressive values shared by all the other figures in the drama, whether loyal or disloyal. The conspiracy is detected by the "cool, stern Salemenes" (II, i, 91), and the epithets indicate how little distinguishable he is from the soldier he exposes. Sardanapalus interrupts the fighting between them and then, ignoring his brother's counsel, pardons the rebels. The intervention wins Arbaces, who exclaims "methought he looked like Nimrod as he spoke," praises the magnanimity by declaring "Semiramis herself would not have done it," and renounces the uprising rather "than live ungrateful" (II, i, 352–373). It is ironic that the priest pledged to revere the sacred names of the race should rebuke Arbaces for this "weakness—worse/ Than a scared beldam's dreaming of the dead,/ And waking in the dark," but his attitude throws light on the king's (II, i, 349–351). Beleses cynically warps the ambiguous omens to serve his ends, but Sardanapalus mocks the religion of his fathers and announces that he will "dispense with/ The worship of dead men" (II, i, 239–240) because he is profoundly haunted by the past; his skepticism, like his effeminacy, is the sign of an effort to escape the heritage of violence he fears in himself. Therefore to be measured favorably against his ancestors carries with it the sinister warning that the pacific demeanor through which he has sought to control his passions is in jeopardy. From the outset Sardanapalus recognizes and struggles against his aggressiveness:

> Ne'er
> Was man who more desired to rule in peace
> The peaceful only: if they rouse me, better
> They had conjured up stern Nimrod from his ashes,
> "The Mighty Hunter!" I will turn these realms
> To one wide desert chase of brutes, who *were*,
> But *would* no more, by their own choice, be human.
> (I, ii, 370–376)

The king's tranquil façade is a vigilant attempt to prevent these forces from erupting, but the psychological defense betrays him when it leads to the unwise pardon of the rebels. Byron's most impressive achievement in the drama is to make the reader aware of the problematical motives beneath unimpeachable sentiments, and to sense that the need of Sardanapalus not to seem angry or vindictive in his own eyes contributes to his unwillingness to punish Arbaces and Beleses as they undoubtedly deserve. The banishment to which he sentences them so chimes in appearance with their expectations of secret assassination that they resume their plans. The very shape of events seems to render charity unviable: Arbaces "even yet repenting must/ Relapse to guilt" (II, i, 455–456), and the king is enmeshed in strife by his commitment to peace. Byron entirely invented this episode, and its disastrous outcome illustrates once again his disbelief in any intermission of the hostilities between men. If the sequence is considered in the context of the works discussed already a fantasy that confirms the misgivings of every Byronic hero is apparent: the experience of Sardanapalus argues that because charity will be repaid with ingratitude harshness is the only mode of survival. The cruel syllogism reflects Byron's difficulty in conceiving of a mean between oppression and passivity, and in this uncompromising formulation the opposite terms are really the same. Sardanapalus becomes in his own words "the very slave of Circumstance/ And Impulse" (IV, i, 330–331) because he will not exert the authority to act, as much as any of his predecessors the prisoner of the unconscious drives that he has failed to work through.

The chief irony of the drama is that Myrrha and Salemenes regard as his salvation the recklessness Sardanapalus displays when attacked, whereas to him it marks the collapse of his desperately maintained ideals. Myrrha joyfully abandons her previous criticism and declares:

> He, who springs up a Hercules at once,
> Nursed in effeminate arts from youth to manhood,
> And rushes from the banquet to the battle,
> As though it were a bed of love, deserves
> That a Greek girl should be his paramour,
> And a Greek bard his minstrel—a Greek tomb
> His monument.
>
> (III, i, 221–227)

Myrrha adds death to the association of sex and war noted above, and the linkage is strengthened in the nightmare Sardanapalus endures at the beginning of Act IV. In a scene that realizes Beleses' taunt to Arbaces he imagines himself at a feast with his ancestors, and wakes terrified to admit to Myrrha that "there was a horrid kind/ Of sympathy between us, as if they/ Had lost a part of death to come to me,/ And I the half of life to sit by them" (IV, i, 124–127). The dream brilliantly manifests the victory of the unconscious over Sardanapalus' attempts at repression, and presents in strikingly naked fashion Byron's own preoccupations. Remembering the significance of the early death of Byron's father, the weight of the detail Sardanapalus tells Salemenes can be understood:

> *Sar.* My father was amongst them, too; but he,
> I know not why, kept from me, leaving me
> Between the hunter-founder of our race,

> And her, the homicide and husband-killer,
> Whom you call glorious.

Sal.   So I term you also,
> Now you have shown a spirit like to hers.
>   (IV, i, 177–181)

The seemingly casual confession is perhaps the most poignant moment in the play, since the disapprobation of his father is a projection of the guilt Sardanapalus feels for having been a truant to the code of the parents he repudiates but stands in awe of. As in Byron's life the early absence of the father leads to an exaggerated sense of the family tradition, so in the drama the parental image is displaced backwards onto Nimrod and Semiramis; the folklore appellation Sardanapalus gives to them, "The Hunter and the Crone" (IV, i, 132), emphasizes their potent status. The reward of his unexpected bravery is at last to win from Nimrod the acceptance he consciously disclaims but inwardly craves; he relates to Myrrha that "The Hunter laid his hand on mine: I took it,/ And grasped it..." (IV, i, 143–144). His reaction to Semiramis is far more charged with anxiety, for the imagined encounter embodies his darkest fears:

> The female who remained, she flew upon me,
> And burnt my lips with her noisome kisses;
> And flinging down the goblets on each hand,
> Methought their poisons flowed around us, till
> Each formed a hideous river. Still she clung;
> The other phantoms, like a row of statues,
> Stood dull as in our temples, but she still
> Embraced me, *while I shrunk from her, as if,*
> *In lieu of her remote descendant, I*
> *Had been the son who slew her for her incest.*
>   (IV, i, 149–158; italics added)

This horrible vision reveals the fundamental inversion on which *Sardanapalus* is constructed. The Byronic hero ordinarily proves his independence of woman by committing himself to a brutal conception of manhood, but it is impossible to differentiate the self from the mother figure by that expedient if she is a byword for violent aggression. Hence if one impulse beneath Sardanapalus' epicene manner is a desire to regress to the safe world of the child, the customary and powerful impulse to rebel against the mother by becoming as unlike her as possible is present here too, only in this case the peculiar situation generated by the "masculinity" of Semiramis requires the effeminacy of her descendant. Ironically, Sardanapalus is never more mother's boy than when he drops the stance of gentleness that was his means of establishing a unique course of conduct and goes forth as the heroic warrior lauded by all. Accordingly, in his nightmare he sees himself as swallowed up by the mother, the nourishing fluids of the womb transformed by ghastly specific parody into poisons that have killed his chance of autonomous adult existence. In resentment Sardanapalus directs the ferocity Semiramis represents against her, and wishfully views himself as her murderer.

In his dream Sardanapalus meets Semiramis when he seeks the "sweet face" of Myrrha, for he gains the love of both women simultaneously by acquiescing to their code of aggression (IV, i, 103).[21] The conjunction underscores their function as the twin aspects of woman, mother and lover, and in turn it enables the reader fully to comprehend the association of sexuality with violence and death. Early in the drama Sardanapalus argues against Myrrha's sanguinary insistence that Arbaces and Beleses be executed by observing that "your sex, once roused to wrath,/ Are timidly vindictive to a pitch/ Of perseverance, which I would not copy" (II, i, 586–588), and a later comment reiterates still more sharply the connection he feels between women and the absence of restraint: "femininely meaneth furiously,/ Because all passions in excess are female..." (III, i, 380–381). Throughout the drama the sensuality imputed to Sardanapalus is less apparent than his desire to remain aloof, and the first two acts show him, in contrast to Antony, resisting rather than succumbing to the blandishments of a woman. It may be inferred from this evidence that just as Sardanapalus is afraid to lose his temper against the rebels so is he afraid to lose his self-possession in the grip of amorous passion. Indeed, the figure of Semiramis declares the equivalence of giving way to violence and giving way to sexuality: the loss of control experienced by the conscious mind is the common term. The equation, rooted in the plot of the play, reveals Byron as well as his fictive character. A fragile ego identity sees itself perpetually threatened by the upsurges of passion, and precisely because Byron's feelings were strong he feared their power to disrupt his precarious stability. The juxtaposition of Myrrha with Semiramis reinforces the impression that Byron views woman's sexuality as an enveloping force capable of dissolving a man's integrity, and the picture of woman-the-devourer is a reflection of the anxieties of Byron's relations with women. In *Don Juan* he turns the irrepressible vitality of passion into a prime source of comedy, but the narrator never ceases to remind the reader that its elemental fury is no less the source of tragic waste in human life. The contrary modes spring from a single assumption, that the ego is too weak to withstand the instinctual drives it is charged with controlling. Byron's characteristic action involves the defeat of the conscious part of the personality by its chthonic roots, and however comic the situation he never portrays it without an undercurrent of fatality.

The other woman in the drama, Zarina, enters immediately after the king's account of his vision, and her delayed entrance completes the triple union of the Queen, Myrrha, and Semiramis. The king's wife is the node of all the ambivalence towards woman conveyed by the play, and in confessing why he neglected her for many years Sardanapalus articulates the pattern that we have repeatedly noticed:

> I was not formed
> To prize a love like thine, a mind like thine,
> Nor dote even on thy beauty—as I've doted
> On lesser charms, *for no cause save that such*
> *Devotion was a duty,* and I hated
> All that looked like a chain for me or others
> (This even Rebellion must avouch); yet hear
> These words, perhaps among my last—that none
> E'er valued more thy virtues, though he knew not
> To profit by them—...
>   (IV, i, 335–344; italics added)

To his hesitant question whether she can forgive him, the "gentle, wronged Zarina," as he calls her, selflessly replies: "I have never thought of this,/ And cannot pardon till I have condemned" (IV, i, 308–309). The speech maps Byron's familiar topography: the suicidal flight of the hero from the idealized woman he desires in order to assert an illusory freedom. On this occasion, however, Byron rings an interesting change on the theme: Zarina comes to bid farewell to Sardanapalus because *she* is fleeing the besieged palace with her sons so that the dynasty may be preserved. The king's concern for the throne is the corollary of his *rapprochement* with his ancestors; he anticipates that if he loses it his sons will forever execrate him: "all Earth will cry out, 'thank your father!'/ And they will swell the echo with a curse" (IV, i, 289–290). Her departure inverts the oedipal triangle as perceived by the child: instead of a mother "deserting" her son for the father it presents a wife deserting the husband for her sons. This state of affairs corresponds to what the son subconsciously wishes, but since the situation in the drama is seen from the point of view of Sardanapalus it reproduces in displaced form the fear of the child that if he asserts his manhood as he desires his mother will abandon him. Zarina wants to stay and has to be wrestled off the stage by Salemenes, but his "fraternal force" merely enacts the king's rejection; in consenting to her withdrawal Sardanapalus has already announced that he "must learn sternness now", and that lethal word signals the approaching end (IV, i, 398). "She's dead—and you have slain her" (IV, i, 417), the king accuses his brother-in-law when Zarina faints, but it is his own steadily emerging masculine will which dooms the sustaining female. With the going of Zarina the play passes into the world of men where no forgiveness is possible and the resentments between generations rage unabated.

The true symbol of womanly value in the play no sooner leaves than her place is taken by its counterfeits; Myrrha reappears and Sardanapalus resumes his benevolent and loving stance. "To me war is no glory," he tells Myrrha, "conquest no renown":

> I thought to have made mine inoffensive rule
> An era of sweet peace 'midst bloody annals,
> A green spot amidst desert centuries,
> On which the Future would turn back and smile,
> And cultivate, or sigh when it could not
> Recall Sardanapalus' golden reign.
> I thought to have made my realm a paradise,
> And every moon an epoch of new pleasures.
> I took the rabble's shouts for love—the breath
> Of friends for truth—the lips of woman for
> My only guerdon—so they are, my Myrrha [*He kisses her.*]
> Kiss me. Now let them take my realm and life!
> They shall have both, but never *thee*!
>
> (IV, i, 511–523)

The deceiving and self-deceived apology confirms Byron's power to present character dramatically; the progression from "peace" to "paradise" to "pleasures" indicates how thoroughly he had mastered the nuances by which speakers are made to reveal themselves by their own words. Sardanapalus hardly admits his errors before he twists the justified self-criticism into a renewed display of selfishness disguised as great passion. The unrestrained wilfulness precludes the

Eden Sardanapalus talks of establishing, and in a few lines it will surface completely and make a mockery of his professed pacifism. He scorns with the fury he had previously condemned the advice of Salemenes to await the rebels' second attack:

> I detest
> That waiting; though it seems so safe to fight
> Behind high walls, and hurl down foes into
> Deep fosses, or behold them sprawl on spikes
> Strewed to receive them, still I like it not—
> My soul seems lukewarm; but when I set on them,
> Though they were piled on mountains, I would have
> A pluck at them, or perish in hot blood!
> Let me then charge.
>
> (IV, i, 556–563)

The many perspectives put forward by the play on this speech elicit a wonderfully complex response. A moralist might see Sardanapalus as the voluptuary rightly threatened with the loss of his throne for shirking responsibility, whereas to his own eyes he appears as an innocent victim forced into war by a dedication to peace. To Salemenes and Myrrha his eagerness for battle atones for his initial passivity, whereas the overblown rhetoric hints that his "courage" is more vicious than his indolence ever was and supports a reading of him as all along the headstrong agent whose libido now at last clearly exhibits its latent violence.

Salemenes is in a sense the first casualty of the metamorphosis he encouraged, for when Sardanapalus takes up his martial legacy Salemenes becomes redundant in the symbolic scheme of the play, and he is killed at the beginning of Act V while standing "upon the same ground" as the king (V, i, 109). Byron heightens the sense of the inevitability of the king's development by the use of an omen, as in *Marino Faliero*: it is evident that the external event manifests the psychological process when, in accord with an ancient augury, the Euphrates suddenly overflows its banks, demolishing the bulwark of the palace and ensuring Sardanapalus' defeat. With much largesse the king dispatches his faithful servants by boat and prepares his grand immolation, but the excess to which he has succumbed flares up once more in his anger at the herald who demands his surrender. Reminded that it would disgrace "the last hours of a line/ Such as is that of Nimrod" to violate a sacred office by killing an unarmed mes-

senger, Sardanapalus rescinds the order of decapitation he has brut-
ally given, saying "My life's last act/ Shall not be one of wrath" (V, i,
329–330; 335–336). Having achieved this uneasy and ambiguous accommodation with his heritage, Sardanapalus readies himself to die.

The conclusion of the drama firmly demonstrates the distance
between the role filled by women in Byron's work and in *All for Love*.
The solemn death of Cleopatra dominates the final moments of Dryden's play (and Shakespeare's), but Byron relegates Myrrha to a subordinate position within the spectacle Sardanapalus arranges for himself. She claims that it is her *"duty"* (V, i, 371) to kindle the pyre he
has had constructed and to join him upon it; in her loyalty the
wished-for counterpart of the duty Sardanapalus resentfully felt he
owed Zarina is recognizable. The resulting suttee suggests rather the
male fantasy of the absolute dependence of women on men for their
identity—the legend relates that Sardanapalus slew his wives and
concubines before his death as a matter of course—than the mutual
end of two equally noble lovers. Yet this very inequality is affecting.
Byron has drawn Myrrha so roundedly that the self-indulgence that
stains the king's return of her fidelity is disturbing in greater or lesser
degree throughout the drama. Because his sincerity is not entirely
trustworthy her death does not grant the tragic sensation of involvement and transcendence experienced with Shakespeare's Cleopatra,
but it does uncomfortably suggest the myriad dishonesties, miscon-
ceptions, and unseen frictions in human relationships.

Sardanapalus' grand conflagration is the climactic emblem of the
equivocal revelations of the play. "My fathers, whom I will rejoin,"
the king begins his last soliloquy (V, i, 422): *Sardanapalus* reaches the
same termination as *Marino Faliero*. Though Faliero shudders at sensuality and rebels in order to protect his authority whereas Sardanapalus appears to be a debauchee who wants only to renounce his
power, both are overtaken by their ambivalent need to prove themselves worthy of their ancestors. Sardanapalus continues:

> the light of this
> Most royal of funereal pyres shall be
> Not a mere pillar formed of cloud and flame,
> A beacon in the horizon for a day,
> And then a mount of ashes—but a light
> To lesson ages, rebel nations, and
> Voluptuous princes. Time shall quench full many

A people's records, and a hero's acts;
Sweep empires, into nothing; but even then
Shall spare this deed of mine, and hold it up
A problem few dare imitate, and none
Despise—but, as it may be, avoid the life
Which led to such a consummation.

                                                    (V, i, 436–449)

The immolation is the apotheosis convention prescribes for the hero of a saga and in conventional terms Sardanapalus has earned it by his bravery, but Byron enables the reader to see, through his proud contemplation of his immortality, that it is also the supreme instance of his exquisite taste for theatrical effect. The king brings himself forward once again as a prince of peace become a sacrificial martyr, but after five acts we understand that the promised land of which he dreams and for which he borrows the Biblical rhetoric of cloud and pillar fails to materialize because of his own Titanic nature. The reader understands, indeed, more than he does, for the protagonists of Byron's dramas move not towards self-knowledge but towards self-revelation. Sardanapalus has little grasp of the forces that undo him, and the reader's position as spectator is to watch the crumbling of the ideal personality he consciously tried to erect for himself under the terrible pressure of his unconscious imperatives. His passions, supported by the demands of the superego, destroy Sardanapalus, but there is a certain pathos to his struggle, and a certain splendid authenticity in his end rises above his effort to give didactic shape to his career. *Sardanapalus* is a "problem," not the easily categorized piece its superficially traditional form suggests, and one that richly represents the tangled springs of human behavior.

The line by Sheridan that Byron selected for the epigraph to *The Two Foscari* encapsulates these themes: "The *father* softens, but the *governor's* resolved." At the center of the drama is the trial of Jacopo Foscari for alleged treason against Venice, over which his father the Doge is required to preside. The situation contains the already familiar elements: a father who figures as the oppressor of his son, and, as in *Marino Faliero* and *Sardanapalus*, a conflict between obligation to the state and private freedom. The outward circumstances of the play might thus be loosely termed political, but it is again striking that Byron imparts little of the information needed to assess the charges and countercharges of the plot. Jacopo is pursued until he dies by Loredano, who thereafter relentlessly forces the resignation of the Doge, knowing it will kill him, because he believes the elder Foscari poisoned both his father and uncle. However, neither Jacopo's guilt nor Loredano's accusation is ever fully clarified, and to a point the inscrutability pays dividends.[22] In the first speeches Byron refers to the torture inflicted upon Jacopo as "the Question," and the recurrent phrase is a sign of the interrogative role the reader must adopt. Because the secondary characters do not wholly comprehend the events before them the drama evolves as much in their uncertain responses as in the clash of the principals, and their attempt to puzzle out the action is the prototype for the reader's. Yet in the end the drama is weakened by the doubts that Byron permits to surround the basic facts of the story, and his want of concern with them alerts the reader that his interests lie elsewhere than in the feud between Loredano and the Foscari.

"I have been so beyond the common lot/ Chastened and visited," Jacopo says sadly in Act IV, "I needs must think/ That I was wicked" (IV, i, 166–168). All Byron's heroes are haunted by this sense of a guilt anterior to any action which drives them toward self-punishment, and here the note of bewildered innocence is not unwarranted: Jacopo is a victim of the hate aroused by his father, and it is thus appropriate that the Doge appear as his persecutor. The Doge seems dimly to realize that Jacopo is his scapegoat; he tells Jacopo's wife Marina that "they who aim/ At Foscari, aim no less at his father" (II, i, 86–87). By his action he in effect consents to the substitution, and when Marina reproaches him for complicity and he replies by arrogating the words of Christ on the cross the bitter variation of Christian symbolism becomes explicit: "I forgive this, for/ You know not what you say" (II, i, 125–126). "You have seen your son's blood flow, and your flesh shook not," she exclaims in horror (II, i, 129), but the Doge feels only that Jacopo is a "disgrace" to their house and it is left to her to insist that the Venetians should "implore/ His grace" for their cruelty (II, i, 171–172). Byron counterpoints the suggestion that the dedication of the Doge to Venice is a secular analogue of the Gospel declaration that God so loved the world that He gave His only begotten Son to redeem it with a characteristic allusion to *patria potestas* hinting at an adversary position devoid of charity: Barbarigo describes the Doge "With more than Roman fortitude . . . ever/ First at the board

in this unhappy process/ Against his last and only son" (I, ii, 24–26).
An Old Testament parallel conveys the Doge's attitude more accurately than the New; it is clear that he has cast himself as the martyr of
the piece in the image of Abraham commanded to slay Isaac:

> I have observed with veneration, like
> A priest's for the High Altar, even unto
> The sacrifice of my own blood and quiet,
> Safety, and save honour, the decrees,
> The health, the pride, and welfare of the State.
>
> (II, i, 255–259)

I do not know precisely how much weight Byron meant us to give to
echoes like these, but their frequency (like his lifelong fascination
with, and opposition to, the intricacies of Christian dogma) testifies to
the appeal made to his imagination by episodes of a son slaughtered
by a father.

The dimensions of the family conflict in *The Two Foscari* extend to
every area of the plot. Jacopo is in prison because he is unable to exist
apart from Venice; already in exile for a previous offence, he opened a
treasonous correspondence in order to be discovered and recalled. He
knows that he will not survive his return but he is compelled to it by
the irresistible impulse that his welcome to death reveals: "my native
earth/ Will take me as a mother to her arms" (I, i, 142–143). Jacopo
exclaims that the brief glimpse of the city he is allowed while out of
his cell makes him feel "like a boy again" (I, i, 93), for to him it
represents the innocent peace of childhood. His happy memories of
swimming in the ocean and racing gondolas along its surface further
illustrate the nature of his desire to regress to a fostering maternal
environment. "I was a boy then," he concludes wistfully, and the
reply of the guard seals the impossibility of ever recapturing that lost
bliss: "Be a man now: there never was more need/ Of manhood's
strength" (I, i, 122–123).

The Doge calls his son's compulsion "womanish," and it is indeed produced by identification with the mother, but he too transfers
to the city the emotional force usually inspired by women. In this
context, as in *Marino Faliero*, the feminine gender customarily employed in referring to Venice acquires special significance. The common usage resonates disconcertingly when at his first appearance the
Doge recounts his service to Venice while the city destroys his son:

> I found her Queen of Ocean, and I leave her
> Lady of Lombardy; it is a comfort
> That I have added to her diadem
> The gems of Brescia and Ravenna; Crema
> And Bergamo no less are hers; her realm
> By land has grown by thus much in my reign,
> While her sea-sway has not shrunk.
>
> (II, i, 17–23)

The language confirms that Venice stands at the apex of an oedipal triangle in which the brand of traitor enforces Jacopo's position as the defeated son and the Doge's eminence magnifies his status as the triumphant father and husband. His rationale for rejecting Marina's plea that he intervene in Jacopo's behalf exposes his complete identification with paternal authority:

> *Doge*   I found the law; I did not make it. Were I
> A subject, still I might find parts and portions
> Fit for amendment; but as Prince, I never
> Would change, for the sake of my house, the charter
> Left by our fathers.
>
> *Mar.*   Did they make it for
> The ruin of their children?
>
> *Doge*   Under such laws, Venice
> Has risen to what she is—a state to rival
> In deeds, and days, and sway, and, let me add,
> In glory (for we have had Roman spirits
> Amongst us), all that history has bequeathed
> Of Rome and Carthage in their best times, when
> The people swayed by Senates.
>
> *Mar.*   Rather say,
> Groaned under the stern Oligarchs.
>
> *Doge.*   Perhaps so;
> But yet subdued the World: in such a state
> An individual, be he richest of
> Such rank as is permitted, or the meanest,
> Without a name, is alike nothing, when
> The policy, irrevocably tending
> To one great end, must be maintained in vigour.
>
> *Mar.*   This means that you are more a Doge than father.
>
> (II, i, 395–413)

The deadly juggernaut the Doge makes of the state is a reflection of the ruthless self-control he practices upon himself, for he loves his son but will not be seen to unbend. "I cannot weep," he tells Marina, "I would I could" (II, i, 78), and the hypersensitivity that perceives sympathy as condescension explodes when she attempts to commiserate: "Pitied! None/ Shall ever use that base word, with which men/ Cloak their soul's hoarded triumph, as a fit one/ To mingle with my name" (II, i, 146–149). The first consequence of such repression is as always the sense of a hostile, determinist universe; "So, we are slaves,/ The greatest as the meanest—nothing rests/ Upon our will," the Doge laments of his self-created Hell (II, i, 357–359). Jacopo's death is the counterpart (and in some measure the result of) his own stifled tenderness. "And this is Patriotism?" Marina asks unbelievingly; "To me it seems the worst barbarity" (II, i, 427–428). She likewise denounces her husband's attachment to Venice as "Passion, and not Patriotism" (III, i, 143), and through her it is realized that the fanatic loyalty to Venice that links the otherwise unlike father and son is the mark of a crisis of which the harshness of the one and the softness of the other are the twin faces.

Marina is a second, sexual focus of the disguised situation expressed in *The Two Foscari*, and she occupies a position congruent to that of Venice in the complex of feelings represented by the two men. On the surface she and the city are polar opposites: whereas Venice is the exalted lady of the Doge and the devouring mother of Jacopo, Marina is the loyal wife of the latter and the courageous antagonist of the former. This symmetry, however, discloses a deeper similarity. Jacopo's weakened condition makes him so dependent on Marina for support, forensic and physical, that she becomes to him the nursing protectress that she is to their children, a portrait of the ideal aspects of the fantasized mother figure even as Venice is of the negative. Yet since the structure of the drama places as much emphasis on the intimacy between Marina and the Doge as on the marriage relationship Jacopo seems to the reader to be in competition with his father for her attention. The advantage he enjoys in our minds by actually being her husband is offset when his early death leaves Marina and the Doge alone together. In the end the Doge too is reduced to dependence on Marina by his grief-stricken collapse and removal from office, and in the configuration of the elderly widower watched over by his son's wife the motif of the redemptive daughter observed throughout Byron as a primary manifestation of his central ambivalence toward women recurs. Indeed, Marina's strength has sinister implications. Marina is proud not to have "left barren the great house of Foscari," but the reader knows too well the connotations of such sternness not to be taken aback when she declares that she refused to cry out in the pain of childbirth "for my hope was to bring forth/ Heroes, and would not welcome them with tears" (I, i, 240–247). The corollary of her maternal fierceness is the terrifying capacity for passion that from Gulnare through Myrrha and Semiramis Byron distrustfully ascribes to his female protagonists. If Marina is the exponent of charity pleading against the savage world of men her instincts also make her a destructive force within that world: "I have some sons, sir,/ Will one day thank you better," she warns Loredano (III, i, 269–270). The anticipation of revenge entails upon future generations the misery that afflicts the Doge and Jacopo, and hints that Marina is a mother who, like Venice, may consume the life of her children.

Byron's characterization of Loredano is the perfect complement to the internal dynamics of the Foscari family. The cynical contempt for legitimacy he displays in answering Barbarigo's objections to the planned deposition of the Doge calls into doubt the elder Foscari's sacramental vision of the immutable institutions of Venice:

> *Bar.*   What if he will not?
> *Lor.*   We'll elect another,
>   And make him null.
> *Bar.*   But will the laws uphold us?
> *Lor.*   What laws?—"The Ten" are laws; and if they were not,
>   I will be legislator in this business.
>
> (IV, i, 36–39)

The Doge's exaltation of the state is cast in a still more ambiguous light when even after this flagrant admission Loredano rebuts Barbarigo's argument that the Doge has already suffered enough in the death of his son by turning against him exactly the principle the Doge invoked in refusing to aid Jacopo, sanctimoniously proclaiming that "The feelings of private passion may not interrupt/ The public benefit" (IV, i, 265–267). The immediate effect of this hypocrisy is undoubtedly to confirm Loredano's wickedness, but with it Byron also reminds the reader that the forms of the state can be manipulated to mask personal ends; the play is less concerned with apportioning individual guilt than with adumbrating the common motivation of the enemies. Like the Doge, Loredano is obsessed with the need to fulfill the imagined expectations of paternal authority; he is driven to retribution by the "hereditary hate" he carries engraved on his tablets, an apt emblem of his psychological fixity. He is a scourge to the Foscari only because he must prove that he is a good son to his own forebears, and his thirst for vengeance will be the inheritance of Marina's children in the next cycle, when the roles of persecutor and victim will appear reversed. The intergenerational continuity of the strife is further evidence for apprehending the warfare between the families as a displaced image of the tensions within the family; it should be observed that in overthrowing the Doge Loredano acts out the resentments against the father that Byron excludes from the portrait of the weakly submissive Jacopo, who is so thoroughly an overshadowed son that he never becomes a man. Just as Jacopo's fate is an instance of the child's worst fears for himself, Loredano's triumph and curious escape from punishment are perhaps to be explained as an image of his wishes.

As the play proceeds it becomes increasingly obvious that the notion of an autonomous state with a will of its own is a convenient fiction men elaborate to conceal their culpable aspirations and impulses. A conversation between Memmo and an unnamed senator invited to lend by their neutral presence an air of disinterestedness to the cabal against the Doge displays the temptation of power clothed in the specious respectability of "duty":

> *Mem.*   As we hope, Signor,
> And all may honestly, (that is, all those
> Of noble blood may,) one day hope to be
> Decemvir, it is surely for the Senate's
> Chosen delegates, a school of wisdom, to
> Be thus admitted, though as novices,
> To view the mysteries.
> *Sen.*   Let us view them: they,
> No doubt, are worth it.
> *Mem.*   Being worth our lives
> If we divulge them, doubtless they are worth
> Something, at least to you or me.
> *Sen.*   I sought not
> A place within the sanctuary; but being
> Chosen, however reluctantly so chosen,
> I shall fulfil my office.
> *Mem.*   Let us not
> Be latest in obeying "The Ten's" summons.

> *Sen.*   All are not met, but I am of your thought
> So far—let's in.
> *Mem.*   The earliest are most welcome
> In earnest councils—we will not be least so.
>
>   (IV, i, 82–98)

Byron deftly imitates the interior duplicity by which the moral sense is laid asleep and equivocation changes into enthusiasm. His demonstration of the pervasive allure of the state as a pliable sanction for individual aggressiveness makes a comment the passage of time renders still more significant than it was in the 1820s. Because of their stunted inner lives the heroes of most of Byron's tales must derive their sense of themselves from the outside; they exist only so long as they are in motion, conducting war and wreaking revenge. Faliero extends this syndrome, and it is because his image of himself requires continuous public confirmation that he cannot accept the distinction Angiolina draws between honor and reputation. The Doge bewails the diminished opportunity to base a public identity on valorous exploits, but as his translation of Steno's insult into an affront to Venice reveals, he compensatorily aggrandizes himself by identifying with the state, an expedient Byron had presciently intuited the conditions of modern life would favor. It may thus be understood how the rebel Faliero foreruns his apparent opposite, Foscari, who defines—and enhances—himself by his exaggerated devotion to Venice. The gambit fails both men, however: Faliero is frustrated by the state's anonymity and finally bows to the weight of established authority, and Foscari's prestige, as Memmo remarks in the first scene of *The Two Foscari,* is that of "a gilded cipher" (I, i, 196). He is defeated by the artful Loredano, whose chicanery shows that in the mass state the grand Titans are superseded by the cunning exploiters of form and ritual.

    The supposed omnipotence men idolize in the state in order to satisfy their own needs levies with growing severity the penalty of psychological evasion as *The Two Foscari* advances. Jacopo is sentenced to fresh exile, and Marina tries in vain to reconcile him to the decree the country he loves passes against him. "Obey her," she urges, " 'tis she that puts thee forth," but he replies despondently, "Ay, there it is; 'tis like a mother's curse upon my soul . . ." (III, i, 185–187). Marina is permitted to accompany him, but the sentence includes the proviso that their sons must remain behind:

Jac.	And must I leave them—*all?*
Lor.	You must.
Jac.	Not one?
Lor.	They are the State's.
Mar.	I thought they had been mine.

(III, i, 386–388)

The restriction is horridly apposite, for it recapitulates Jacopo's self-destructive exaltation of Venice; in the fate of his children the negative aspects of the mother figure represented by the city win out over Marina, their complement and double. Divorced thus from his maternal native land, forced to abandon his father and sons, weakened from the torture that is the embodiment of these spiritual sufferings, Jacopo dies. The Doge throws himself prostrate on the body in sincere grief, but Marina's sharp remark enables the reader to see beyond the pathos of the situation and comprehend the Doge's responsibility for the anguish he suffers:

> Aye, weep on!
> I thought you had no tears—you hoarded them
> Until they are useless; but weep on! he never
> Shall weep more—never, never more.

(IV, i, 214–217)

The half-buried echo of Lear's words over the body of the daughter his folly has destroyed points up the Doge's collaboration in the circumstances of which outwardly he is only the victim; the source of his misery is the sternness he cherishes in himself and its reflection, the state.

The last act fully discloses the pernicious hollowness of the ideal to which the Doge has given himself. The Ten force him to abdicate, and the common usage he employs as he resigns the ducal ring and bonnet returns the reader to the fundamental level of the drama: "The Adriatic's free to wed another" (V, i, 192). An otherwise gratuitous conversation with Memmo renders the oedipal content still more explicit:

| Doge. | Methinks I see amongst you A face I know not.—Senator! your name, You, by your garb, Chief of the Forty! |
| Mem. | Signor, I am the son of Marco Memmo. |

> *Doge.*   Ah!
> Your father was my friend.—But *sons* and *fathers*!
> (V, i, 195–199)

His tormentors hypocritically insist that the Doge leave the palace with an honorary escort, but in a final terrible irony he dies when he hears the bell announcing his successor. Having repressed the areas of the self that lay outside his office, the Doge no longer has any existence apart from it. The Ten decree magnificent obsequies, and though Marina rightly protests that the elaborate courtesy mocks them, the irony cuts in the other direction as well: it is in the name of such insubstantial grandeur that the Doge sacrificed his family and, at last, himself.

"What I seek to show in *The Foscaris*," Byron told Murray, "is the *suppressed* passion..." (*LJ* 5: 372). The multiple repressions of the drama offer the most complete illustration of the conflict that dominates Byron's imagination: through them may be seen from all angles the resentful, helpless son and the rigid posture he adopts in defense, together with the awesome mother whom he alternately desires and fears.

4

Rebels Cosmic and Domestic

*A*t the end of January 1821, two weeks after he had begun *Sardanapalus,* Byron noted in his diary plans for three more tragedies, including "Cain, a metaphysical subject, something in the style of Manfred, but in five *acts,* perhaps, with the chorus" (*LJ* 5: 189). He turned to the project only when *The Two Foscari* had been completed, and by then his enthusiasm for the regular drama had been weakened by the poor reception given the London production of *Marino Faliero. Cain,* begun on July 16 and despatched to England September 10, consequently was written in three acts only and fell into "the Manfred metaphysical style... full of some Titanic declamation" (*LJ* 5: 368). When he switched to the freer form, cannily citing the little-known "mystery" as precedent, Byron relinquished the hope he had expressed of setting an example to reform the English stage (*LJ* 5: 347). The differences between the ostensibly neoclassical dramas and the various modes with which he experimented thereafter, however, do not extend to theme. The common protagonist of all the plays is the Titanic rebel, and Cain, discontented with "the politics of Paradise" (*LJ* 5: 368), is a direct descendant of Faliero and Foscari.

Scholarship has assiduously documented the eclectic assemblage of sources on which Byron drew in *Cain,* but the profusion of influences reinforces the impression that he was hardly concerned to conduct a rigorous investigation in theology.[1] To approach the drama, as did its first shocked readers, as literally an essay in metaphysics is to miss the point, which is that Byron's ironic revision of divine history is the culmination of his recurrent human themes.[2] The drama is foreshadowed by the frequent allusions to Cain in the tales, for Byron had long since taken the first son, living in painful proximity to the Eden he is forever denied, as the archetype of his heroes, aggrieved by their sense of irreparable loss and undeserved suffering.

If the events recorded in Genesis are compared with the interpretation Byron gives to them, the animosity towards Adam that without scriptural evidence he attributes to Cain is immediately noticeable. "Toil? and wherefore should I toil?" Cain demands in his first soliloquy: "because/ My father could not keep his place in Eden?" (I, i, 65–66). The note of filial resentment is accentuated in the encounter Byron invents between Cain and Lucifer before the murder of Abel. The archangel cleverly exacerbates Cain's malaise by a prophecy that, though anachronistic, is highly revelatory of his author's concerns: "Perhaps he'll make/ One day a Son unto himself," Lucifer says of God, "—as he/ Gave you a father—and if he so doth,/ Mark me! that Son will be a sacrifice!" (I, i, 163–166). The speech neatly fuses God and Adam as the objects of Cain's resentment; the loveless despot depicted by Lucifer, ruling in "unparticipated solitude" and miserable despite his omnipotence, is the familiar paternal imago. Lucifer, the primordial rebel against the Father, seems to have achieved the independence Cain desires, and, as Cain's response to this diatribe indicates, he is seductive because he gives body to Cain's unvoiced hostility: "Thou speak'st to me of things which long have swum/ In visions through my thought" (I, i, 167–168). In Byron's treatment of Cain's motivation anger towards his father is so prominent that the sibling rivalry associated with the myth recedes into a secondary effect; indeed the frustration that goads Cain to slay his brother arises in part from impatience with the docile acquiescence in the principles of patriarchal subordination that Abel displays in deferring to him:

> *Abel.*   Brother, I should ill
> Deserve the name of our great father's son,

> If, as my elder, I revered thee not,
> And in the worship of our God, called not
> On thee to join me, and precede me in
> Our priesthood—'tis thy place.
>
>   (III,i, 195–200)

The relationship between Cain and Lucifer enables Byron to illustrate in full the familiar central pattern of rebellion and stalemate, for the two seem successive stages of the same character. Since Lucifer exemplifies Cain's bitter aspirations, Cain—and the reader—can gauge them by evaluating their results in him. Cain soon discovers that the promise of freedom Lucifer tenders him is only the illusion that enwraps an inescapable servitude:

> *Cain.*   Why should I bow to thee?
> *Luc.*   Hast thou ne'er bowed
>   To him?
> *Cain.*   Have I not said it?—need I say it?
>   Could not thy mighty knowledge teach thee that?
> *Luc.*   He who bows not to him has bowed to me.
> *Cain.*   But I will bend to neither.
> *Luc.*   Ne'er the less,
>   Thou art my worshipper; not worshipping
>   Him makes thee mine the same.
>
>   (I, i, 314–320)

Lucifer's assertion of triumph is the outward sign of the afflictions of self-consciousness in Byron's work, nowhere more sharply expressed than in this drama: the self-consciousness that distinguishes Cain from those around him is the consciousness of a self tormented by its own separateness and horrified by the shrunken solipsism it contemplates.

Cain experiences what Manfred declares figuratively: the Tree of Knowledge is not that of Life. Lucifer entices him less by offering to better his condition than by intensifying his dissatisfaction. In Act II Lucifer exhibits to Cain a vast panorama of an extinct pre-Adamite creation; "the object of the Demon," Byron explained to Murray, "is to *depress* him still further in his own estimation than he was before, by showing him infinite things and his own abasement, till he falls into the frame of mind that leads to the Catastrophe . . . from the rage and fury against the inadequacy of his state to his conceptions . . . (*LJ* 5:470). Lucifer achieves his end, but Cain's acute intelligence discovers the limitations of his mentor. He finds the glittery revelations "inferior still to my desires and conceptions" and remains unintimidated by the domineering manner of the archangel:

> Luc.   What are they which dwell
> So humbly in their pride, as to sojourn
> With worms in clay?
> Cain.   And what art thou who dwellest
> So haughtily in spirit, and canst range
> Nature and immortality—and yet
> Seem'st sorrowful?
>
>   (II, i, 82–86)

"I seem that which I am," replies Lucifer: the Devil is the sole Byronic actor to make that statement, and it betrays his rigidity.

Cain invariably has the last word in his debates with Lucifer, who must sophistically evade his questions or confess his impotence. At the close of the second act he unwittingly reveals the perpetual round of destruction to which he has doomed himself and which he would have Cain share. Cain has intuited that "though proud," Lucifer has a superior:

> Luc.   No! By heaven, which he
> Holds, and the abyss, and the immensity
> Of worlds and life, which I hold with him—No!
> I have a Victor—true; but no superior.
> Homage he has from all—but none from me:
> I battle it against him, as I battled
> In highest Heaven—through all Eternity,
> And the unfathomable gulfs of Hades,
> And the interminable realms of space,
> And the infinity of endless ages,
> All, all will I dispute! And world by world,
> And star by star, and universe by universe,
> Shall tremble in the balance, till the great
> Conflict shall cease, if ever it shall cease,
> Which it ne'er shall, till he or I be quenched!
> And what can quench our immortality,
> Or mutual and irrevocable hate?
>
>   (II, ii, 426–442)

This rodomontade, and especially the frenzied rush of qualifications and contradictions at the climax, uncovers the desperation of the speaker and the futility of the course he advocates. Having already succeeded in aggravating Cain's discontent and having forfeited his pose of aloof superiority, Lucifer vanishes from the play.

It is puzzling that a speech as evidently muddled as Lucifer's is not greeted with the derision it merits from a mind as analytic as Cain's, and that unfulfilled expectation points to a central feature of the drama. The meaning of *Cain* is larger than can be articulated by any of the imperfect dramatis personae: only the reader is in a position to comprehend the full significance of the action, and he can do so only when he learns to infer as much from what is left unsaid as from what is uttered. Byron speaks as it were over the heads of his characters, dropping hints directly to his audience, so that writer and alert reader join in a fellowship of privileged understanding largely denied Cain. Cain, however, does see through Lucifer's boasts, and to grasp why he can expose the fallacies of the archangel yet fall prey to his designs is to approach the deepest level of the play.

Lucifer reinforces Cain's desire to assert himself, but his rhetoric makes a second, subtler appeal at the same time. Cain is temperamentally gentle, sensitive to the beauties of nature, and eager to realize for man the paradisal world he imagines: "I thirst for good," he cries (II, ii, 238). This thwarted idealism, to which Byron's letter to Murray explicitly ascribes Cain's unhappiness, has a particular psychological basis.[3] Alienated from his family by the contempt of the self-aware man for the unthinkingly pious, Cain is gnawed by the attendant feelings of loneliness. Lucifer's invocation of an "unbounded sympathy of all/ With all" who suffer "in concert," making endurable the innumerable pangs he blames on the "Indefinite, Indissoluble Tyrant" unerringly reaches Cain's unrequited need of mutuality (I, i, 152–161). "Never till/ Now met I aught to sympathise with me," Cain poignantly confesses, and then defensively insists: "'Tis well—I rather would consort with spirits" (I, i, 189–191). The abrupt shift in tone reveals the Titanic bravado of the Byronic hero as the cloak of his starved craving for acceptance. Cain easily penetrates the specious reasonings that constitute Lucifer's first line of attack, and he gradually discerns that the glimmer of fraternity that has subliminally attracted him is equally deceptive. In one of the most moving exchanges of the play Cain recognizes the impoverished isolation of the archangel:

> *Luc.*   I pity thee who lovest what must perish.
> *Cain.*   And I thee who lov'st nothing.
>   (II, ii, 337–338)

That his understanding should not avail him marks the fatalistic view of character on which Byron builds his drama: intellectual self-knowledge alone cannot alter behavior, for the will is the prisoner of the emotional imperatives of the self.

The Manicheanism that the play argues in the rationalistic patterns of an exercise represents the formalization of much more tangled impulses: the perpetual war between Lucifer and God is the unrelenting strife that for Byron typifies the world of men. Throughout the play Cain oscillates between the rival claims on his allegiance made by Lucifer and by his wife, Adah, for as always in his work Byron counterpoints the stark vision with that of the nurturing woman whom the hero condescends to and loves. The two vary in proportion to each other: the more savage the world of men, the more nurturing the female figure. The Biblical story afforded Byron an occasion sanctioned by tradition to elaborate the fantasy of incestuous bliss to which he returns again and again, since Cain's wife is of necessity also his sister. He develops an extended picture of their peaceful domesticity and sets it off against Lucifer's knowing remarks that future ages will regard innocent unions like theirs as sinful (I, i, 362–380), rejecting the distance made available by dramatic form for direct communication of his urgent personal preoccupations.

A simple yet important change in the chronology of the original emphasizes the underlying configuration. Antedating the birth of Cain's son Enoch enables Byron to present Adah in a fully maternal role, and simultaneously provides an appropriate locus for any regressive tendencies. In previous works the desire to retreat from the harsh conflicts of adulthood to the secure, mother-protected condition of infancy was often expressed by the hero himself, and his natural ambivalence towards it resulted in the violent alternations of tone already traced: Enoch supplies a vehicle to convey the desire in its purest form and thus lessens the pressure on Cain. Lastly, the presence of Enoch permits Byron to show Cain as both son and father and thereby to complete his scheme.

In an early encounter Lucifer expounds the dubious antinomy between love and knowledge on which he thrives and demands that Cain choose. Adah entreats him to choose love, and he replies that he loves nothing but her:

> *Adah.*   Our parents?
> *Cain.*   Did they love us when they snatched from the Tree
>   That which hath driven us all from Paradise?

Adah.   We were not born then—and if we had been,
           Should we not love them—and our children, Cain?
Cain.   My little Enoch! and his lisping sister!
           Could I but deem them happy, I would half
           Forget—but it can never be forgotten
           Through thrice a thousand generations! never
           Shall men love the remembrance of the man
           Who sowed the seed of evil and mankind
           In the same hour! They plucked the tree of science
           And sin—and, not content with their own sorrow,
           Begot *me*—*thee*—and all the few that are,
           And all the unnumbered and innumerable
           Multitudes, millions, myriads, which may be,
           To inherit agonies accumulated
           By ages!—and *I* must be the sire of such things!
                                 (I, i, 433–450)

Cain's ready sympathy and the resentment that militates against it both shine forth in this passage. Cain rejects his parents because they have deprived him of Eden, but the misery he generously wishes not to entail on his descendants is nothing but the projection of his anger. He half-conceives that if Enoch were able to forgive, the endless sequence of recriminations he anticipates would be broken, but since he cannot himself forgive Adam he is incapable of believing in the forgiveness of others. When his despair is increased by Lucifer's wounding display of the realm of death in Act II Cain calls down on his children the woe he reproaches Adam for having inflicted on him:

Luc.   Dost thou curse thy father?
Cain.   Cursed he not me in giving me my birth?
           Cursed he not me before my birth, in daring
           To pluck the fruit forbidden?
Luc.   Thou say'st well:
           The curse is mutual 'twixt thy sire and thee—
           But for thy sons and brother?
Cain.   Let them share it
           With me, their sire and brother! What else is
           Bequeathed to me? I leave them my inheritance!
                            (II, ii, 22–29)

The intergenerational antagonism repeatedly witnessed in Byron is formulated here with symmetrical clarity, and Cain is its helpless victim.

Lucifer advises Cain that "to form an inner world/ In your own bosom" is the sole means of bearing the anguish he has abetted (II, ii, 463–464). The echo of *Paradise Lost* resounds ironically because like all of Byron's principals Lucifer is tortured precisely by the absence of the integrated, self-sustaining identity for which Milton's Adam must strive. Were the stability Lucifer recommends available to Cain the archangel would not have gained a disciple.

In her attempt to comfort Cain Adah too employs a Christian vocabulary (without the duplicity of Lucifer), but her appeal to the chief article of the creed is repugnant to him. She counsels the creation of another Paradise and atonement for their parents' error:

> Cain.   What is that
> To us? they sinned, then *let them* die!
> Adah. Thou hast not spoken well, nor is that thought
> Thy own, but of the Spirit who was with thee.
> Would *I* could die for them, so *they* might live!
> Cain. Why so say I—provided that one victim
> Might satiate the Insatiable of life,
> And that our little rosy sleeper there
> Might never taste of death nor human sorrow,
> Nor hand it down to those who spring from him.
> Adah. How know we that some such atonement one day
> May not redeem our race?
> Cain.   By sacrificing
> The harmless for the guilty? What atonement
> Were there?
>
>   (III, i, 75–88)

Cain condemns the doctrine of vicarious atonement the instant he embraces it because the prefiguration of Christ reawakens the lethal suspicion at the core of his dismay: that he is a son who has been sacrificed for his father. In the tableau of Cain meditating on his tranquilly dozing child Byron captures the fundamental issue of the drama: whether the son will survive. Enoch, who has not a single word to speak, who has neither control over nor even consciousness of his destiny, is the emblem of the play's deepest concerns.

Enoch alone can release Cain from becoming the target of his son's hate, as Adam is of his, but only if Cain first interrupts the cycle by casting off the resentments that oppress him. Though Cain scorns Adah's hope of a redeemer the example of her selflessness temporarily abates his truculence. Encouraged by her loving maternal devotion and persuasive mildness, Cain joins her in pronouncing a benediction on their son:

> Cain.   Bless thee, boy!
> If that a mortal blessing may avail thee,
> To save thee from the Serpent's curse!
> Adah.   It shall.
> Surely a father's blessing may avert
> A reptile's subtlety.
> Cain.   Of that I doubt;
> But bless him ne'er the less.
>   (III. i. 156–161)

This doubting act of faith resolves for a brief moment the conflicts in the drama. Cain's invocation of happiness for his son can indeed mitigate the consequences of the Fall, since it puts a stop to the oedipal struggle that *is* the "Serpent's curse" in Byron's universe. For a little space Cain becomes the rare, precious figure yearned after in all Byron's works: the benevolent father.

Such a state of remission is transient, however; Cain achieves his precarious calm only in the fostering company of Adah, and cannot maintain it apart from her. When she leaves with Enoch so that Cain and Abel may perform their religious rites his habitual self reasserts its dominance and the catastrophe rapidly ensues. The awful consequences of the ferocious and unyielding drives of the human personality manifest themselves not only in the primal fratricide (the murder of Abel is the apposite end of the sacrificer of flesh), but also in the anathema Eve hurls at her remaining son. Our first mother appears as the negative of the potent figure whose positive is Adah: she is the dread woman who excommunicates man from joy, exemplified by the beginning of her terrible crescendo and the three lines which Byron, obviously engaged by the imprecation, added as "clinchers" after he had already forwarded the finished manuscript to Murray (*LJ* 5: 361):

> May all the curses
> Of life be on him! and his agonies

> Drive him forth o'er the wilderness, like us
> From Eden, till his children do by him
> As he did by his brother!...
> May the grass wither from thy feet! the woods
> Deny thee shelter! earth a home! the dust
> A grave! the sun his light! and heaven her God!
>
> (III, i, 421–425; 441–443)

Eve's forecast of the next revolution of the cycle in which Cain will be the sufferer reiterates the scenario of unhappy masculine aggressiveness that in Byron rules man's behavior. Lucifer and the God he execrates are the reciprocal faces of this masculine aggressiveness: the aspiring rebel is the projection of Cain's desires even as the stern tyrant he imagines set against him is the projection of his resentments.

Eve's grim prophecy is not the only voice the reader hears as the action closes. Through the introduction of an Angel of the Lord Byron considerably expanded the account given in Genesis of Cain's punishment, and the revisions illuminate once again for the reader the possibilities of reconciliation.[4] Most significant is the stress Byron lays on the Angel's consoling reassurances to Adah that revenge will not be taken on her husband:

> *Angel.*   Thou hast slain thy brother,
> And who shall warrant thee against thy son?
>
> *Adah.*   Angel of Light! be merciful, nor say
> That this poor aching breast now nourishes
> A murderer in my boy, and of his father.
>
> *Angel.*   Then he would but be what his father is.
> Did not the milk of Eve give nutriment
> To him thou now seest so besmeared with blood?
> The fratricide might well engender parricides—
> But it shall not be so—the Lord thy God
> And mine commandeth me to set his seal
> On Cain, so that he may go forth in safety.
> Who slayeth Cain, a sevenfold vengeance shall
> Be taken on his head. Come hither!
>
> *Cain.*   What
> Wouldst thou with me?
>
> *Angel.*   To mark upon thy brow
> Exemption from such deeds as thou hast done.
>
> (III, i, 484–499)

By presenting the reader with Enoch's potential parricide and equating it with Cain's own crime Byron emphasizes the vicious circle of the play, but it is now broken by the intervention of the Angel. Cain's "exemption" (the word is Byron's) is a miracle of divine grace, and in Cain's departure with his wife and son Byron gestures toward the forever unrealized hope that, granted so signal an indulgence, man will rise above himself and not re-establish the pattern.

Yet *Cain* is the saddest of Byron's works, for Cain's obtuse inability to comprehend the absolution awarded him is his most tragic example of human rigidity. Reduced like many of Byron's Titans to succor from the faithful maternal woman, Cain continues to envision himself as the victim of an implacable God, and his self-pity is the final note of the play:

> *Cain.*   O Abel!
> *Adah.*   Peace be with him!
> *Cain.*   But with *me*!
>   (III, i, 561)

The characteristically anticlimactic conclusion underscores Cain's failure to learn from his harrowing experience. In Cain's moment of generosity as a father and in the pardon by the Father which parallels it Byron depicts the remedy for the ills he narrates. Byron's play is moving, however, because the career of the gloomy hero who dominates it suggests a profoundly pessimistic denial of the assumption which justified Freud in placing his labors among the healing arts: that lucid, perceptive analysis could lead to psychic amelioration. *Cain* unfolds in a moment of prehistory, as it were, before the decisive act through which the protagonist defines himself forever as the first murderer. The former worlds which Lucifer shows Cain in the second act are the magnified image of the transformation of the infinite potential of the future into the dead fixity of the past which Cain himself falls prey to. The drama is thus the inverse of *Don Juan,* in which Byron discovers that by rewriting the past he can re-open the future and preserve himself from the determinism which enshrouds Cain.

"*Cain,*" declared Shelley, "is apocalyptic, it is a revelation never before communicated to man."[5] Shelley's praise was surely welcome to Byron, but the play is apocalyptic only in its unveiling of the resistance to regeneration impacted in the personality. Its parergon, *Heaven and Earth,* carries Byron's somber exegesis of Biblical history through Cain's descendants to the Flood, a further repetition of the Fall. Byron's diagrammatic construction here lays bare his constant themes but diminishes the complexity that elsewhere invests them with dramatic life.[6] Anah and Aholibamah, Cain's grand-daughters, have forsaken their mortal lovers Japhet and Irad, Noah's sons, for Azaziel and Samiasa, two of the "sons of God," who, according to the passage of Genesis on which Byron founded his plot, "saw the daughters of men that they were fair; and . . . took them wives of all which they chose" (VI, i–ii). The sisters display the typical polarities of Byron's women: meek, merciful love in Anah and passionate fierceness in Aholibamah. Their complementary relationship is thrown into relief by the antiphonal pairing of their speeches (e.g.: I, i, 36–80, 81–134; I, iii, 610–649, 650–677). Despite their very different characters the sexuality the sisters possess in common is as always in Byron an ambivalent quality: their attractiveness causes the angels to disobey God and lose title to eternity, and Byron's sketch of a continuation indicates that both women were to drown in the chastising deluge.[7]

The central consciousness of the play is the pathetic Japhet, who can neither win Adah for himself nor soften his father sufficiently to obtain inclusion in the Ark for her. The patriarch is a stern figure rebuked for his lack of compassion, a fit representative of the God Byron implies. In this tale of divine wrath the threatening father who darkens Byron's works acquires supreme incarnation in Jehovah, and Japhet's bafflement is the inevitable corollary. The destruction of the earth is presented as the vengeful act of a distant deity, and even so unimpeachable a member of the heavenly hierarchy as Raphael sympathizes with Satan and hints that he is unforgiven because of God's obduracy (I, iii, 554–585). The protagonists of the earlier plays are overtaken by a ruin that symbolically reflects their psychology but in *Heaven and Earth* the apparently innocent are crushed with the guilty by the absolute triumph of masculine power.

Titanic defiance seems more futile than ever in this dying environment, and except for Aholibamah its place is taken by the elegies for mankind and for the natural beauties soon to be overwhelmed which permeate the drama. The longing backward gaze throughout

Byron is epitomized in Anah's rejection of salvation for herself if others must die: "What were the world, or other worlds, or all/ The brightest future, without the sweet past—" (I, iii, 434–435). This melancholy past-centredness sharply distinguishes *Heaven and Earth* from the contemporary lyrical drama it outwardly resembles, *Prometheus Unbound*: Byron's sense of lost bliss is not lightened by any Shelleyan glimpses of restoration. The situation of the defeated son at the heart of the play is lit up in the confrontation between Japhet and the mother who beseeches him to rescue her infant son. Japhet's inability to protect the baby is a sign of his own cancelled future, for his arbitrary preservation offers no prospect of a meaningful adult life. The final word of the drama is his lament that he must continue to exist:

> To die! in youth to die!
> And happier in that doom,
> Than to behold the universal tomb,
>   Which I
> Am thus condemned to weep above in vain.
> Why, when all perish, must I remain?
> (I, iii, 924–929)

Japhet's plight encapsulates the feelings of despair known by all the lost sons who are Byron's heroes.

There are two suggestions in the play of alternatives to its cosmic impasse: the voice of faith that rises over the floods to affirm the divine will (I, iii, 883–904) and Japhet's allusions to an ultimate redemption (I, iii, 193–203). These undoubtedly explain why Byron called *Heaven and Earth* "very pious" (*LJ* 6: 31), but they are isolated. Their ineffectuality left the drama open to charges of blasphemy in Byron's day, and, more damagingly, precludes the clash of viewpoints that might have vivified it. Its one-sidedness, however, is the work's most revealing aspect. Byron began composition on October 9, 1821, in the midst of one of his periodic depressions, and he told Medwin that it "occupied about fourteen days." He "talked of writing a second part," but confessed "that it was only as Coleridge promised a second part to 'Christabel.'" His never writing it may have had motives more fundamental than declining interest, since when Murray balked at publication Byron determinedly transferred the play to John Hunt. The cause seems inherent in the drama itself:

the vision of a world crushed by an angry Jehovah already completed Byron's fantasies of malign paternal power.

Werner is at once the first and the last of Byron's finished plays, and so offers a microcosm of his dramatic universe. It is based on "Kruitzner, or The German's Tale," which is contained in Volume IV of *The Canterbury Tales* by Harriet Lee and her sister Sophia. Byron read the novel shortly after its appearance in 1801, and at thirteen was inspired to attempt a dramatization that, as he later recalled, he "had sense enough to burn." The impression made by the tale was lasting, however: in 1815 while on the Drury Lane Committee Byron again tried to turn the story into a play "for the house," and had written several hundred lines when interrupted by the scandalous separation from Annabella. The stubborn fascination exerted by the novel persisted during the succeeding busy years; on October 9, 1821, the day he began *Heaven and Earth,* Byron wrote Murray for the materials of a fresh start:

> Don't forget to send me my first act of *Werner* (if Hobhouse can find it amongst my papers)—send it by post (to Pisa); and also cut out Sophia Lee's "German's tale," from the *Canterbury Tales,* and send it in a letter also.
>
> (*LJ* 5: 390)

Reacquaintance did not disappoint Byron, and he told Medwin subsequently: "There is no tale of Scott's finer. . . . I admired it when I was a boy, and have continued to like what I did then. This tale, I remember, particularly affected me."[8] The MS. of the 1815 effort could not then be located, but Byron was undeterred; he set about writing on December 18 and finished all five acts within a month, discovering as he proceeded that he "perfectly" remembered many lines from his earliest adolescent version.[9]

Two impulses are discernible in Byron's renewed endeavor to transform Miss Lee's clumsily handled story into an effective drama. His resumption of a work begun before his disillusionment with Drury Lane and admittedly designed for production seems a deliberate bid for the theatrical success refused *Marino Faliero.* As was his custom, Byron announced in the preface that "the whole is neither intended, nor in any shape adapted, for the stage," but its harmony with popular taste was obvious and earned *Werner* a substantial record of performance. [10] The enigmatic, guilt-ridden protagonist, hinting at his sins to a priest and flaring up in histrionic confrontations with all around him, is a role tailored for a star wanting to score "points." Byron compellingly unfolds the murder mystery plot, embellishes it with duels, and gives scope to the scenic elaboration cherished by nineteenth-century audiences in the contrasted settings of the action, a decaying provincial palace complete with secret passage and a "large and magnificent Gothic Hall in the Castle of Siegendorf, decorated with Trophies, Banners, and Arms of that Family." The Gothic elements Byron had abjured in recent years recall *Manfred*, begun not long after his previous effort to dramatize "Kruitzner." In both instances the emotional excess encouraged by the genre seems to have provided a conventional outlet for very personal expression. He wrestled with Miss Lee's mediocre tale off and on for twenty years, and this prolonged engagement points to an involvement more intricate than the desire for recognition as a playwright which is the immediate cause of *Werner*. The tenacious hold upon his imagination enjoyed by "Kruitzner" is explained by its moral: the sins of the fathers shall be visited upon the sons. If it is understood that a confirmation of his own psychodynamics might easily appear to Byron as an external cause, his statement in the preface to *Werner* that the tale "may, indeed, be said to contain the germ of much that I have since written" is the conclusive evidence for the oedipal themes at the core of Byron's work.

The themes of *Werner* are characteristic, but the coloring shows some new lights. Siegendorf is a penurious Bohemian aristocrat disinherited long since by an unforgiving father for the rash acts of his youth, chief among them his match with a beautiful but poor foreigner, Josephine. This blocking figure has just died when the play opens, and Siegendorf hopes at last to claim his position. He has never ceased to lament the loss of his "wealth, and rank, and power" (I, i, 78), what his wife perceptively describes as "these phantoms of thy feudal fathers" (I, i, 137), and there are traces in his conduct toward her in the first scene of a resentment that his love cannot wholly eradicate. His wishes are frustrated anew by a powerful cousin, Baron Stralenheim, who covets the lands and vacated title for himself, and to that end misuses his authority, persecuting Siegendorf and forcing him to hide under the pseudonym of Werner. Stralenheim's intervention merely repeats the exclusion originally imposed by the elder Siegendorf; in the 1815 draft Werner laments: "My father's wrath extends beyond the grave,/ And haunts me in the shape of Stralenheim!" (I, i, 18–19). Thus doubly barred from his rightful legacy and bereft even of his name, Werner is a type of the son too weak to establish his identity while his father lives.

Werner is not the only son in the play, and significant perspectives are added by the already noticed phenomenon of duplication. Werner and Josephine, fleeing from the representative of parental opposition, are themselves parents in search of missing offspring. They have a child, Ulric, whom the elder Siegendorf relented so far as to raise as his own, but the boy, re-enacting his father's wildness, vanished shortly before the old man's death. Ulric and Werner are son and father, but to the head of the clan they stand in the same filial relationship, and it is the complex modulation of their roles that energizes the drama.

To the decrepit manor where Werner has taken refuge circumstances bring Stralenheim, rescued from drowning in the upset of his carriage at a river-crossing by two passing strangers, Gabor the Hungarian and, as Act II discloses after suspenseful delay, the sought-for Ulric. The coincidence strains credulity, and its very improbability prompts a question of its function. A well-known passage of Freud brilliantly illuminates its significance, especially when the place filled by Stralenheim is remembered:

> In actual fact the "rescue-*motif*" has a meaning and history of its own, and is an independent derivative of the mother-complex, or more accurately, of the parental complex. When a child hears that he *owes his life* to his parents, or that his mother *gave him life*, his feelings of tenderness unite with impulses which strive at power and independence, and they generate the wish to return this gift to the parents and to repay them with one of equal value. It is as though the boy's defiance were to make him say: "I want nothing from my father; I will give him back all I have cost him." He then forms the phantasy of *rescuing his father from danger and saving his life*; in this way he puts his account square with him. This phantasy is commonly enough displaced on to the emperor, king or some other great man; after being thus distorted it becomes admissible to consciousness, and may even be made use of by creative writers. In its application to a boy's father it is the defiant meaning in the idea of rescuing which is by far the most important; where his mother is concerned it is usually its tender meaning.[11]

These insights permit the connection of Ulric's gesture to the struggles of other Byronic heroes to achieve autonomy, and are corroborated as the hostile motives Freud hypothesized beneath a surface benevolence gradually manifest themselves in the drama.

By his familiarity with the secret passage Werner gains access to the room where the exhausted Stralenheim is sleeping, and though tempted to murder his enemy he only steals a rouleau of gold to pay for his journey to safety. The following morning Ulric arrives, and, his lineage unknown to the Baron as the Baron's pursuit of his father is unknown to him, is commissioned to investigate the robbery. Ulric thus unwittingly becomes the hunter of his father, producing a situation that literally renders the deepest level of the drama. The happiness of their subsequent surprise reunion after twelve years of separation is destroyed when, still ignorant of who has committed it, Ulric denounces the theft. Werner confesses and eloquently defends himself against his son:

> Ulric, before you dare despise your father,
> Learn to divine and judge his actions. Young,
> Rash, new to life, and reared in Luxury's lap,
> Is it for you to measure Passion's force,
> Or misery's temptation? Wait—(not long,
> It cometh like the night, and quickly)—Wait!—
> Wait till, like me, your hopes are blighted, till
> Sorrow and Shame are handmaids of your cabin—
> Famine and Poverty your guests at table;
> Despair your bed-fellow—then rise, but not
> From sleep, and judge!
>
> (II, ii, 100–110)

He concludes:

> . . . there are crimes
> Made venial by the occasion, and temptations
> Which nature cannot master or forbear.
>
> (II, ii, 147–149)

By depicting him as a sensitive soul driven to dishonesty this speech is calculated to win the audience's sympathy for Werner, and Ulric, now apprised of Stralenheim's machinations, vows to aid his escape. Once more he figures as savior, this time directly of his parents. He gives Werner a diamond formerly his grandfather's to bribe the guards and obtain transportation; his possessing the stone emphasizes that his grandfather's power has passed to him. Despite the assistance Werner fears that his son condemns him, and he implores Ulric not to despise him:

> *Wer.* Oh, do not hate me!
> *Ulr.*   Hate my father!
> *Wer.*   Aye,
> My father hated me. Why not my son?
> *Ulr.* Your father knew you not as I do.
> *Wer.*   Scorpions
> Are in thy words! Thou know me? in this guise
> Thou canst not know me, I am not myself;
> Yet (hate me not) I will be soon.
> *Ulr.*   *I'll wait!*
> In the meantime be sure that all a son
> Can do for parents shall be done for mine.
>   (III, i, 228–235)

This pathetic colloquy replays Werner's subjection to the elder Siegendorf and attests to the complete reversal of the positions of Werner and Ulric: by saving Werner Ulric accomplishes the son's desire to surpass and dominate the father. An instructive comparison with *Manfred*, which suggests itself at this point, measures the changes in Byron since the shattering events of 1816. His earlier protagonist owes his life to the Chamois Hunter and is humiliated by the rescue; his only compensation is to condescend to the hunter. When the Abbot, his spiritual father, offers divine salvation, Manfred's need to prove his self-sufficiency requires that he reject him too. In the last scene of the revised version Manfred demonstrates a kind of equality with the impressively solid Abbot, but it is at the price of his life, and there is no vision before 1822 of a son victorious like Ulric.

The relations between father and son are disrupted again at the instant of flight. Ulric excitedly informs Werner that Stralenheim has been killed and demands to know whether he is the assassin. The second aspersion of his rectitude angers Werner, but Byron subtly interweaves a tacit admission of his repressed desires into his plea of innocence:

> If I e'er, in heart or mind,
> Conceived deliberately such a thought,
> But rather strove to trample back to hell
> Such thoughts—if e'er they glared a moment through

The irritations of my oppressed spirit—
May Heaven be shut for ever from my hopes,
As from mine eyes!

(III, iv, 43–49)

Ulric withdraws the imputation and Werner's suspicions fall on Gabor the Hungarian, whom Stralenheim had accused of the robbery. Werner, knowing that the other was maligned, had sheltered him in the concealed passageway, but with such heavy-handed warnings not to explore its turnings—"who knows it might not/ Lead even into the chamber of your foe?"—as to reveal a half-conscious wish to provoke Gabor to the murder he did not have the daring to attempt himself (III, i, 96–97). The pervasiveness of filial resentment in every part of the drama is illustrated by lines that Byron singled out to recite to Medwin from Gabor's soliloquy: as he counts the hours in darkness Gabor meditates that each clang of Time's clock "takes something from enjoyment" but "the knell/ Of long-lived parents finds a jovial echo/ To triple time in the son's ear" (III, iii, 1–12).[12] Gabor proceeds toward Stralenheim's room, but the scene closes before he reaches it, and as he has fled the palace when Ulric discovers Stralenheim's corpse, Byron neatly tantalizes the reader's curiosity about the culprit. Ulric urges Werner to depart and profit from the removal of his enemy, and by promising to settle everything quiets his objection that flight at this juncture will stain his reputation. The act ends on his pious proclamation that "To save a father is a child's chief honour" (III, iv, 168).

By the beginning of Act IV Byron has thus fulfilled the expectations aroused by his creaky plot: parents and child have been reunited, Ulric has proved himself a model son, and as if by providence the trappings on which the inwardly insecure Werner relies for his identity have been restored to him, making him at last Count Siegendorf. But Byron prepares the happy outcome only to snatch it away, and in so doing he first engages sympathies and then forces an examination of the assumptions on which they are based.

The mythical dramas allowed Byron little scope for social criticism, but that concern returns with the realistic, historical mode of *Werner*. The aristocratic status Werner hungers for allies him with a class which the drama repeatedly characterizes as cruel or fatuous. In a long soliloquy in the first act Josephine decries the oppression "Of feudal tyranny o'er petty victims" and regrets her husband's yearning to take his place among the "despots of the north" (I, i, 697–730); her words are immediately followed by Werner's entry with the gold he has stolen, a perfect example of the moral ambiguity of his pride in birth. Gabor laments the degeneration of the "brave chivalry... of the good old times" (II, i, 324–325) and protests the "trampling on the poor" by the nobility (I, i, 656). The grand assembly of the aristocracy that Werner rapturously describes in the last act is no more to Josephine than a tedious ritual—"Well, Heaven be praised! the show is over" (V, i, 14)—and to the servants who are required to march in it nothing seems worse than forming "the train of a great man,/ In these dull pageantries" (V, i, 12–13).

The later acts of the play further ask the reader to consider Werner's complicity in the death that has brought his good fortune. He attempts to expiate the robbery by giving the coins he purloined to a monastery, but his heavy sense of guilt is out of all proportion to the sole criminal act for which he is strictly responsible. The obscure feeling of accountability that haunts him grows rather from the correspondence of Stralenheim's murder with his own wishes; his plan to marry Ulric to the slain man's daughter, Ida, is evidently an effort to atone the wrong he unconsciously blames on himself. Ida is the one major addition Byron made to Miss Lee's tale, and she is yet another variation of the motif of the redemptive daughter.

Whatever uncertainty may remain about the nature of the motives for which Werner punishes himself is dispelled when Gabor reappears amid the festivities. In an effective *coup de théâtre* he clears his name by convincingly demonstrating that Ulric is the murderer; aghast, Werner exclaims "God of fathers!" (V, i, 335), and then, in the most pregnant speech in the play, reveals that at the moment of the assassination he had "horrid dreams": "I dreamt of my father—/ And now my dream is out!" (V, i, 357–360). Byron could hardly declare more emphatically that the killing of Stralenheim is a displaced realization of Werner's repressed filial rage, carried out essentially by his double, since Ulric occupies a position identical to his in respect to the elder Siegendorf. Without remorse Ulric avows his culpability; his only emotion is wonder that his father had not deduced it long before. Werner's ignorance is easily explained by the speeches quoted above, and witnesses the fine consistency of Byron's characterization. Werner's glorification of the aristocracy is symptomatic of his general psychic strategy of coping with oppression by identifying with his oppressor, instead of fighting him as Ulric does. Werner's meager self-respect depends on not admitting to consciousness the hostility the murder expresses, and what he denies in himself he is precluded

from observing in others. "Parricide!" he cries out as Ulric coolly
schemes the disposal of Gabor (V, i, 423), and the stigma is symbolically if not literally true: it correctly describes the motives of the crime
already committed, and indicates that in consequence of his identification with paternal authority Werner has made himself their next
object. His reunion with Ulric is a deadly confrontation with his own
buried self, who inexorably rises to terrify him when he ceases to be a
son and becomes Count Siegendorf. The repressed returns with
primitive starkness as Ulric vindicates himself by exactly repeating his
father's words:

> *Who* proclaimed to me
> That *there were crimes* made venial by the occasion?
> That passion was our nature? that the goods
> Of Heaven waited on the goods of fortune?
> *Who* showed me his humanity secured
> By his *nerves* only? . . .
> The man who is
> At once both warm and weak invites to deeds
> He longs to do, but dare not. Is it strange
> That I should *act* what you could *think*? We have done
> With right and wrong; and now must only ponder
> Upon effects, not causes.
>   (V, i, 441–455)

"Ida *falls senseless*—Josephine *stands speechless with horror*," reads Byron's last stage direction, and the play closes with Ulric's flight to the
outlaw bands he clandestinely leads and Werner's despairing recognition that his dynastic aspirations are blasted: "Now open wide, my
sire, thy grave;/ Thy curse hath dug it deeper for thy son/ In mine!—
The race of Siegendorf is past" (V, ii, 64–66). Werner's collapse at
Ulric's revelation is only the outward completion of the psychic
suicide he chose in disowning his aggressive energies, reducing himself to a passive, querulous victim, but like all Byron's protagonists he
is blind to the inner source of his misfortunes. His ascription of them
to a father's curse even as Ulric charges his crimes to his father makes
up a double portrait of the figure of the blighted son that obsessed
Byron.
    This ending requires attentive consideration, however, especially
in the ways it diverges from the original. In Miss Lee's novel Kruitzner retains power and his fugitive son is inadvertently killed in a

skirmish with hussars whom he has sent to police his borders. The freedom Byron accords Ulric is a remarkable contrast to this crude poetic justice, and it appears still more surprising when compared to the severely constricted fates allotted the sons in the preceding dramas. It would be foolish to seek a particular cause for the relative enlargement Ulric enjoys, but Byron's life had become happier in the months since *Heaven and Earth*. In November he had moved to Pisa, joining the Shelleys and their friends there and renewing his intimacy with Teresa after the weeks of separation resulting from the exile of the Gambas from Ravenna. Comfortably settled for the first time with his mistress, who had quit her much older husband for him and gained the sanction of *il Papa* to do so, Byron was living in circumstances that suggestively parallel the fantasies detectable in his works.[13] Wherever the explanation lies, Ulric achieves an ambivalent success beyond the reach of his fellow alienated Titans: in the final scenes of the play he undoes his father and establishes his independence. He drops the pose of the dutiful son and like Selim and Hugo steps forth in his true rebelliousness, to witness more potently than they could to the suppressed resentments Byron invariably discovers beneath filial obedience. The motives Freud observes in the rescue motif fully emerge in Ulric's justification for the murder of Stralenheim: "As stranger I preserved him, and he *owed me/ His life:* when due, I but resumed the debt" (V, i, 462–463). This hostility, vented initially on a surrogate, now finds its real target and Ulric contemptuously abandons his beseeching father:

Sieg.   Stop! I command—entreat—implore! Oh, Ulric!
          Will you then leave me?
Ulr.   What! remain to be
          Denounced—dragged, it may be, in chains; and all
          By your inherent weakness, half-humanity,
          Selfish remorse, and temporizing pity . . .
              No, Count,
          Henceforth you have no son!
Sieg.   I never had one;
          And would you ne'er had borne the useless name!
          Where will you go? I would not send you forth
          Without protection.
Ulr.   Leave that unto me.
          I am not alone; nor merely the vain heir
          Of your domains; a thousand, aye, ten thousand
          Swords, hearts, and hands are mine.
                       (V, ii, 33–46)

"Henceforth you have no son!": Ulric's words express the inverse of his meaning, which is that after this rejection of his heritage for an authority based on his own accomplishments he will have no father. Werner's well-meaning offer of protection reflects once again the parental imago from whom he has never been able to emancipate himself, but Ulric, in Freud's phrase, strives to become the father of himself. It may be speculated that his bleak triumph accounts for much of Byron's attraction to "Kruitzner."

Ulric's wilful exile to his private army comes full circle to the stern warrior-outcasts of the oriental tales, but Byron now provides an etiology of his hero that impressively deepens the characterization. The oedipal conflicts that motivate his protagonist are visible only obliquely and imperfectly in early works like *The Giaour* and *Lara*; there are many reasons for his having adopted the discontinuous narrative mode of the tales, but part of its appeal to Byron may have lain in his discovery that through it he might simultaneously confront and conceal the psychological stresses that generated the poems. The results are largely artistically successful, but at a price: the reader responds to the spectacular events he relates but can only guess at their springs. Time seems to have brought Byron sufficient composure to explore his situation: in *Werner*, years after he had reshaped his own childhood and marriage in the opening cantos of *Don Juan*, he presents his hero in the environment that molds him. Ulric's predecessors loom large because they stand in isolation, but what they gain in awesomeness they lose in credibility; Ulric, in contrast, forms part of a complexly realized picture of family psychodynamics, and the ampler context conduces to better understanding.

The increased comprehension is effectively illustrated by one respect in which Ulric is more alone than his forerunners, his departure without a woman to solace him. Like them he is diffident towards the woman who adores him, but *Werner* furnishes the materials to uncover the roots of this typical pattern. Ida has been all but adopted by Josephine's maternal love (V, i, 14–74) and she is the bride selected by his father. This close association with the parents from whom he is trying to break free makes it impossible that Ulric should reciprocate her affection, and her role thus brings into sharper focus a threatening aspect possessed in common by Byron's women. The extensively depicted family relationships of *Werner* repeatedly illuminate Byron's other works in this fashion, and give a richly detailed picture of the habitual workings of his imagination. Ulric, though he defeats his father, remains entrapped in the futile conflicts that for Byron symbolize the world of men. As Stralenheim says in Act II, recognizing his affinity with Ulric and hoping to engage him in his service, war is the natural condition of this world: "peace/ Is but a petty war . . . . War will reclaim his own" (II, i, 169–172). Ulric makes war "for himself" (IV, i, 37), pursuing it with complete indifference to cause, as if it were simply a more exciting chase. His murder of the man he has just rescued displays his utter amorality, and indeed the forces that drive him rise from depths of the personality untouchable by the persuasions of morality. His declaration to Werner that "we have done with right and wrong" casts as a psychological imperative Lucifer's proclamation of the end of metaphysical absolutes: "Were I the victor, *his* works would be deemed/ The only evil ones" (*Cain*, II, ii, 445–446). The full analysis of *Werner* brings greater knowledge to the reader but no remission of strife for Byron's characters.

It is through its effect on the reader that Ulric's escape is especially provocative. Punishment of the villain permits an audience to distinguish itself from him and thus flatters its moral superiority, and Byron's refusal to meet our expectations should direct us rather to recognize ourselves in Ulric's hostility. The conclusion rebounds against us by asking that we admit the probable presence in our own minds of the desires for which we want Ulric punished. "In the crowd," the comic steward Idenstein has already joked,

> your thief looks
> Exactly like the rest, or rather better:
> 'Tis only at the bar and in the dungeon,
> That wise men know your felon by his features; . . .
> (II, i, 206–210)

The challenge to complacent assumptions runs throughout the play and is social as well as personal. Stralenheim's servant Fritz equates the "soldiers and desperadoes" of the black bands Ulric leads in their ravages to a list of celebrated generals:

> After all,
> Your Wallenstein, your Tilly and Gustavus,
> Your Bannier, and your Torstenson and Weimar,
> Were but the same thing upon a grand scale; . . .
> (II, i, 138–141)

The insistence that society's outlaws and its heroes are identical is a colloquial, satiric counterpart to the statements of Lucifer and Ulric, and reveals the filiation of attitudes and techniques between *Werner* and *Don Juan*. "Had Buonaparte won at Waterloo," the narrator of Byron's epic comments in Canto XIV,

> It had been firmness; now 'tis pertinacity;
> Must the event decide between the two?
> I leave it your people of sagacity
> To draw the line between the false and true,
> If such can e'er be drawn by Man's capacity:...
> (XIV, 90)

Beneath the surface differences the dramas and *Don Juan* are continuous, and Byron's adaptation of melodrama shows its beholders not monsters and saints, but themselves.

The Deformed Transformed is in many ways the most surehanded of Byron's plays even in its unfinished state. Byron fluidly mixes chorus and song with dialogue that ranges from familiar conversation through stately description, and counterpoints the voice of aspiration with the mocking commentary of the devil who is the instigator of the action. The devil's sardonic repartee clashes dramatically against the other principals, and his wit manipulates the reader's responses to their heroic savagery at the sack of Rome in 1527. The satiric deflation of conquest hypocritically justified by religion is a vision like that of the Ismail cantos of *Don Juan*, composed at the same time (1822), and the drama also sheds revealing light on aspects of Byron's self-presentation in the greater work.

The central event of *The Deformed Transformed* is the devil's obliging metamorphosis of the hunchbacked Arnold into "the beauty of the host" (I, ii, 220) he yearns to become. Byron declares in the preface that the incident is founded on *The Three Brothers*, a novel by Joshua Pickersgill; according to Mary Shelley "this had long been a favourite subject with Lord Byron," and she recalled his mention of it in Switzerland in 1816 (*Poetry* 5: 474 n. 2). If, as is probable, Byron read Pickersgill's novel at a time near its publication in 1803, then it, like "Kruitzner," belongs to his adolescence, when the developmental strains normal to that period would have intensified the shame he always felt in connection with his lameness. The return for his final plays to two works which had powerfully affected him earlier in his life suggests that in his maturity Byron was at last able to examine the traumas to which they are intimately related.[14]

Arnold is on the verge of suicide when the devil arrives in answer to his wishes. The cause of his self-hatred appears with unmediated clarity in the interchange with his mother that opens the play:

> Bertha.   OUT, Hunchback!
> Arn.   I was born so, Mother!
> Bertha.   Out,
>   Thou incubus! Thou nightmare! Of seven sons,
>   The sole abortion!
> Arn.   Would that I had been so
>   And never seen the light!
> Bertha.   I would so, too!
>   But as thou *hast*—hence, hence—and do thy best!
>   That back of thine may bear its burthen; 'tis
>   More high, if not so broad as that of others.
> Arn.   It *bears* its burthen;—but, my heart! Will it
>   Sustain that which you lay upon it, Mother?
>   I love, or, at least, I loved you: nothing
>   Save You, in nature, can love aught like me.
>   You nursed me—do not kill me!
>   (I, i, 1–12)

For an author to transcribe himself thus undisguisedly is startling, and the arduous progress towards self-understanding it attests must never be underestimated. The personal revelations of *Manfred* do not penetrate beyond the incest with Augusta: the deep-lying needs which produced the affair make their presence felt, but surface only in displaced forms and remain in an obscurity the play cannot disperse. In these lines, by contrast, Byron reaches the most profound and painful stratum of his being and brings it to conscious scrutiny, shielded only by a character transparent to contemporary readers who were accustomed to refer all his personae to himself. This capacity to meet his anxieties relatively directly and simultaneously to face his audience without the obfuscating and self-aggrandizing postures of the oriental tales, *Manfred*, and *Childe Harold*, says much about the gains of Byron's later years.

As Arnold discriminates by beauty rather than bravery among the Worthies of the ancient world from whom he is to choose his ideal shape he plainly reveals the fixation on the mother that underlies the myriad motives acted out by Byron's Titanic protagonists. "I ask not/

For Valour, since Deformity is daring," he explains to his benefactor (I, i, 313–314), but the remediable physical defect that has captured critics' attention wounds him less in itself than the loss of his mother's love. Moore quoted *The Deformed Transformed* in recalling the passage from Byron's *Memoirs* in which he "described the feeling of horror and humiliation that came over him, when his mother, in one of her fits of passion, called him 'a lame brat'" (*Poetry* 5: 477 n. 1); the *Memoirs* were burnt by Byron's executors after his death, but the drama preserves the record of the lasting psychological damage inflicted by Mrs. Byron. "I could have borne/ It all," Arnold maintains, "had not my mother spurned me from her" (I, i, 342–343), and the hopes he cherishes break out at the first sight of himself as Achilles: "I love, and I shall be beloved!" (I, i, 421). To his chagrin Arnold watches the devil assume his castoff body and learns that he will have him forever at his side: the inseparability of his old and new selves reveals Byron's belief that the stamp imprinted on a man's character in childhood could not be erased by a mere exchange of outward shapes. If Arnold's metamorphosis is characterized as wish-fulfillment on Byron's part it must be added that he immediately exposes its inadequacy.

The explicit double of the devil is the culmination of Byron's tendency to embody the warring divisions of the self in independent actors.[15] In *The Deformed Transformed* this recurrent psychological pattern serves a wider purpose, for the constant attendance of the devil on Arnold in his original ugliness reinforces the emphasis Byron had placed since *Childe Harold* on the carnage the glorification of battle conceals. "The mild twins—Gore and Glory," the devil observes, unintentionally describing his relationship to Arnold (II, ii, 12). In *Childe Harold* Byron named Napoleon a "bastard Caesar": even the touchstone is devalued when the devil in his grotesque incarnation adopts the name Caesar, and his choice marks Byron's ultimate reduction of martial fame. Throughout the play he consistently subverts the conventionally heroic. The heroes whom Arnold thirsts to emulate are invoked as "Demons... who breathed to destroy" (I, i, 174–181); Achilles is declared a true "Titan" (I, i, 294), but the word loses its gloss when applied equally to the brutal invaders of Rome (I, i, 186).

The thematic coherence of the play belies its apparent formal looseness. Arnold's view of Rome as the magnificent center of empire and church is set against the devil's reminder that "Rome's earliest cement/ Was brother's blood" (I,ii, 83–84). The devil's epigram gives utterance to the ubiquitous nostalgia that locates the origin of civilization in the guilty consequences of the Fall: Romulus, like Cain in Judaeo-Christian myth, first slew his brother and then, like Cain's descendants, instituted the city. Rome, which Byron had once represented as the measure for Manfred and the goal of his own pilgrimage, reverts to the emblem of this incessant masculine rivalry. Arnold, the scorned sibling warned by his mother to "call not thy brothers brethren" (I, i, 24), is the fitting head of the attackers whom the Chorus of Spirits in Part II greets as the avengers of Remus (II, i, 84). Embarked upon his dream of violence, he is caught up in its momentum like Sardanapalus and Juan until his fury provokes an admonition from the devil himself:

> I gave thee
> A form of beauty, and an
> Exemption from some maladies of body,
> But not of mind, which is not mine to give.
> (II, ii, 15–18)

It only seems a paradox that the aim of Arnold's slaughter, not wholly recognized by himself, should be the recovery of the serenity associated with mother-love. The real desires to which reckless bravery is but the means appear when Arnold saves a Roman maiden, Olimpia, from a crowd of threatening soldiers, exactly as Juan saves Leila from the Cossacks. This renewed instance fully discloses the tender aspects of the rescue motif shown by Freud. Arnold falls in love with Olimpia, but she remains indifferent. In the fragmentary third part of the drama Arnold confesses his sense of betrayal to Caesar, and in this disappointment speaks the lament of the child still frustrated in his attempt to replace his father and possess his mother's love: "I saved her life, too; and her Father's life,/ And Father's house from ashes" (III, 55–56). "You seek for Gratitude," Caesar replies,

> But *found* would it content you? would you owe
> To thankfulness what you desire from Passion?
> No! No! you would be *loved*—what you call loved—
> *Self-loved*—loved for *yourself*—for neither health,
> Nor wealth, nor youth, nor power, nor rank,
> nor beauty—
> For these you may be stript of—but *beloved*
> As an abstraction—for—you know not what!
> These are the wishes of a moderate lover—
> And *so* you love.
> (III, 57–67)

The perceptive and worldly-wise devil knows and accepts what Arnold has not yet learned to endure: that the longings for a vanished union that torment him are beyond the power of any other woman to satisfy.

An outline of Part III of *The Deformed Transformed* suggests that Byron intended Olimpia to remain unmoved by Arnold's "heat/ Promethean" (III, 88–89). Eventually Arnold was to become "jealous of himself under his former figure, owing to the power of intellect," and this surprising reversal witnesses in miniature the evolution of Byron's poetic stance. The analysis of the needs that produce Titanic defiance enables Byron definitively to declare its inevitable failure to satisfy them, and so to reject its dangerous fascination in favor of the protective distance from ruinous engagement maintained by wit. The fall of Rome, which had formerly been the topic of Byron's grandest but most despairing rhetoric, is to Caesar merely a "comic pantomime" (II, iii, 32). Arnold's final subordination to Caesar parallels that of the "hero" to the narrator of *Don Juan*, but Caesar, the "universal sneerer," lacks the expansiveness of his creator. In Arnold *The Deformed Transformed* shows Byron bare, as it were: a portrait at once true, and yet so stripped as to be false, lacking as it does the transforming fictions he composed to dress himself.

PART III: DON JUAN: *THE SELF DEPLOYED*

5

The Byronic Hero as Little Boy

*N*o contemporary reader of the first canto of *Don Juan* alive to current gossip could have failed to notice that the ostensibly independent characters of the story all reveal Byron. Anonymous publication provided him the opportunity not to hide himself but rather to facilitate self-expression and to tease his audience. Byron is the narrator (by the end of the canto the few attempts to establish a persona distinct from himself are abandoned), the unhappily married Don José victimized by a bluestocking wife, and also Juan, the sexually precocious youth under the care of a widowed mother. Only a critical method flexible enough to regard such divided self-presentation as a legitimate subject of inquiry will reach the center of *Don Juan*: a reader who excludes on principle Byron's tantalizing play with the demarcations between biographical revelation and fiction sacrifices the essential quality of the poem.

In a paper on developments in therapeutic technique entitled "Remembering, Repeating and Working-Through" Freud observes that some patients who have no conscious knowledge of their past nonetheless reveal it to the analyst:

... we may say that the patient does not *remember* anything of what he has forgotten and repressed, but *acts* it out. He reproduces it not as a memory but as an action; he *repeats* it, without, of course, knowing that he is repeating it. . . .

As long as the patient is in the treatment he cannot escape from this compulsion to repeat; and in the end we understand that this is his way of remembering. . . .

We must be prepared to find, therefore, that the patient yields to the compulsion to repeat, which now replaces the impulsion to remember, not only in his personal attitude to his doctor but also in every other activity and relationship which may occupy his life at the time—if, for instance, he falls in love or undertakes a task or starts an enterprise during the treatment. The part played by resistance, too, is easily recognized. The greater the resistance, the more extensively will acting out (repetition) replace remembering.[1]

In the light cast by Freud the relationship of Juan and the narrator can be approached. The anxieties Byron remembers and reflects upon in reviewing his life, Byron-as-Juan acts out, or, to phrase it differently, Byron remembers by letting Byron-as-Juan act out.

The central critical issue raised by Byron's repetitions here presents itself. To the degree that his plots return again and again to the same situation Byron appears trapped in a neurotic compulsion to act out without understanding his dilemma. This assessment is offset, however, by the increasing fullness of exploration made possible by the detachment he is generally able to maintain in *Don Juan*. The free play of the poem permits him to contemplate his anxieties and not merely remain subject to them. What Byron-as-narrator recollects from the past loses its forbiddingly determined shape when it is transferred to Juan, and as it unfolds with unrestricted potential moment by moment in his present it acquires lively immediacy. The reader participates in each new incarnation of the old predicament, and looks forward eagerly to future ones. Like Leporello's catalogue aria in *Don Giovanni*, Juan's serial re-enactments present compulsive repetition as comic reaffirmation.[2]

A comparison with Wordsworth is again instructive. Looking back on his childhood days in *The Prelude*, Wordsworth discovers that they are so far removed from his present state "that, musing on them, often do I seem/ Two consciousnesses, conscious of myself/ And of some other Being" (II, 31–33). His poem is an attempt to bridge that discontinuity through memory: as the poem proceeds the adult Wordsworth constantly reinterprets the frightening moments of his childhood as the benevolent ministry of nature, "all gratulant if rightly understood" (XIV, 387). By its conclusion Wordsworth has fabricated a connection that is satisfying to him. In the words of the "Ode: Intimations of Immortality," Wordsworth declares the "vanishings" and "misgivings" of the child to be "the master light of all our seeing," and the inchoate apprehensions "before which our mortal Nature/ Did tremble like a guilty thing surprised" he represents as the indication of "high instincts." Both the Ode and *The Prelude* resolve the dismay they initially record by thus subsuming it within the "philosophic mind." *Don Juan* illustrates equally firmly an awareness that "the child is father of the man," but it gives full play to the negative aspects of that inheritance which Wordsworth is concerned to minimize. For Wordsworth the traumatic events of youth are hailed as "spots of time" that disclose a rich meaning to later contemplation: Byron enshrines his trauma in Juan, whose arrest is permanent. Byron's younger and older selves, his "two consciousnesses" of Juan and the narrator, are nominally discrete, so that childhood experience is denied the positive qualities Wordsworth ascribes to it, and the poem implies a view very different from Wordsworth's belief in the coherent growth of the personality. The narrator, a victim of indigestion and metaphysical doubt, enjoys no sense of a central self, and Juan enters wholly into each fresh experience because he has almost no memory, remaining so passive that he may scarcely be said to develop a character.

Byron's permanently divided consciousness yields no integrated self, but it offers enhanced dramatic possibilities. Wordsworth movingly confesses in *The Prelude* that the "hiding-places" of his power were gradually receding from him (XII, 277–286), and the loss is the corollary of his successful ordering of his past. As he translated bewilderment into reassurance he simultaneously diminished the intensity of the recollections from which his poetry sprang: the imperturbable solidity achieved after great struggle by the man Wordsworth, attested by all who knew him after the early years of the century, closed off the peculiar unease that had been the strength of the poet. The double mode of Byron's retrospection enables him to relate the conflicts of his past in their original clarity and vitality, thus avoiding the fate Wordsworth laments and that he too had risked in striving for the premature synthesis of the exalted lyric voice in Cantos III and IV of *Childe Harold*. The perspective gained by locating his anxieties in Juan let Byron approach them as a joke and, thus defended, work them through rather than repress them. Juan's retreat from prominence before the ever more poised narrator of the astonishingly fertile last cantos is the sign of the genuine integration Byron's initial presentation of himself as split had helped him to achieve. It must be observed, nonetheless, that Byron exists in the poem as the continually shifting web of relations between Juan and the narrator. Should the two ever have wholly converged, or should Byron ever have identified with either alone, the poem would have stopped: Juan without the narrator is fixed, the narrator without Juan is a shell (hence it is appropriate that he not carry Byron's own name).

Manfred and the later cantos of *Childe Harold* suffer because their personal material is undigested: in effect they are insufficiently autobiographical and hence imperfectly fictional. In the first canto of *Don Juan*, by contrast, Byron depicts the formative events of his life, his experiences as son and husband, but so thoroughly rearranged as to raise a private past into a public fiction. The impulses behind the rearrangement are the key to the poem, for in retelling in this oblique fashion the circumstances of his childhood and marriage Byron is able to construct an ideal version of them, one that is favorable to the ego whose fragility is betrayed by the divided self-presentation. His spoof of the shorthand accounts of Alfonso's suit for divorce (I, 189) undercuts the pretension to truth of nominally factual reporting, and thus slyly insinuates the equal veracity of his mode. He confronts the traumas that obsess him, but at a safe remove: what Byron-as-Juan painfully endures, Byron-as-narrator rises above, turning to comedy the bitterest elements of his own life and indeed narrating them as if they were not part of *his* life at all. The narrator, above the action and exercising supreme control over it, is an image of Byron as he would like to be, a self-reassuring demonstration that he was master of the problems that tormented him. The opening canto of *Don Juan* is the work of a man still possessed by the resentments that have obscurely governed his life, but it should be understood as an effort to exorcise them through the magic gesture of art: to neutralize them by exploring their causes, expressing them fully, and then converting them to fiction.[3]

Previous treatments of the Don Juan materials present from the outset the fully-formed libertine associated with the legend.[4] By showing Juan in his childhood Byron demythologizes the story and gives instead a psychological sketch of the effects of environment on character. The tale is less a chronicle of Juan's actions than of his education, and it is scarcely an exaggeration to say that Juan's education is his experience with women.[5] His early life is dominated by his mother, Inez, whom Byron modelled principally on his wife: the allusions to Inez's mathematical bent and to Samuel Romilly, who had acted for Lady Byron in the separation, are there to be acknowledged (I, 12–15). Byron drew on his own marriage in painting the quarrels between Inez and Don José, and details like Inez's spiteful attempt "to prove her loving lord was *mad*" as Lady Byron had done, make the parallel explicit (I, 27). In this scheme Byron figures as Don José, but the reader recognizes at the same time that Juan is placed by José's death in a situation identical with Byron's first years: Juan left with Inez recapitulates Byron brought up by his mother. The compound of his wife and mother in Inez is profoundly significant. The presentation of himself as simultaneously the son and husband of this woman suggests that at some not wholly conscious level Byron descried at last the shadowy motives underlying the extraordinary behavior he exhibited during his marriage and the anguish of the separation. He seems in his analytical division of himself to intuit that the crisis of his relationship with Annabella grew out of much earlier psychic conflicts with his mother, and thus brings to the surface the true nature of the dilemma at which in 1816–1817 *Manfred* had only hinted.

The deliberately emasculated education to which Inez subjects her son exposes her sexual hypocrisy, but Byron also intimates the deeper strands of her character that generate it. Although Inez is not a sympathetic figure, it may be wondered how much of her fanatic prudery is the natural reaction of a neglected wife whose husband maintains two mistresses. The lack of affection in her life produces a corresponding concentration on Juan, as Mrs. Byron's did on young Byron. Her determination to preserve his naiveté springs in part from fear that his nascent adolescent sexuality will lead him too away from her:

> Young Juan now was sixteen years of age,
> Tall, handsome, slender, but well knit: he seemed
> Active, though not so sprightly, as a page;
> And everybody but his mother deemed
> Him almost man; but she flew in a rage
> And bit her lips (for else she might have screamed)
> If any said so—for to be precocious
> Was in her eyes a thing most atrocious.
>
> (I, 54)

Inez's desire to have Juan taught all the skills of manhood while yet insisting that he remain a child points to a type-constellation larger than the personal satire of this canto: the overly protective mother and the son whom she will at all costs make "quite a paragon" (I, 38) but keep utterly dependent on her.

It is inevitable that Juan should seek to establish his autonomy, and Inez's desire to manage him by suppressing his sexuality pits her against a force to which she herself is prey. In *Don Juan* sexual passion is "the controlless core of human hearts" (I, 116), continually breaking through the tidy patterns our conscious, social selves impose on it, refusing to be stultified and reasserting its turbulent primacy. Through the narrator's ironic disclaimer the reader learns that Inez's kindness to Julia is a pretense aimed at quashing scandal:

> Some people whisper (but, no doubt, they lie,
> For Malice still imputes some private end)
> That Inez had, ere Don Alfonso's marriage,
> Forgot with him her very prudent carriage;
>
> And that still keeping up the old connection,
> Which Time had lately rendered much more chaste,
> She took his lady also in affection,
> And certainly this course was much the best; . . .
>
> (I, 66–67)

When Inez's prudery collides with the resentment that she cannot admit at having been supplanted by a younger woman, the emotional power of the latter triumphs. She throws Juan and Julia together:

> Perhaps to finish Juan's education,
> Perhaps to open Don Alfonso's eyes,
> In case he thought his wife too great a prize.
>
> (I, 101)

The affair does "finish" Juan's education, but only in the sense that it terminates Inez's careful sheltering: in a perfect satiric example of the self-defeating nature of repression, she becomes the agent of the catastrophe she most wished to avert.

At the moment of the lovers' tryst the narrator comments that " 'T was surely very wrong in Juan's mother/ To leave together this imprudent pair" (I, 110). The remark emphasizes the paradox of Juan's position. On the one hand he frustrates his mother by his success with Julia and so gains a vengeful independence of her, but on the other he merely acts out one of her desires. The aside underscores for the reader the recognition that Juan's first sexual encounter, which should be his initiation into manhood, is only an extension of his mother's dominance. There is no evidence that Juan realizes how thoroughly he has been manipulated, but his failure to attain freedom sets forth the pattern the poem will repeat again and again.

Juan's independence is further limited by the evolution of Julia, who is unlike Byron's later women in that the more she talks the less complex she becomes. Her tirade upon the night of discovery is magnificently theatrical, but it is of a familiar type. Byron's tour de force consists in part of making acceptable the reduction of a three-dimensional personage to a stock *intrigante.* The reduction is necessary if the narrative is to advance, since it would be too harsh to abandon a fully sympathetic character as callously as the poem drops Julia. The lovers are initially apprehended as equally young and innocent, but Byron continually suggests the extent of Julia's sophistication. When he retracts because it is "trite and stupid" (I, 55) a simile declaring Julia's charms as natural to her as his bow to Cupid he prepares further qualifications. The narrator retains sympathy for Julia by depicting her as the victim of her passions and incapable of preventing the hypocrisy she practices since "Passion most dissembles" (I, 73), but the similes he employs implicate her in a world much more ambiguous than Juan's. Her effect on him is compared to the wiles of Armida, Tasso's wicked sorceress (I, 71), and her bower is said to be as pretty "as e'er held houri in that heathenish heaven" described in Moore's erotic verse (I, 103). Over their first embrace falls the light cast by the narrator's sardonic reflection that "a good deal" of love "may be bought for *fifty* Louis" (I, 108). Though Julia feels no wrong when her "conscious heart" (I, 106) glows in her cheek, the reader questions an innocence that has been likened to the complacency with which Christians burn heretics (I, 83). After such broad hints that Julia's self-deception is either wilful or of a moral blindness that approaches culpability the reader should not be surprised by her marvelous but equivocal apotheosis at the end of the canto.

The revelation of Julia's character, her vain delight in her many admirers and the boast of an "old and deaf" confessor intended to prove her devotion but suggesting the opposite (I, 147), shows Juan as still the pawn of an older woman. Despite Juan's sexual vitality the affair rather impairs than fosters his growth into independence. The narrator calls him a "poor little fellow" (I, 86), and Julia's maid Antonia, "an adept" (I, 140), wonders at her mistress's passion for "a child" with a "half-girlish face" (I, 171–172). Juan remains passive, not speaking throughout the canto. In what is to become his characteristic situation, he is saved from discovery by the ingenuity of the two women, but their protection also stifles his freedom. When Alfonso enters the boudoir Juan is effectively absent from the scene, bundled up in the bed, "half-smothered" by the women who shield him (I, 165), and then crammed in a closet.

If one postulates with Northrop Frye that the archetypal comic resolution displays the defeat of the blocking figures and the formation of a new society around the united lovers,[6] then the ending of Canto I is a mixed resolution. The blocking figure is defeated, insofar as Alfonso is "pommelled to his heart's desire" (I, 184), and, like Inez, brings about his own downfall, the public confirmation of his cuckoldry. But it is equally true that the love of Juan and Julia is broken off, and that aspect bears examination. It is typical of Byron's poem that the husbands and fathers who interpose between Juan and his lovers, however much they may be characterized as fools, triumph over him. This pattern does more than emphasize Juan's unheroic weakness: it is congruent with the melodramatic and tragic works already examined, and it clarifies the nature of Byron's comedy. Juan's enforced departure from Spain appears comic less because it is an escape from Alfonso's persecution than because it is a welcome release from the constriction threatened by Julia. Juan's near-suffocation in the bedclothes symbolizes the dangers her attractiveness poses, and he must leave if he is to achieve the freedom to act for himself. Since Byron-as-Juan does not have the strength to emancipate himself, Byron-as-narrator intervenes, immuring Julia in a convent and thus keeping the poem comic.

The circumstances in which Byron places Juan permit an understanding of the causes of his subordination to women: Byron's reflection on his childhood shows not only a dominating mother but also a lack of any men who might provide models of adulthood. Juan's father is dead, and Alfonso is not only a fool but also a rival. The tutor Inez selects to guard Juan in his travels is, like all her education, unfit to conduct him to manhood. Pedrillo's academic knowledge is no aid in a shipwreck, and Juan must save the man who stands to him *in loco parentis:*

> Juan got into a long-boat, and there
> Contrived to help Pedrillo to a place;

> It seemed as if they had exchanged their care,
> For Juan wore the magisterial face
> Which courage gives, while poor Pedrillo's pair
> Of eyes were crying for their owner's case: . . .
>> (II, 56)

Even Pedrillo's *Imitatio Christi,* his meek death to sustain his starving companions, instead brings agony to those who feast on his corpse, a further instance of Byron's hostility to the Christian myth of the sacrificed son. Pedrillo's passing marks the end of the outward constraints Inez exerts on Juan, but the pattern of maternal dominance is fixed.

Juan supersedes his tutor and arrives on Haidée's island tested like a hero and ready to begin anew. The narrator insinuates that Juan has gone beyond an unselfconscious innocence like Haidée's (II, 172), but despite his greater experience the configuration of son and mother reasserts itself. Underneath its surface freedom *Don Juan* displays a determinist view of character: Pope's "ruling passion" is given a foundation in psychological development. The plenteous food, warmth, and affection that Haidée generously gives Juan make his stay in the cave a return to the all-nourishing womb, and Byron insists that this shelter is also a confinement. He conveys its double nature in a characteristically rapid series of incongruous similes:

> An infant when it gazes on a light,
> A child the moment when it drains the breast,
> A devotee when soars the Host in sight,
> An Arab with a stranger for a guest,
> A sailor when the prize has struck in fight,
> A miser filling his most hoarded chest,
> Feel rapture; but not such true joy are reaping
> As they who watch o'er what they love while sleeping.
>> (I, 196)

Haidée's love is a maternal tenderness for the "helpless" (II, 197) dependent who reposes in her care, "hushed as the babe upon its mother's breast" (II, 148). Juan's sleep is an infantile regression from his fortitude in the shipwreck, as moribund as the state from which Haidée revived him. "She,/ Who watched him like a mother" (II, 158), is from the outset associated with death; because she is so appealing the threat she represents is lethally tempting. Even as she resuscitates Juan her "small mouth/ Seemed almost prying into his for breath" (II, 113). She wraps his sleeping body against the cold

> ... closer, lest the air, too raw
> Should reach his blood, then o'er him still as Death
> Bent, with hushed lips, that drank his scarce-drawn breath.
> (II, 143)

Here enveloping protection becomes suffocation, and what were only undertones in Juan's affair with Julia become prominent. The syndrome is familiar: no sooner does Byron endow a woman with extraordinary powers than she becomes a threat to the hero. Because Juan is so close to Byron, the rebound is particularly forceful, and the violent shifts in tone stigmatized by many critics in Byron's treatment of this episode mark the depth of his investments in it. Byron's initial description of Haidée is filled with menace:

> Her hair, I said, was auburn; but her eyes
> Were black as Death, their lashes the same hue,
> Of downcast length, in whose silk shadow lies
> Deepest attraction; for when to view
> Forth from its raven fringe the full glance flies,
> Ne'er with such force the swiftest arrow flew;
> 'T is as a snake late coiled, who pours his length,
> And hurls at once his venom and his strength.
> (II, 117)

The serpent in Eden is internal: Haidée appears as death because Byron perceives the longings for retreat she embodies as inimical to the adult independence he also cherishes. Through Juan he elaborates a fantasy of recapturing lost childhood bliss, and in his capacity as the completely free storyteller he extricates him from its powerful spell with the return of Lambro.

Juan's stature on the island derives entirely from his position as Haidée's consort, and the spectacular court they hold in Canto III is based on Lambro's accomplishments, not his own. The rumor of Lambro's death which precedes their celebration is perhaps the plainest instance of wish-fulfillment in Byron: his lovers can rejoice fully only when the intimidating father who opposes them has been miraculously removed. His repeated reminders that "they were children still,/ And children still they should have been" (IV, 15) enforce the regressive quality of Juan's attachment to Haidée. The "one star sparkling . . . like an eye" (II, 183) which oversees their kiss seems a figure of the poet himself, indulging from a safe distance in the union of son and mother he has depicted. His invocation of the Madonna in the Ave Maria stanzas accentuates the maternal quality (III, 101–103). The idyll represents Byron's deepest yearnings, but his imagination of the scene immediately releases his darkest fears. Byron describes Haidée and Juan as "happy in the illicit/ Indulgence of their innocent desires" (III, 13), and the import of the paradox, which has seemed merely facile to some critics,[7] is easily understood when it is seen in psychological rather than moral terms. Juan has in effect stolen Haidée from Lambro, and his temerity incurs the wrath Byron invariably associates with any attempt to challenge a father. The oral fears of being swallowed by the mother are succeeded by oedipal ones of being crushed by the father. Almost as if he felt the need for expiation, Byron has Lambro return to punish the lovers. Haidée's dream, in which Juan's face gradually metamorphoses into the presence of her father (III, 31–35), renders explicit the rivalry of father and lover often met before in Byron, and the encounter of the two ends as always with the defeat of the son. Juan is entirely unable to maintain himself against paternal authority: despite Haidée's intercession he is disarmed and despatched to a slave ship in three stanzas.

Haidée would not have become pregnant in the conventional romance to which this episode is kin, and her pregnancy reveals her essentially maternal nature. Her death without giving birth, like her swallowing-up of Juan, emphasizes that the nurturing feminine qualities that make the island a paradise are also inhibiting. Byron exploits the pathos of the sudden interruption of the lovers' joy and of Haidée's death, but the termination is evidently necessary if Juan is to be propelled on further adventures. The exigencies of plot, however, are not the sole forces shaping Byron's authorial choices. It is a nice critical question whether the involvement in his story the narrator conveys is merely feigned by Byron in order to heighten the reader's response, or whether it is the sign of an unresolved tension in Byron himself. No absolute solution to the riddle is possible, but in the narrator's deliberate, ironic dismissal of Juan the strong identification that requires the rejection can be detected: "Here I must leave him, for I grow pathetic,/ Moved by the Chinese nymph of tears, green tea!" (IV, 52). In the previous stanza the narrator has contrived to blame Juan's misfortunes on Haidée: "Wounded and chained, so that he cannot move,/ And all because a lady fell in love" (IV, 51). This distortion, presenting Juan as the passive victim of the woman who loves him, is like that in *Mazeppa*, discussed above (p. 102): it indicates once again the ambivalent consequences of Juan's absorption in Haidée, from which Byron as narrator both dissociates himself and rescues Byron-as-Juan. The uneasy attitude to women visible in these lines, springing from fear of maternal dominance, is responsible for the fate meted out to Haidée. Byron moves his hero as in the tales from the regressive fantasy dear to him to the world of men, but the rejection of the supportive, enclosing feminine environment is accompanied by nostalgia for the peace possible within it. Haidée's death is recorded in an elegiac stanza (IV, 71), but the narrator abruptly closes his lament and returns to Juan with an admission in which Byron himself seems to be heard:

> But let me change this theme, which grows too sad,
> And lay this sheet of sorrows on the shelf;
> *I don't much like describing people mad,*
> *For fear of seeming rather touched myself—*
> Besides, I've no more on this head to add;
> And as my Muse is a capricious elf,
> We'll put about, and try another tack
> With Juan, left half-killed some stanzas back.
>
> (IV, 74; italics added)

There is no equivalent series of engagements and emphatic disengagements in so brief a space in the later cantos of *Don Juan:* after this point pathos is replaced by more aggressive stances toward the reader, and the narrator's voice becomes increasingly steady as the poem proceeds.

In the first four cantos Byron rapidly and indirectly reconstructs major portions of his life and career. As already seen, Juan's experiences comment on both his childhood and his marriage, and Juan's expulsion from Spain parallels his own exile from England. Indeed, Juan's cry, "Farewell my Spain! a long farewell!'", cut short by retching, stands in parodic relation to Byron's own voyages as described in Cantos I and III of *Childe Harold*, especially "Childe Harold's Goodnight" in Canto I: "Adieu, adieu, my native shore." The vision of withdrawal to a maternal harmony that in the tales compensates for disasters in the world of men is developed in its purest form when Haidée's island succeeds Spain, and then abandoned again in her death and Juan's second sea journey.[8] The cantos cannot be taken as literal autobiography, but their very departures from strict accuracy enlarge their interest from another perspective. They offer a revealing picture not of Byron's outer, but of his inner, life: his sense of himself and of his past in 1818–1819. Almost a year, however, elapsed between the composition of Canto IV and the start of Canto V, and when Byron resumed *Don Juan* in the autumn of 1820 his position had changed. The writing of Canto IV in November 1819 coincides with the arrival of Count Guiccioli in Venice, ending a six-week period in which Byron and Teresa had been alone together at La Mira and the Palazzo Mocenigo. After some terrible rows Byron saw his lover leave his house with her husband, a scene that suggestively resembles Juan's relinquishment of Haidée to Lambro. The narrator's sentiments that it is better for Juan and Haidée to be separated than to endure the diminution of their love in time no doubt echo the rationalization Byron put on his own sudden loss of Teresa, but the depression was too serious to avert. He had counselled acquiescence to the demands of propriety, in part because continuation of the affair would openly declare him a *cavalier servente* and he resisted the regular attachment it implied. His frequent mockery of the institution in *Beppo* and his letters shows his fear of seeing himself as the "supernumerary slave" of a woman.[9] The alternative, however, was worse: to Hobhouse he confessed that he felt "so wretched and low—and lonely—that I will leave the country reluctantly indeed" (*BLJ* 6: 244). A wry letter to Kinnaird testifies that the new disappointment in love was intensified by Byron's interpretation of it as a repetition of the hurt of his marriage: "the Country has become sad to me,—I feel alone in it—and as I left England on account of my own wife—I now quit Italy for the wife of another" (*BLJ* 6: 241). The proposed voyage illustrates the same reaction of flight from his troubles that Byron had fallen back on in 1816, but it was not to happen for some years. For the moment he remained with Teresa: "I have not been able to find enough resolution to leave the country where you are, without seeing you at least once more:—perhaps it will depend on *you* whether I ever again shall leave you" (*BLJ* 6: 258). Though his grumblings at *serventismo* persisted, when Byron returned to *Don Juan* a year later the liaison with Teresa was an established feature of his life. His choice of Teresa is perhaps the strongest confirmation of the applicability to Byron of Freud's remarks in "A Special Type of Choice of Object Made by Men." Byron was entranced by her combination of convent decorum and uninhibited sexuality, a paradox of Italian women

which matched the bifurcation of his own maternally-centered views
of female sexuality. In her tolerant and unwavering love he found the
kind of affection he had always sought, and her marriage to the much
older and saturnine Count Guiccioli added to her appeal. By taking
Teresa from him Byron achieved his fantasies of rescue and triumph
over another man.

In Byron's initial happiness with Teresa the disquiet of Cantos III
and IV abated. An index of the altered mood is the figure of Johnson,
the Englishman with whom Juan is bound in the Turkish slave market
at the beginning of Canto V:

> "Pray, sir," said Juan, "if I may presume,
> What brought you here?"—"Oh! nothing very rare—
> Six Tartars and a drag-chain -"—"To this doom
> But what conducted, if the question's fair,
> Is that which I would learn."—"I served for some
> Months with the Russian army here and there;
> And taking lately, by Suwarrow's bidding,
> A town, was ta'en myself instead of Widdin."
>
> "Have you no friends?"—"I had—but, by God's blessing,
> Have not been troubled with them lately. Now
> I have answered all your questions without pressing,
> And you an equal courtesy should show."
> "Alas!" said Juan, "'t were a tale distressing,
> And long besides."—"Oh! if 't is really so,
> You're right on both accounts to hold your tongue;
> A sad tale saddens doubly when 't is long.
>
> (V, 15–16)

The formality of Juan's address hints to the reader that Byron is
parodying an epic *topos*. In an epic that began conventionally *in medias
res* Johnson's inquiry would furnish the opportunity for the usual
retrospective account of the hero's adventures, but Byron's com-
mencement *ab ovo* has foreclosed that possibility, and Johnson's lack
of concern with what the reader already knows is the result. Moreover, a full response to Johnson would ask of Juan a small-scaled
spiritual autobiography that he does not possess the self-awareness
to compose, let alone make into the inclusive and brilliant meditation
the narrator has fashioned.

Johnson remains an apparent false start in the poem, but he is
nonetheless significant in its thematic pattern. He is the first man

Juan has met who is neither a rival nor much older—he is thirty (V, 10)—and he is therefore a possible friend and model as well as father figure. Juan is easily drawn into conversation by Johnson's hearty, open nature. His cheerful account of his three wives and his unassuming stoicism counteract Juan's despair. Though the narrator will endlessly question how one knows the "right point of view," Johnson's commonsensical belief that wisdom is gained only through adversity is a moral of the poem, its secular equivalent to the theodicy of *Paradise Lost:*

> "All this is very fine, and may be true,"
> Said Juan; "but I really don't see how
> It betters present times with me or you."
> "No?" quoth the other; "yet you will allow
> By setting things in their right point of view,
> Knowledge, at least, is gained; for instance, now,
> We know what slavery is, and our disasters
> May teach us better to behave when masters."
>
> (V, 23)

Heretofore, Juan has lived only in the present; in Johnson's measured resumé of his own disillusionments he witnesses a maturity that can come only by learning from the past. From Johnson's calm preparedness for whatever may come he might learn to look ahead, and to consider the future without anxiety. Johnson has the foresight to correct Juan's rash impulse to attack Baba and flee the harem in which they are imprisoned, observing what Juan has never considered, that they do not know the way out. After their escape Johnson continues as Juan's mentor, introducing him to Suwarrow and then to war itself, the test of his manhood against men as his sexual escapades are its test against women. During the siege of Ismail he exemplifies the balance of discretion and valor wanting in Juan, retreating in order to rally while Juan thoughtlessly advances, loses his way, and endangers his life under the sway of his thirst for glory (VIII, 52). Even John Johnson's name—literally, John son of John—emphasizes his affinity with Juan: he is Juan as he might grow up to be. (The parallels are close and numerous: e.g., Juan is about to have his third affair, Johnson has had three wives.) At the same time, his perseverance, bravery, and ironic detachment make him the double of the narrator, his surrogate within the action. However, since Byron has replaced the conventional counterpointed pair of picaro and ser-

vant with the narrator and Juan, and his scheme depends on maintaining their separation, there is no place for such a mediating (and
duplicating) figure. Johnson serves his function—about which more
shortly—and disappears.

The presence of a worthy and encouraging male figure, contrasting sharply with the hostile men who usually confront Byron's
heroes, offsets the humiliating emasculation visited upon Juan by the
eunuch Baba, who overrides his protests and dresses him as a harem
girl. The transformation marks the uncertainty of Juan's sexual identity, and represents the collapse of the masculine image Byron's
heroes have struggled to preserve. In Byron's world sexual roles are
not determined by genes alone, but by power: as Juan is helpless, he
becomes a woman. Concurrently, the beautiful Gulbeyaz who has
purchased him becomes masculine because of her position. She is
described as "imperious" and self-willed (V, 110–111), exactly like
Napoleon or the heroes of Byron's tales. Like them, she commands
love and treats its objects like slaves: that is, like women—hence
Juanna.

The reversal of roles contributes to one of Byron's most subtly
ironic visions of the Fall, the archetypal event whose implications will
be discussed in the next chapter. Johnson jokingly urges Juanna to
keep her chastity "though Eve herself once fell" (V, 84), and it is
Gulbeyaz who assumes the figure of Satan:

> Her form had all the softness of her sex,
> Her features all the sweetness of the Devil,
> When he put on the Cherub to perplex
> Eve ....
>
> (V, 109)

Disaffected by her peremptory manner, Juan refuses to succumb.
Thus Juanna does not "fall," as did Julia and Haidée, but her resis-
tance does not proceed from innocence or mortal rectitude. In a
Benthamite age Byron's satire is a reminder that actions give no clue
to motives; Juanna's chastity is fed by a pride more vainglorious than
Eve's:

> ... he had made up his mind
> To be impaled, or quartered as a dish
> For dogs, or to be slain with pangs refined,
> Or thrown to lions, or made baits for fish,

> And thus heroically stood resigned,
> Rather than sin—except to his own wish: . . .
>
> (V, 141)

Gulbeyaz's tyranny over Juan is another image of the threatening woman; the closeness of the scene to Byron's own fears is betrayed by a feeling interjection of the narrator's: "She was a Sultan's bride (thank Heaven, not mine!)" (V, 111).[10] It is not surprising therefore that Juan relents as soon as Gulbeyaz restores the customary notions of masculine and feminine by beginning to weep. The episode comes to a brilliant conclusion with the simultaneous arrival of the Sultan, as if evoked by Gulbeyaz's vacating the male prerogative. Her authority is in fact only a reflection of his: his appearance forces both Gulbeyaz and Juan—whom he mistakes for a pretty girl, accentuating Juan's impotence (V, 155)—into the role of women, and so the rendezvous remains unconsummated.

Juan's humbling transvesture is a start on the path to self-consciousness because it draws a distinction between external appearance and internal identity. His resistance to Gulbeyaz is the first instance in which he views himself from the outside and gropes to make a choice, however melodramatically. His increasing self-reliance is evident during the night he spends in the harem. Juan's affairs with Julia and Haidée show him passive, constricted, or in a deathlike sleep. He now becomes active, capitalizing on his feminine disguise to approach Dudù secretly and successfully. Her Rubens-esque form, placid nature, and likeness to a "soft landscape of mild earth" (VI, 53) suggest once more a maternal Venus, but for the first time Juan displays the traditional masculine initiative. Though Juan wholly succeeds only in a situation in which there are no other men to hinder him, the reassertion of his sexuality demonstrates that masculinity can be as effectively maintained through wit and skill as through the limited conception of "sternness" to which the heroes of the tales are committed: Juan's clever manipulation of his circumstances is a sign of his creator's transferred identification, from the Titans to the adroit improvisor of *Don Juan*. Artifice converts Juan's anxiety-provoking reduction into a triumph, and so the specter of the Fall dissolves into a comic anecdote of sensual dream followed by earthy gratification, the only unambiguously joyful treatment of sex in the poem.[11]

Juan's fitful progress toward autonomy is hastened by his experiences in battle, the quintessence of the violent conflicts inherent in

the world of men. Byron permits Juan to act out the rescue fantasy
already considered: Juan fights off two Cossacks who are about to kill
a Turkish girl of ten, and while Johnson is concerned solely with
plunder, he pauses to guarantee her safety (VIII, 101). In this work
where Byron-the-narrator exults in his control Byron-as-Juan obtains
without difficulty the status that painfully eluded the heroes of Byron's less comically distanced writings: he surpasses his father figure.
As if to confirm that his usefulness is at an end, Johnson vanishes
from the poem and Juan himself assumes the role of father by adopting the orphaned Leila, in whom Medwin saw Byron's own daughter
Allegra.[12] In this incident the close alliance between the rescue fantasy and the motif of the redemptive daughter is clear. Juan's rise to
eminence in the world of men taints him with its savagery, and
naturally produces the complementary desire to return to the tranquil
bliss the child knew with his mother. A clue to the underlying
mother-son relationship expressed in inverted form in the relationship of Leila and Juan is the narrator's insistence on calling her an
"infant," despite her age: the repeated usage emphasizes the need to
exclude any trace of an unsettling sexuality from Juan's affection for
her.[13]

Juan's thoughtless courage in the siege is a dubious quality: it
wins him a place in the world of men, but his glory is the kind the
narrator denounces, and it does not alter the pattern of his dealings
with women. After the battle cantos Juan never again encounters men
threatening to him, but he is far from free of threatening women.

Juan's ambivalent changes are accelerated in St. Petersburgh,
whose sterile imitation of life Byron captures in a precise epithet,
summing it up as a "pleasant capital of painted snows" (IX, 42). Its
ruler, Catherine the Great, is psychologically the least interesting of
Byron's women. He accords her little physical description and makes
no attempt to individualize her: she is the mere emblem of appetite,
the "grand Epitome" of lust and war (IX, 57). Perhaps it is because
Byron could not risk an extended portrait of a sexually devouring
woman that he does comparatively little with Catherine, despite his
fascination. As early as Canto II, in the midst of the Haidée idyll,
Byron had intimated the connection between sexual drives and violence by an offhand allusion to Pasiphae (II, 155). Later he suggests
that the siege of Ismail could have been prevented had the needs that
provoked it been directly satisfied in a meeting between Catherine
and the Sultan: "she to dismiss her guards and he his Harem,/ And
for their other matters, meet and share 'em" (VI, 95). The sublimation

of sexual desires into aggression is neatly stressed when their looting exhausts the Russian soldiers too much to rape the expectant and disappointed Turkish matrons (VIII, 128–132). The connection of lust and war thus displayed is elaborated in the court of Catherine. Her unbroken procession of gigantic and faceless lovers betrays the essential nature of appetite. Because lust recognizes nothing beyond its own compelling drives and obliterates all individual distinctions in seeking satisfaction it is directly related to the destructiveness of war. Anterior to this portrayal is a view of sexual and aggressive passions as equally inimical to the stability of the ego. Juan initially returns Catherine's lust with the undiscriminating sexual intensity of adolescence, as automatically as he had fought at Ismail:

> ... he was of that delighted age
> Which makes all female ages equal—when
> We don't much care with whom we may engage,
> As bold as Daniel in the lions' den,
> So that we can our native sun assuage,
> In the next ocean, which may flow just then—
> To make a *twilight* in, just as Sol's heat is
> Quenched in the lap of the salt sea, or Thetis.
>
>   (IX, 69)

The allusive texture in which the *doubles-entendres* of this stanza are clothed is unusual in these cantos, where the language is generally coarse. The numerous genital puns are a gauge of the depersonalization.

The theme that passion is hostile to true human relationships, brought to the fore at St. Petersburgh, runs throughout *Don Juan*. Its propositions are too rigidly antithetical to adjust to the complicated demands men and women make of each other. Haidée's lineage begins in Fez, "Where all is Eden, or a wilderness" (IV, 54); Gulbeyaz creates either "A kingdom or confusion anywhere" (V, 129). The women of *Don Juan* inherit the syntax that earlier had belonged to Byron's heroes, and the common trait is further evidence of Byron's equal wariness toward the imperatives of (masculine) ambition and (feminine) passion. Drives break down the sheltered area in which play is possible and a self can be freely constructed. The narrator, defending himself against charges of cynicism, proposes that the lesson of *Don Juan* is that it shows the unhappy consequence of the inability to temper desire:

The Nightingale that sings with deep thorn,
Which fable places in her breast of wail,
Is lighter far of heart and voice than those
Whose headlong passions form their proper woes.

And that's the moral of this composition,
If people would but see its real drift;—...
                                                    (VI, 87–88)

The parade of moderation is self-protective: while he sends Juan into
the situations most problematical for him Byron-as-narrator counters
their turmoil by striking an unflappable Horatian stance.

Juan's rise at court extends and darkens the qualities of his relationship to Gulbeyaz. He is bought by the Empress as he was bought
by the Sultana, and this time he does not resist. Juan internalizes his
slavery, acquiescing in his reduction to an exploitable commodity.
The sexual roles are again reversed: with full complicity he becomes a
prostitute selling himself to a wealthy protector, lapsing into a dependent position Byron bluntly characterized to Medwin as "man-
mistress to Catherine the Great."[14] The ambiguous but there muffled
implications of the luxury Juan enjoys with Haidée come into relief.
Juan is increasingly assimilated to a commercial society that substi-
tutes cash for love. The narrator says that he grows "a little dissi-
pated" (X, 23) and falls into "self-love" (IX, 68), which is to say that
he judges himself as others judge him and accepts as if true the high
valuation he owes to chance. Catherine's gifts block his achievement
of independent adulthood, and with fine irony Byron conjoins the
two most threatening women in Juan's life thus far by having Inez
write to praise Catherine's "*maternal* love" (X, 32).[15]

A yearning for innocence preserves Juan from entire subjection.
"In Royalty's vast arms he sighed for Beauty," the narrator comments
(X, 37), but he can do nothing against Catherine, the archetype of the
devouring mother whose fierce embrace unmans her son. He falls ill
from her attentions and the doctors prescribe travel, but that familiar
remedy is only a palliative. Juan leaves Spain to pursue his education
less corrupt than the society he escapes; he leaves Russia for his
health carrying his infection within. Circumstances force him to quit
Julia and Haidée, but he leaves unencumbered, free to begin afresh;
he leaves Catherine as her ambassador, to be fully accepted by the
highest circles of England's crass society and to become the focus of
its marriage-mart.

The uncompleted state of *Don Juan* makes speculation hazardous, but internal developments and Byron's comments to friends forecast Juan's involvement in a new scandal and consequent expulsion from England.[16] Juan's experience would thus parallel Byron's in 1816 and return the poem to its starting point in the autobiographical materials contained in Juan's departure from Spain. The several evocative heroines of the final cantos are headed by Adeline Amundeville. Adeline's casuistry in regard to her feelings for Juan recalls Julia, but whereas Byron lessens Julia's complexity he endows Adeline with potential richness. The justly-praised champagne simile (XIII, 37–38), ending with the comment that "your cold people are beyond all price,/ When once you've broken their confounded ice," hints that Adeline's emotions may erupt through her impeccable exterior, prompting an ambiguous "fall" upwards into sincerity even as they undo her. The unexamined jealousies which, presuming on the objectivity of forty days' seniority, Adeline misrepresents to herself as "maternal fears/ For a young gentleman's fit education" (XIV, 52), imperil Juan's precarious autonomy in familiar fashion. Her dazzling performance at the electioneering dinner she hosts illustrates her deftness at maneuver and corroborates the narrator's warning that she will be "the fair most fatal Juan ever met" (XIII, 12). Juan is encroached upon also by the exuberant Duchess of Fitz-Fulke. In a symmetrical reversal of Juan's transvesture in the harem Fitz-Fulke exploits the superstition of the Black Friar and dresses herself as a man to entangle Juan in an affair.

The incipient relationship between Juan and Aurora Raby seems unlikely to survive the assaults of two such aggressive women. A Catholic like Juan, Aurora is guarded by that difference from the artificiality of English society, as is Leila by her Moslem faith. "She looked as if she sat by Eden's door," the narrator says (XV, 45), and though he differentiates her from Haidée the likeness is apparent. Her purity renews in the increasingly jaded Juan "some feelings he had lately lost,/ Or hardened" (XVI, 107) and rouses him to activity. Once more the determinedly pregenital character of Juan's affections is noticed: Byron indicates more than Adeline's cattiness when in a speech of hers he rhymes "Raby" to "baby" (XV, 49). This glimmer of a tender relationship is cut across by the Duchess's escapade. The metamorphosis of the chilling phantom of the Friar into gloriously voluptuous flesh is a measure of the life-enhancing energies of *Don Juan*, but also of the anxieties that recur in the plot. Juan's encounter with the Duchess leaves him "wan and worn" the next morning (XVII, 14), as debilitated by her as by Catherine. The narrator's directing attention to Juan's "virgin face" (XVII, 13) is no mere arch dig in the ribs: Juan's passivity may be a kind of innocence, but it is far more ominously the weakness of a man no more able to control his destiny than a child subject to his mother's whims.

The configuration taken by Juan's experiences from Inez to Fitz-Fulke is that of a passive boy and a domineering mother. That is perhaps no revelation, and it is equally a critical commonplace to talk of the sovereign authority the narrator of *Don Juan* wields over his creation. It has been less appreciated, however, that Byron's ostentatious display of authorial command is complementary to the particular stressful psychological materials of the story. Yet even the reader who accepts the contention that Juan's career repeatedly re-enacts the domination of a son by his mother may be unconvinced that there are intimate links between his specific inadequacies and the Byron recognized in the narrator. Some observations in C. G. Jung's essay "Psychological Aspects of the Mother Archetype" may offer further persuasion:

> The effects of the mother-complex differ according to whether it appears in a son or a daughter. Typical effects on the son are homosexuality and Don Juanism, and sometimes also impotence. In homosexuality, the son's entire heterosexuality is tied to the mother in an unconscious form; in Don Juanism, he unconsciously seeks his mother in every woman he meets. . . .
>
> Since a "mother-complex" is a concept borrowed from psychopathology, it is always associated with the idea of injury and illness. But if we take the concept out of its narrow psychopathological setting and give it a wider connotation, we can see that it has positive effects as well. Thus a man with a mother-complex may have a finely differentiated Eros instead of, or in addition to, homosexuality. . . . This gives him a great capacity for friendship, which often creates ties of astonishing tenderness between men and may even rescue friendship between the sexes from the limbo of the impossible. He may have good taste and an aesthetic sense which are fostered by the presence of a feminine streak. Then he may be supremely gifted as a teacher because of his almost feminine insight and tact. He is likely to have a feeling for history, and to be conservative in the best sense and cherish the values of the past. . . .
>
> In the same way, what in its negative aspect is Don Juanism can appear positively as bold and resolute manliness; ambitious striving after the highest goals; opposition to all stupidity, narrow-mindedness, injustice, and laziness; willingness to make sacrifices for what is regarded as right, sometimes bordering on heroism; perseverance, inflexibility, and

toughness of will; a curiosity that does not shrink even from the riddles of the universe; and finally, a revolutionary spirit which strives to put a new face upon the world.[17]

Jung's categorizations of masculine and feminine may be challenged as unduly prejudicial without at all weakening the essay. Anyone familiar with Byron's life as recorded in Leslie Marchand's fine biography may easily adduce evidence to support the applicability of these remarks. They penetrate the anomalies and apparent contradictions Byron presents, and, more important, they point beyond biography to comprehension of the structure of *Don Juan*. It cannot be said, for example, that Juan seeks his mother in every woman he meets, even unconsciously: he is too much a pawn of the story, too lacking in purpose and volition, to attribute to him the motivation proper only to a three-dimensional character. The mother complex Jung describes, however, may seem by inference a probable hypothesis about Byron himself, and it undeniably suggests a common ground for the fixity of Juan and the audacity of the narrator.

In Byron's early tales ostensibly mimetic narrative repeatedly modulated into a prolonged gaze at an unchanging crisis. The two modes, sequential narrative and lyric plaint, were in continual conflict, with plot forever yielding to static monologue. What Wordsworth remarked of his own poems in the Preface to the *Lyrical Ballads* is equally germane to Byron's works: it is the feeling which gives importance to the situation, and not the situation to the feeling. In this regard the difficulties the narrator of *Don Juan* experiences in trying to tell his story are perfectly genuine, because Byron's commitment to action and narrative is offset by the contrary urge toward expression typified by Manfred's cry, "My pang shall find a voice." In *Don Juan* Byron solves, or at least suspends, the problem by centering his poem on the narrator. Juan's adventures provide movement while the narrator self-consciously makes the contemplative impulse which had obstructed narrative into his most fertile subject. Freud saw the oedipal triangle as momentous because it marks the child's entry into his society: in *Don Juan* the rhythm of Juan's falls and the narrator's rescues of him, the recurrent plot envisioned in everwidening, ever refined contexts, reveals the very kernel of Byron's conception of himself and his stance in the world.

6

History and Allusion

The psychological configuration
on which *Don Juan* rests influences every facet of the poem, but it
would be less interesting if it only recorded a stage in Byron's personal development. Though Byron tapped the deepest layers of his
unconscious in Juan and the narrator, in embodying portions of himself in these independent characters he enlarged them into figures of
wider import. The quotation from Jung in the last chapter describes
an affinity between regressive impulses and an interest in history,
and Byron's reworking of his own past in *Don Juan* is significantly
paralleled by his treatment of literary and cultural history.

Central to both *Childe Harold* and *Don Juan* is Byron's attempt to
construct a public identity for himself, in *Childe Harold* III–IV by synthesis and in *Don Juan* by fragmentation and re-creation. The identity
is "public" in two closely allied but distinguishable ways. The figure
Byron presents in both poems is Byron as he wishes to appear, the
definitive interpretation of himself and his notorious doings. Yet

Byron seeks not merely to establish an authorized version of his past and personality, but also to place the identity he invents in European history. His self-definition requires that he connect himself with the men and events that have shaped his culture and that he become influential equally with them: he studies history in order that he may enter it.

Don Juan is marked by a mode of incessant but curiously casual, apparently inconsistent, allusion that differentiates it from the grave, heroic invocations of the later *Childe Harold*. This technique, often set down to Byron's putative neoclassicism, is in fact very different from Augustan formal imitation. A brief and necessarily general comparison between certain uses of the past in Byron and in his eighteenth-century predecessors brings into focus Byron's success in connecting his private history with larger meanings.

The doctrine of imitation was fundamental to Augustan poetics: it provided the writer with a stylistic model and an ethical context. The rewards of an ostensible adherence to tradition were not restricted to relatively straightforward if subtle enhancements of meaning; as W. K. Wimsatt suggests, the Augustan poets are often at their best when subverting their proclaimed literary standards and making them the vehicle of exuberant, imaginative play.[1] To be effective, however, parody depends on knowledge of the originals, and by mid-century the strategies the Augustan poets employed to enlarge their meaning, their very language and procedures, were becoming unavailable.[2]

Byron's approach had to be different. Even in the first two cantos of *Childe Harold* his determination to overcome the limitations of space and time and omnivorously to draw history and as much of the world as he knew into his poem is evident. On the surface the poem is a simple narrative of a journey from the western to the eastern end of the Mediterranean. The reader's sense of chronology is more complex, however, since the progress eastward is also a regression in time. There are two eras mingled in Spain, with the recent Peninsular Campaign overlaid on the Medieval and Renaissance wars of Moslem and Christian.[3] As the poem moves on it carries the reader further back, to the primitive world of the Suliotes and the origins of Western civilization in ancient Greece. A second look at the stanzas on Marathon discussed earlier (II, 88–92; pp. 31–32) prompts further reflections about time and place in this pilgrimage. If it is asked where these stanzas are located, the answer seems easy—"at Marathon"—and the passage gains greatly from the sense of a "here" defined for the reader by his knowledge of the narrator's actual travels. Yet the physical description is not particularized, and the "Marathon" Byron evokes is less a point in space than a moment in history. And yet again, for all its vividness the passage is less an attempt to capture the individual qualities and specific details of a precise moment than it is an allusion to an event that has already become a "magic word." In that regard, "Marathon" has neither time nor place: it is a figurative complex of values. If it is asked "what is the time of *Childe Harold*?", a proper response is that the time is always the present of the narrator who remembers and re-enacts the past.[4] Byron replaces the conception of the past as essentially a static comparative framework to be *imitated*, whether respectfully or in parody, by a past that is to be directly *re-experienced*.

Childe Harold, especially but not exclusively in the fourth canto, provides a re-reading of figures and monuments of Western culture which through its own vitality preserves their significance. The later eighteenth century feared that the weight of history had begun to inhibit poetic originality: Byron demonstrates that it could yet serve. The poem makes the past available to the informed imagination so that it can contribute to self-knowledge in the present; the four cantos taken together witness the continuity of Western history. The "I" of the poem expands to become the register of that meaning: Byron makes of himself a mythic exemplar.

The method has nonetheless a powerful limitation. Imaginative participation in a cultural continuum does not wholly mitigate the reality of the present. There remain two realms: the realm of significance is the timeless world of figurative value that the past has become; the narrator stands fixed on a blank and now insignificant plain. Byron's historical consciousness repeatedly leads to despair because it increases his awareness of the disparity between the present and the world of value he can imagine, whether in memory or prophecy. The disjunction the Augustans perceived primarily in cultural terms Byron expresses in anxious personal accents: he attributes it to the individual's own mutability and mortality. He attempts to transcend these limitations by identifying himself with the unchanging forms of nature and art, but the attempts prove futile and provoke fresh cries of despair. The conclusion of the fourth canto bares man's tenuous relationship to the "Images of Eternity" he can envision from his prison in a world of flux.

If man's own mutability and mortality are the villains of *Childe*

Harold, they are the heroes of *Don Juan*, which warns against the dangers of fixity and paradoxically suggests that the way to conquer time is not to seek the stillness of the Apollo Belvedere but to give oneself to motion. "Now there is nothing gives a man such spirits," the narrator comments, "As going at full speed—no matter where its/ Direction be": "the great *end* of travel," he reflects, "is driving" (X, 72). *Childe Harold* labors to assimilate the past, but the victories its reverence achieves intensify the narrator's frustrations. By strategies which tend to diminish its coherence *Don Juan* alleviates the difficulties inherent in trying to summon "the past" into the present as if it were a closed, self-contained code of meaning. Through parody, fragmentation, doubt, and exaggerated disharmonies Byron lightens the burden of the past while yet building upon its foundation. His wide-ranging allusions display his mastery of tradition and establish his title as an innovator from within rather than an ignorant iconoclast from without. The techniques are disintegrative, but their intentions and ends are positive: they clear space for Byron to advance his present artistic concerns and simultaneously renovate a tradition that had become either unavailable or oppressive.

The complementary nature of Byron's two activities should now be apparent. In converting the events of his childhood and marriage into the comic adventures of Juan Byron steps free of their crippling influence, transforming what he experienced as a fate imposed on him or a lost bliss for which he yearned into a rich body of material he could shape according to his deliberate poetic purposes. He similarly breaks up the reputations and works of classical authors, the authority of great men, and all other forms of solemnly received meaning in order to be relieved of their pressure. The nose-thumbing carries its own anarchic pleasures, but it also makes part of a constructive effort to bring the fixed past alive by an act of imagination.[5]

Stanzas 122–123 of Canto I, immediately preceding the exposure of Juan in Julia's bedroom, afford an extended illustration of Byron's allusive technique. Two minor allusions in these stanzas typify the problems of discrimination that study of the texture of Byron's verse encounters. Is the phrase "us youth" in I, 125 (quoted below), one of Byron's favorite epithets, *calculated* to remind the reader of the desperate, aging Falstaff of *2 Henry IV*? And, whether deliberate or automatic, how much does it add to the reader's sense of the sordid world depicted in the stanza? Another occasion for tact is presented by stanza 123:

'T is sweet to hear the watch-dog's honest bark
Bay deep-mouthed welcome as we draw near home;
'T is sweet to know there is an eye will mark
Our coming, and look brighter when we come; . . .

J. C. Maxwell has observed that this is Byron's memory of a passage
from a novel he loved, *The Vicar of Wakefield:*

> And now my heart caught new sensations of pleasure the nearer I ap-
> proached that peaceful mansion. As a bird that has been frightened from
> his nest, my affections outwent my haste, and hovered round my little
> fireside with all the rapture of expectation. I called up the many fond
> things I had to say, and anticipated the welcome I was to receive. I
> already felt my wife's tender embrace, and smiled at the joy of my little
> ones. As I walked but slowly, the night waned apace. The labourers of
> the day were all retired to rest; the lights were out in every cottage; no
> sounds were heard but of the shrilling cock, and the deep-mouthed
> watch-dog at hollow distance.
>
> (ch. 22)

Maxwell does not comment upon it, but the context in which
Goldsmith sets this image of domestic peace qualifies it in a fashion
that gives point to Byron's echo. The vicar utters the sentiments as he
returns home with his daughter Olivia after her seduction by Thorn-
hill, and he will arrive to find his house in flames. Despite its surface
tranquility the allusion implies a situation of a "fallen woman" and
blasted hopes that, if recognized, prepares the reader for Byron's
denouement.[6]

The casual and buried character of these allusions makes one
wary of too rigidly claiming significance for them, but the echoes of
Paradise Lost are more prominent. The central stanza of the passage
sets forth Byron's version of the Fall:

But sweeter still than this, than these, than all,
Is first and passionate Love—it stands alone,
Like Adam's recollection of his fall;
The Tree of Knowledge has been plucked—all's known—
And Life yields nothing further to recall
Worthy of this ambrosial sin, so shown,
No doubt in fable, as the unforgiven
Fire which Prometheus filched for us from Heaven.

(127)[7]

It is perhaps because the metaphor of the Fall itself is so obvious, yields so much so readily, that readers have had little curiosity to inquire more deeply about Byron's use of Milton in this episode. The stanza just cited is the culmination of a six-stanza pattern that begins:

> —'T is sweet to hear
> At midnight on the blue and moonlit deep
> The song and oar of Adria's gondolier,
> By distance mellowed, o'er the waters sweep;
> 'T is sweet to see the evening star appear;
> 'T is sweet to listen as the night-winds creep
> From leaf to leaf; 't is sweet to view on high
> The rainbow, based on ocean, span the sky.
>
> (122)

The extended anaphora should recall to the reader Book IV of *Paradise Lost:*

> Sweet is the breath of morn, her rising sweet,
> With charm of earliest Birds; pleasant the Sun
> When first on this delightful Land he spreads
> His orient Beams, on herb, tree, fruit, and flow'r
> Glist'ring with dew; fragrant the fertile earth
> After soft showers; and sweet the coming on
> Of grateful Ev'ning mild, then silent Night
> With this her solemn Bird and this fair Moon....
>
> (641–648)[8]

Byron thus intimates a comparison between prelapsarian Adam and Eve and Juan and Julia, but it is necessary to observe that this parallel is drawn on the night of their discovery in November and not at their first spontaneous embrace in June, when it might have been more fit. By his sly fuss about the "liberty" his muse takes in leaping ahead six months Byron brings to the fore the duration of the affair. This emphasis on time is crucial, for however innocent Juan and Julia were at the outset, the continuance of the liaison makes conscious adulterers of them. Byron implies this progression by the increasing crassness of his catalogue:

> Sweet is a legacy, and passing sweet
> The unexpected death of some old lady,

>   Or gentleman of seventy years complete,
>   Who've made "us youth" wait too-too long already,
>   For an estate, or cash, or country seat,
>   Still breaking, but with stamina so steady,
>   That all the Israelites are fit to mob its
>   Next owner for their double-damned post-obits.
>   (125)

One of the recurrent themes of *Don Juan* is its insistence that innocence and experience are stages in the temporal succession by which the poem is haunted. Byron's expansive verse, flowing rapidly from the peaceful landscape of stanza 122 to the money-hungry, unfeeling society of stanza 125, reproduces the evolution of Juan and Julia towards an ambiguous sophistication. Moreover, the verse generalizes that movement and makes it representative of an entire culture, just as Julia's accelerated transformation from chaste twenty-three to accomplished *intrigante* acquires resonance through the shift from allusions to Milton's Eve to the world of Restoration comedy.

In none of the editions of *Don Juan* with which I am familiar is the allusion to *Paradise Lost* annotated, and it is undeniable that the tenor of Byron's references to the Fall is apparent even when the specific echo remains unheard.[9] Byron's allusions typically occupy a secondary position, perhaps so that he would not appear more learned than a gentleman should, perhaps because he knew that he could not rely on his readers to catch them. To miss them, however, is to miss Byron's precise tone and meaning: to miss the skillful reinterpretation of a *topos* is to lose the very literariness of his art. Through the parallel of Juan and Julia to Adam and Eve Byron shapes his reader's response to their affair by casting the appealing lovers in the role of the primal sinners. In this schema Juan's enforced departure from Spain is the counterpart to the expulsion from the Garden, and it is tempting to judge the horrors of the shipwreck as the condign retribution Juan must suffer for transgression, a temptation Byron increases by numerous references to Dante.[10]

Juan seems to undergo a purgatorial death-by-water to be reborn, cleansed, on Haidée's pastoral island. The second canto, however, displays numerous allusions to other Old Testament stories of fall and exile which diminish his culpability. In stanza 16 his sorrows are compared to the laments of the Jews during the Babylonian Captivity, a comparison whose gravity has already been proleptically qualified by the narrator's appropriation in stanza 7 of the same psalm to make a lightly suggestive compliment to the beauty of Spanish women. Allusions to the Flood run throughout the second canto, from a parallel between Juan's ship, "the holy *Trinidada*," and the Ark, to Noah's Dove and the rainbow of the Covenant. Byron's immediate rhetorical point is ironic, to stress the disjunction between the providential universe represented by these signs and the world of meaningless event experienced by his characters, but there is a provocative refinement. Noah was the good man whom God saved from the destruction visited upon the corrupt earth, and Byron's employment of the Old Testament parallel thus deflects attention from Juan's "sins" onto the hypocrisies of Spanish society. Within this framework, Juan is no more than an innocent scapegoat for the scandal-loving world that produced him.

The conflation of these two stories is not systematic, but it repays attention. Scriptural exegesis aligned the Fall and the Flood, seeing in the second a renewed proof of the depravity of man of which the first is the archetype. Byron, in contrast, exploits their differences to multiply the interpretations to his story.

Nowhere is Byron's free raiding of the past more apparent than in the description of the siege of Ismail in Cantos VII and VIII. In a note to *English Bards and Scotch Reviewers* Byron observed that "as the *Odyssey* is so closely connected with the story of the *Iliad*, they may almost be classed as one grand historical poem," and in *Don Juan* he blends the two works. Juan's adventures parallel Ulysses' wanderings and the siege of Ismail parallels the battle for Troy. The episode thus corresponds to the wars of traditional epic, but by a telling compression it serves simultaneously as another component of epic: the voyage to the underworld. It should be noted, however, that the underworld Byron depicts is not the classical one but the Christian: the province of Satan where the wicked are eternally punished. The substitution seems so natural that its effects have been overlooked.

Byron begins with an allusion that establishes the battle as an inverted creation: "'Let there be Light! said God, and there was Light!'/ 'Let there be Blood!' says man, and there's a sea!" (VII, 41). Offhand but continuous Biblical allusion reinforces the literally infernal nature of war: to choose but two instances out of many, the anticipation in the Russian camp is contrasted to the "marriage feast" of Revelation (VII, 49), and the siege ladders are contrasted to the ladders Jacob saw ascending to heaven (VII, 52). The most oblique and many-layered allusion occurs when Juan rescues Leila from the Cossacks:

When Juan caught a glimpse of this sad sight,
I shall not say exactly what he *said,*
Because it might not solace "ears polite;" . . .

(VIII, 93)

The narrator outdoes Pope's sycophantic chaplain "who never men-
tions Hell to ears polite" by omitting the word entirely.[11] Byron's
deference to the sham purity of his audience mockingly exemplifies
the words of Voltaire quoted in the preface to these cantos: "Plus les
moeurs sont dépravés, plus les expressions deviennent mésurées; on
croit regagner en langage ce qu'on a perdu en vertu." This indirect
allusion is surrounded by others far more forceful which unrelent-
ingly demand that the reader recognize the true brutality of war. The
narrator says that the carnage "made some *think,* and others *know,* a
hell come" (VIII, 42). He concludes his image of destruction with a
bitter picture of the victorious Christian cross "red with no *redeeming
gore*" (VIII, 122), illuminated only by slaughter and fire.

Byron gains several ends by his sleights-of-hand in this episode.
By describing the battle as hell he nominally fulfills the requirements
of epic form in a manner satisfactory to a rationalist age which no
longer found the conventional voyage to the underworld credible.
The translation of the battle scenes into an underworld, together with
the substitution of a Christian for a classical underworld, further
makes the chilling comment that man's blindness and violence are
such that the Christian notion of hell is only a metaphor for the life he
creates every day around him on earth. Byron does not represent a
mythic place comfortably remote from the reader, but actual events
which the reader tolerates and presumably even applauds as glorious. His use of the second person precludes any evasion of responsibility: "I sketch your world exactly as it goes" (VIII, 89).

Byron's juxtaposition of the Christian and classical frameworks in
order to multiply his perspectives and make the reader reflect is
epitomized in the most grotesque event in *Don Juan:*

A Russian officer, in martial tread
Over a heap of bodies, felt his heel
Seized fast, as if 't were by the serpent's head
Whose fangs Eve taught her human seed to feel;
In vain he kicked, and swore, and writhed, and bled,
And howled for help as wolves do for a meal—
The teeth still kept their gratifying hold,
As do the subtle snakes described of old.

> A dying Moslem, who had felt the foot
> Of a foe o'er him, snatched at it, and bit
> The very tendon which is most acute—
> (That which some ancient Muse or modern wit
> Named after thee, Achilles!) and quite through't
> He made the teeth meet, nor relinquished it
> Even with his life—for (but they lie) 't is said
> To the live leg still clung the severed head.
>
> (VIII, 83-84).

This hideous incident asks the reader to recognize that the courage and thirst for fame that impelled a classical hero are in Christian terms a sign of man's fallen condition. Throughout these cantos, the narrator plays off these conflicts in our heritage against one another, arguing within the classical context that the unglamorous modern soldiers are as heroic as the ancients, and then adopting a Christian stance, denouncing the falsity of epic values and insisting on the pernicious effects of praising them. Apologizing for having recounted this circumstance, he declares:

> But then the fact's a fact—and 't is the part
> Of a true poet to escape from fiction
> Whene'er he can; for there is little art
> In leaving verse more free from the restriction
> Of Truth than prose, unless to suit the mart
> For what is sometimes called poetic diction,
> And that outrageous appetite for lies
> Which Satan angles with for souls, like flies.
>
> (VIII, 86)

The narrator's attitude to the dependence of epic poetry on "the blaze/ Of conquest and its consequences" (VIII, 90) for its materials descends from Milton, but he is pragmatic rather than dogmatic. Since religion or any dogma can easily be perverted into a justification for barbarity, as the Christian conquest of the Moslems demonstrates, the narrator adheres only to the "fact," setting one interpretation of it next to another to prevent any complacent certainty, exploiting the disjunction in values to emphasize the absurd waste of war.

Byron's satiric comparison of the siege of Ismail and the fall of Troy is double-edged: it both deflates modern combat and charges Homer with fraudulently ennobling the actions of the Greeks and

Trojans. This doubleness suggests another "fact": that Ismail *is* Troy—in modern terms and as it would appear to a modern sensibility. The identity reveals the fresh shadings of the treatment of time in *Don Juan*. The voyage of the enslaved Juan past Troy provokes from Byron a regretful observation of the transience of glory:

> The situation seems still formed for fame—
> A hundred thousand men might fight again,
> With ease; but where I sought for Ilion's walls,
> The quiet sheep feeds, and the tortoise crawls;
>
> Troops of untended horses; here and there
> Some little hamlets, with new names uncouth;
> Some shepherds (unlike Paris) led to stare
> A moment at the European youth
> Whom to the spot their school-boy feelings bear;
> A Turk, with beads in hand, and pipe in mouth,
> Extremely taken with his own religion,
> Are what I found there—but the devil a Phrygian.
>
> (IV, 77–78)

The scene is structurally congruent with the stanzas on Marathon at the close of Canto II of *Childe Harold* and it may be noted again that whereas the stanzas state that time effaces glory the statement is qualified by the memory of the youth in the scene and of the narrator himself. So far the two poems are the same, but *Don Juan* converts Time the Destroyer into Time the Evolver: Juan is soon freed from captivity and he enters a world that is the new Troy, becoming himself the Paris lacking at the original locale. Byron knows this palingenesis is neither the heroic age reborn nor the revolution he prophesied and assisted; he also knows that it is probably very much like the reality of the heroic age before it was transformed by Homer's art. The applicability of Homeric allusion to Juan's deeds at Ismail effectively implies an evolutionary world in which basic drives and situations are forever assuming new shapes yet remain recognizably continuous.

The most intriguing and revelatory example of Byron's revision of classical materials in *Don Juan* is the employment of the *Odyssey* in Cantos II and III. Childe Harold's wanderings through picturesque Mediterranean landscapes occasionally echo the adventures of Ulysses (see p. 33); a more personal use is evident in *Beppo* (1817), where the *Odyssey* figures not prominently but suggestively in the atmosphere of the protagonist's homecoming (cf. p. 99). It is easy to understand why in the years after his separation Homer's domestic epic especially attracted Byron. His epithet of "Clytemnestra" for Annabella dramatizes his view of his position: throughout the *Odyssey* Homer contrasts Ulysses' reception to Agamemnon's, and the image of Ulysses' return to Ithaca to find Penelope ever constant reflected the desires of a man who saw himself betrayed by a treacherous wife and exiled from England. To an adult re-reading the *Odyssey* for the first time since childhood it is extraordinary to discover that the adventures he chiefly remembers are a minor part of the poem and function mostly as impediments to the hero's central urge to regain his hearth and land. The poem assures us that even if we have spent several years with Calypso and Circe we can go home again, and to Byron engaged in Venetian debaucheries that assurance must have exerted a strong appeal. Like many Romantics, Byron was drawn less to the *Aeneid* and its picture of the founding of a new society than to the rhythms of exile and return in the *Odyssey*.

Juan's arrival half-drowned on Haidée's island and her subsequent care of him recapitulate Ulysses' landing on Scheria and discovery by Nausicaa in Books V and VI of the *Odyssey*. Thus much is obvious, but Byron makes more complex use of the parallel than has yet been remarked. Like Joyce's reworking of the incident a hundred years later, the affair between Haidée and Juan is an actualization of the sexuality latent in Homer's narrative. Nausicaa is impelled to the beach where she encounters Ulysses by a dream of marriage, and many ancient critics were prompted to question her modesty when she exclaims over a stranger: "O heav'n! in my connubial hour decree/ This man my spouse, or such a spouse as he!"[12] Nausicaa's unwillingness to accompany Ulysses to her father's court involves them both in some duplicity, and those who found excessive the concern for reputation she alleges in justification were quick to wonder whether circumstances were as decorous as they seem. Perhaps therefore Byron should be seen in the Haidée episode as presenting his view of what "really" happened between Nausicaa and Ulysses: as in the siege of Ismail, relating a literal "fact" that Homer glossed over.

The narrator's hints of what awaits Lambro bring Byron's subtlest development of Homer:

> An honest gentleman at his return
> May not have the good fortune of Ulysses;

> Not all lone matrons for their husbands mourn,
> Or show the same dislike to suitors' kisses; . . .
>
> (III, 23)

This allusion unobtrusively but completely rearranges the Homeric parallel by identifying Haidée with Penelope and Juan with the offensive suitors at Ithaca.[13] The light cast by the *Odyssey* thus clarifies the psychological materials previously discussed. It presents Juan's love for Haidée as rivalry for the wife of an older man, thereby confirming that the symbolic importance of daughters in Byron's writings is a displacement of conflicts with the father over the mother. Lambro's horror at learning that he is presumed dead and that his beloved has already taken a lover is an inversion of the child's feeling that he has been abandoned for his father, but the scene tells also on its surface level. From Lambro's point of view Haidée is an unredemptive daughter, and his emotions have a counterpart in the experience of every doting father on his daughter's wedding day. The *Odyssey* illuminates *Don Juan*, but the illumination is mutual: Byron's poem places its ancestor in a perspective that enables the reader to discern multiple correspondences between the suitors, Ulysses' slaughter of them, and the reader's own inner life.

The condensation of the Scherian and Ithacan episodes of the *Odyssey* functions in several ways. In Homer Nausicaa and Penelope are separate individuals, but Byron's conflation makes them rather stages in time: moving inward from beach to palace Nausicaa grows into Penelope, and an unfaithful Penelope to boot. The obsession with time produces a radical alteration in the conception of ethical norms. Homer represents the contrast between faithful and faithless wife as a polar opposition between Penelope and Clytemnestra, but in *Don Juan* this static and absolute distinction dissolves into succession within a single life:

> In her first passion Woman loves her lover,
> In all the others all she loves is Love,
> Which grows a habit she can ne'er get over,
> And fits her loosely—like an easy glove,
> As you may find, whene'er you like to prove her:
> One man alone at first her heart can move;
> She then prefers him in the plural number,
> Not finding that the additions much encumber.

'T is melancholy, and a fearful sign
Of human frailty, folly, also crime,
That Love and Marriage rarely can combine. . . .

There's something of antipathy, as 't were,
Between their present and their future state;
A kind of flattery that's hardly fair
Is used until the truth arrives too late—
Yet what can people do, except despair?
The same things change their names at such a rate;
For instance—Passion in a lover's glorious,
But in a husband is pronounced uxorious.

All tragedies are finished by a death,
All comedies are ended by a marriage;
The future states of both are left to faith. . . .

(III, 3, 5-6, 9)

Byron degrades the notion of stability to a trick of genre because his exacerbated consciousness of the enigmas of human growth and human relationships precludes any permanence. The integrity of character is obliterated: any character at any moment may metamorphose into its opposite. The processes by which two characters condense into one, or one splits into two, as Byron splits into Juan and the narrator, are reciprocal, since, as Wordsworth observed in lines already quoted from *The Prelude*, a man contemplating his past may see himself as almost two persons. In *Don Juan* the only escapes from the tormenting flux of one's own personality are to die, as Haidée dies, or to develop the resiliency to surmount and enjoy the flux, as the narrator does.

The many levels of time in this passage are the determining features of its structure. The "honest gentleman" who will be cuckolded on his return (III, 23) exists neither in the plane of Homer nor in the plane of Juan's adventures, set in the late eighteenth century, but in Byron's present reflections on the woes of marriage. Stanza 23 implies that it is a contemporary Penelope who would be unchaste, using the mock-epic contrast to reinforce a satire on current mores. According to logic the assertion that inconstancy is universal contained in stanzas 3 through 9 should undercut this attack, since by denying the possibility of a virtue like Penelope's it denies the standard on which the satire is based. The inconsistency, however, is not immediately noticed because Byron situates the comments in different time-sequences: one is a comparison of past and present, and the other the fluctuations of a single life. The double-time thus makes possible Byron's combination of moral satire with cynicism and skepticism.

The manifold strata of time in *Don Juan*, created in part by the technique of allusion, add important dimensions to the relationship between Juan and the narrator. Here, in a stanza already quoted, is another conflation of classical and Christian models:

> But sweeter still than this, than these, than all,
> Is first and passionate Love—it stands alone,
> Like Adam's recollection of his fall;
> The Tree of Knowledge has been plucked—all's known—
> And Life yields nothing further to recall
> Worthy of this ambrosial sin, so shown,
> No doubt in fable, as the unforgiven
> Fire which Prometheus filched for us from Heaven.
>   (I, 127)

The myths of Prometheus and Adam are alike in that both seek to account for the self-consciousness that alienates man from his surroundings.[14] The same gift that divorces man from nature, however, also enables him to devise means to subject it to his control, and according to Aeschylus Prometheus is the founder of all man's arts and sciences. In the following stanzas Byron explores this ambivalent heritage by a review of recent inventions: vaccinations, artillery shells, the guillotine, and other "opposite discoveries" (I, 129). At the opening of Canto X he repeats the association of technological gains with the Fall:

> When Newton saw an apple fall, he found
> In that slight startle from his contemplation—
> 'Tis *said* (for I'll not answer above ground
> For any sage's creed or calculation)—
> A mode of proving that the Earth turned round
> In a most natural whirl, called "gravitation;"
> And this is the sole mortal who could grapple,
> Since Adam—with a fall—or with an apple.
>
> Man fell with apples, and with apples rose,
> If this be true; for we must deem the mode
> In which Sir Isaac Newton could disclose

Through the then unpaved stars the turnpike road,
A thing to counterbalance human woes:
For ever since immortal man hath glowed
With all kinds of mechanics. . . .

(X, 1–2)[15]

Christian tradition offered as consolation for the Fall the view that it
might be regarded as fortunate because it led to Christ, the New, or
Second, Adam. Through the redeemer Christianity offers a restoration of the original harmony of Eden; *Paradise Lost*, for example, while
it does not exhibit the apocalyptic renovation of the visions of Blake
and Shelley, does extend the hope of a "paradise within . . . happier
far." Byron's conceit, however, involves incommensurable terms: to
borrow a phrase from elementary arithmetic, his proposition is not an
instance of apples and apples but of apples and oranges. Technological advances are not equivalent to the prelapsarian unified consciousness, and Byron's ironic list of destructive inventions signals the end
of the Baconian dream that Eden could be reclaimed through science.
Whatever the other recompense, in Byron's schema the divided consciousness is permanent. The simple asymmetry conceals a terrible
irony: man's intellect can show him that he has fallen, but never lead
him to reintegration. The Promethean fire therefore remains "unforgiven," a dubious possession that we must "endure," as Byron had
earlier declared in *Childe Harold* (IV, 163).

The allusions to Prometheus and Adam suggest that *Don Juan* is
not only epic action and Romantic introspection but also a version of
history: the history of consciousness seen as a movement from a past
hypostatized as univalent, conscious only of the present, hence innocent, to the ambiguities and temporal self-consciousness of the
modern era. Byron's formulation of the Fall emphasizes the fall into
time, and as Juan stumblingly proceeds from his rapturous initiation
with Julia and Haidée to his blasé participation in the society of Re-
gency England his career seems loosely representative of man's
spiritual history as Byron views it. Yet if Juan's life begins to appear as
an epitome of Western man the cause lies less in his development
than in the ever-expanding reflections the narrator attaches to him.
Though Juan inhabits the actual, realistically detailed world of the late
eighteenth century, he represents the mental world of ancient epic as
Byron here pejoratively conceives it. In his adventures up to and
including the siege of Ismail Byron depicts the conventional actions of
epic, and, more important, the relatively straightforward motives of

epic: Juan is courteous to women, strong in adversity, unhesitatingly brave in battle, and so forth. To the end Juan retains the passivity that is his peculiar form of unselfconsciousness: it is the narrator who supplies the laminations of meaning in his story as he reflects upon it from his uneasy vantage in the later stages of a process governed by no teleology or eschatology other than increasing self-consciousness.

Toward the close of the first canto the narrator expresses his sense of the changes wrought by time:

> No more—no more—Oh! never more on me
> The freshness of the heart can fall like dew,
> Which out of all the lovely things we see
> Extracts emotions beautiful and new,
> Hived in our bosoms like the bag o' the bee.
> Think'st thou the honey with those objects grew?
> Alas! 't was not in them, but in thy power
> To double even the sweetness of a flower.
>
> No more—no more—Oh! never more, my heart,
> Canst thou be my sole world, my universe!
> Once all in all, but now a thing apart,
> Thou canst not be my blessing or my curse:
> The illusion's gone for ever, and thou art
> Insensible, I trust, but none the worse,
> And in thy stead I've got a deal of judgment,
> Though Heaven knows how it ever found a lodgment.
>   (I, 214–215)

If he apprehends these lines as personal statement alone the reader will be forced to conclude with Harold Bloom that they are vastly inferior to Coleridge's "Dejection: An Ode,"[16] but in *Don Juan* elements of autobiography become signs of a general cultural condition. Even the avarice much extolled by the narrator in the later cantos is the vice appropriate to his commercial age. Throughout, his sophistication, detachment, and abstracting, skeptical intelligence are the qualities which led eighteenth-century critics to doubt that poetry could survive in a rationalized, specialized, modern civilization. The growth of the narrator from passion to judgment outlined in these stanzas is co-ordinate with, and representative of, the poem's view of history; the stanzas should be compared with Bishop Hurd's nostalgia for the world of romance destroyed by reason: "what we have gotten by this revolution is a great deal of good sense. . . . What we have lost is a world of fine fabling." No doubt Byron accepted the commonplace view of history as a movement from innocence to self-consciousness because it offered a cultural parallel to the private experience his regressive desires liked to imagine: the narrator's sentiments express in a lighter fashion the pains of growth which torture Harold, Manfred, and Byron's other early personae.

It is important, however, to put the issue the right way round. Byron does not trivialize history in *Don Juan*, but makes himself as narrator the inclusive figure of his age. It should be noted too that the fluid intermingling of his personal past with the history of the race is finally liberating. The procedure clearly identified Eden with childhood, and the very clarity of the identification permitted Byron to treat his longings as childish. Thus characterized, the phantom of bliss that in its disguised form rules his first work and the vanished glories idealized in *Childe Harold* lose some of their sway. In the end what initially appears a degenerative view of evolution makes room for a more outgoing and confident poetry. These concerns culminate in Byron's great rehandling of the *ubi sunt* motif at the close of Canto IX (76–86):

> Some who once set their caps at cautious dukes,
> Have taken up at length with younger brothers:
> Some heiresses have bit at sharpers' hooks:
> Some maids have been made wives, some merely mothers:
> Others have lost their fresh and fairy looks:
> In short, the list of alterations bothers.
> There's little strange in this, but something strange is
> The unusual quickness of these common changes.
>
> Talk not of seventy years as age; in seven
> I have seen more changes, down from monarchs to
> The humblest individuals under Heaven,
> Than might suffice a moderate century through.
> I knew that nought was lasting, but now even
> Change grows too changeable, without being new:
> Nought's permanent among the human race,
> Except the Whigs *not* getting into place.
>
> I have seen Napoleon, who seemed quite a Jupiter,
> Shrink to a Saturn. I have seen a Duke
> (No matter which) turn politician stupider,
> If that can well be, than his wooden look.
> But it is time that I should hoist my "blue Peter,"
> And sail for a new theme:—I have seen—and shook

To see it—the King hissed, and then caressed;
But don't pretend to settle which was best.
                                                    (XI, 81–83)

In these lines Byron turns the nostalgia that broods over his work into
a convention that he can comically manipulate, and the convention
points the personal feeling outward and universalizes it.

The passage captures the bewilderment of an England involved
abroad in the sudden international realignments brought about by
Napoleon's rise and fall, and bedeviled at home by demands for social
and political reorganization. It brilliantly and concisely expresses the
mood of a period that Carl Woodring, following many historians, has
characterized as the age of acceleration.[17] Yet the *ubi sunt* itself possesses a stability which counteracts the dizzying rush of life it records.
"Change grows too changeable, without being new" is the old prov-
erb, "Plus ça change, plus c'est la même chose," in Byron's particular
accent. Though the stanzas are dominated by transience they testify
as well to the second half of the aphorism. "Nought's permanent
among the human race,/ Except"—and the exception satirically demonstrates continuity. The ironic example is less forceful proof in itself
than in the convention it revitalizes, for by making it come alive again
Byron shows the reader the constant core beneath the radical surface
alterations of human experience.

On a larger scale, Byron creates by his juxtaposed allusions a
speculative dialogue between the Christian and classical values,
revealing their common questions and enabling their different accounts of man to challenge and illuminate each other. While easing its
oppressive weight, Byron's allusive mode places the reader in history, opposing its enlarging context to the solipsistic self-
consciousness of his age. If Byron warns the reader to doubt Homer
and implies that there never could have been a paragon like
Penelope, he at the same time reminds him that there remains a
profound human need to fantasize an example of enduring love,
however the shapes projected by that need may vary. He narrates
Haidée's idyll not as a matter of belief but as fiction which the mea-
gerness of reality, in Freud's grim phrase, makes necessary if man's
emotional and imaginative hunger is to be satisfied:

Oh beautiful! and rare as beautiful!
But theirs was Love in which the Mind delights
To lose itself, when the old world grows dull,

> And we are sick of its hack sounds and sights,
> Intrigues, adventures of the common school,
> Its petty passions, marriages, and flights,
> Where Hymen's torch but brands one strumpet more,
> Whose husband only knows her not a whore.
>
> (IV, 17; italics added)

In Haidée's palace there appears a sycophantic poet: he would appear in England as a radical turned reactionary like Southey, in Germany as an ersatz Goethe, in France a *chansonnier*. "He was a man who had seen many changes," says the narrator,

> And always changed as true as any needle;
> His Polar Star being one which rather ranges,
> And not the fixed—...
>
> (III, 80)

Yet this opportunistic hack recites one of Byron's most powerful revolutionary lyrics, "The Isles of Greece." Or does he? "Thus sung, or would, or could, or should have sung,/ The modern Greek..." (III, 87). Because the oral manner of *Don Juan* converts readers into hearers, Byron's relationship to his audience is almost identical to the hack-poet's, who is the inadequate counterpart of Demodocus and the bard at Ithaca who keep heroic tradition alive in the *Odyssey*. If contemporary court poets are too corrupt to fulfill this function, Byron himself will enact it. "Thou shalt believe in Milton, Dryden, Pope," he declares in the first canto (I, 205), and this unsolemn but serious parody is a chart of his course. He mocks tradition, but carries it forward. "I twine/ My hopes of being remembered in my line/ With my land's language," Byron confesses in *Childe Harold* (IV, 9), and the connection he avows between his poetic activity and his family tradition is significant. His relationship to his poetic predecessors is marked by the same ambivalence as his relationship to his forebears: the figures by whom Byron refuses to be bound are the models of his emulation, the foundations on which he stands.

7

The Fictions of Reality

*I*n the opening cantos of *Don Juan* the reader's primary sense is of an onrushing narrative, of adventure succeeding adventure with hectic pace. Though given the impression of rapidly unfolding action, the reader should distinguish it from the narrator's stance toward his story. For stanza after stanza he abandons Juan to pursue his own interests, yet in regard to the story he often claims that he would rather have had matters otherwise but cannot deviate from the facts. This fixity corresponds with the fixity of Juan's character; it is only the telling that Byron can make protean. Since, however, Juan's career is the vehicle by which Byron records his own present consciousness from moment to moment, *Don Juan* has neither a decisive center to which all questions of meaning may be referred nor a firm closure.[1]

Don Juan is open-ended in a second sense, dependent on the first. The forward movement of the poem tends to unsettle what has passed, for it presents a series in which each new event implicitly redefines the preceding ones and there is no final term to make the pattern unambiguous. A complete vision of Juan's life is never given, and this is not merely a function of the poem's unfinished state. Had Byron finished *Don Juan* by following his protagonist to his end, even this natural conclusion might deliberately have been reduced to a "weak" resolution. The enigmatic last words of the *Ode on a Grecian Urn* and the doubting query of the *Ode to a Nightingale* are but two examples of the Romantic mode of imitating the fullness of experience by a suggestive rather than a summary close. They do not declare an end: they merely send us through the poem again in quest for understanding. *Don Juan* might have reached a kindred, perfectly satisfactory artistic resolution that would have left all the narrator's riddles unanswered. The dynamic of the poem is that as the reader follows Juan's adventures forward he must at the same time move backward to reconsider what he has already seen, and through it Byron manipulates our responses in time as he manipulates history and his own past.

The first pair of incidents in the poem illustrates this process. The reader of Canto I and II encounters a relatively familiar structure.[2] Juan's voyage from the hypocritical world of Spain to the island of purity and love comfortably fulfills conventional expectations of a nostalgic, satiric contrast between artificial society and unspoiled nature. Hurried along by the rapidity of the story, and influenced in what he notices by his stock notions of idyll, the reader is likely to overlook the complicating hints the narrator lets slip about Haidée; indeed Byron's surprise depends on the reader's traditional "set" being so strong that certain details do not immediately register. The metamorphosis of the island into a luxurious court in Canto III therefore comes as a shock that forces the reader to re-examine his preconceptions. The realization that innocence and experience are separated only by a brief instant of time is strikingly brought home to him. Upon meditation the absolute contrast he had first perceived between the sophisticated lady and nature's child is replaced by recognition of their likeness. He remembers that Haidée is a "Lady in the land" (II, 116), who, like Julia, has "rejected several suitors, just to learn/ How to accept a better in his turn" (II, 128). Her ancestry is Moorish (IV, 54), as is Julia's (I, 56). Haidée's knowing and practical maid Zoe, who occasions the maxim "a virgin always on her maid relies" (II, 131), is reminiscent of Julia's maid Antonia, the "adept" who conceals Juan. As the poem advances the parallels between Juan-Julia-Antonia-Alfonso and Juan-Haidée-Zoe-Lambro become as marked as the differences, and when the reader realizes the threat posed by Haidée to

Juan's independence it alters his retrospective estimation of Julia as well as his appraisal of Haidée. By the time of Haidée's death and Juan's departure on the slave ship early in Canto IV the two affairs which had seemed opposites assume the aspect of equivalents.

The reader's experience in these cantos is paradigmatic of his experience in *Don Juan*. Byron juxtaposes Juan's affairs with Julia and Haidée and asks the reader to determine their relationship. As in life subsequent discoveries alter our apprehension of events already in the past, so Byron forces the reader continually to construct and readjust his sense of Juan's actions. The narrator's comments control the response, but they complicate rather than simplify the contrast between "nature" and "society," "innocence" and "experience." There is no univocal emphasis: Byron does not lecture, he teases us out of thought with his presentation of the inevitable process Juan's adventures represent. The essence of the poem, moreover, lies in just this teasing. Byron entices the reader to dispose the events and characters according to some conventional scheme, and then disrupts it: no sooner is a new synthesis made than the next episode requires a reconsideration. By the middle of the fourth canto the reader has learned to suspect his own facile assumptions, and Byron's claim to be a serious moral poet rests on having produced this recognition. The most reprehensible figure in *Don Juan* is Suwarrow, because he only sees "things in the gross,/ Being much too gross to see them in detail" (VII, 77), and it is that blindness from which Byron would save his reader.

The second pair of episodes in *Don Juan* is symmetrical with the first. Juan passes from the haughty Gulbeyaz, twenty-six and married to the fifty-nine-year-old Sultan, to the seventeen-year-old "child of Nature" (VI, 60), Dudù; compare Julia, twenty-three and wed to the fifty-year-old Don Alfonso, and Haidée, also seventeen. In the glimpse of Gulbeyaz giving a hypocritical welcome to her husband and enduring a wretched night thinking of Juan as the Sultan sleeps unwittingly by her side Byron makes the reader aware of the ugly facets of adultery that he suppressed in treating the affair with Julia as comic. The narrator's generalizing comments (VI, 14–25) lessen the distance between reader and characters by bringing them closer to everyday experience, so that whether the reader identifies with cuckold or cuckolder his response includes the fear that he is a potential victim of a like situation: the laugh is no longer as free as it was in the first canto. The different responses Byron elicits from the exactly parallel Julia-Alfonso and Gulbeyaz-Sultan scenes demonstrate his repeated assertion (stated most clearly in regard to Troy and Homer) that the understanding of reality is a function of perspective. He shows that the intensity of art is achieved by selection and overcomes that restriction by leading us through a re-vision of the same complex, emotionally charged human relationship.

The analogy between Haidée and Dudù created by the narrative pattern again changes the view of an earlier heroine. The reader's expectations (or hopes!) that the wicked Lord Byron's description of a Turkish harem will be salacious are not wholly fulfilled: Byron first celebrates the high-spirited chattering childishness of the odalisques—"like birds, or boys, or bedlamites broke loose" (VI, 34)—rather than their eroticism, and when they retire to bed he stresses their silent purity. They are "like flowers of different hue, and clime, and root,/ In some exotic garden sometimes found" (VI, 65), and the accumulation of organic imagery eventually persuades the reader that the harem is not a decadent antithesis of Haidée's island but its counterpart, perhaps even a more natural Eden. Certainly Dudù, despite her role, is more completely a "child of Nature" (VI, 60) than Haidée: the narrator ascribes to her the unselfconscious goodness of the "Age of Gold" (VI, 55), and there is no question of aristocratic rank or previous suitors to sully her genuine naiveté. When she undresses before Juan "in perfect innocence" (VI, 60) the irony thrusts at the situation, not at her character. The interlude between Dudù and Juan is the only unqualifiedly happy expression of sexuality in the poem, and if the conversion of the libidinous fantasy of a harem into a prank played by children on the "Mother of the Maids" (VI, 46) reflects Byron's familiar obsessions, it does something else too. The surprising discovery that a harem girl can be as pure, or purer, than an "island virgin" (II, 142) is a warning against judging by appearances.

The most interesting cross references in the equation Julia: Haidée :: Gulbeyaz : Dudù arise from comparison of the extreme and mean terms with each other, a comparison which further reveals the diagrammatic regularity of Byron's story. Dudù's stammering explanation of her dream is parallel to Julia's tirade in her bedchamber (as it is also to Haidée's dream). It is no more honest, strictly speaking, but the bashfulness and astonishment are sincere, and so Dudù succeeds where Julia fails. The reader's initial impression of Gulbeyaz is the antipodes of his initial impression of Haidée: the queen who commands against the girl who serves. Byron complicates the contrast, however: the court into which Juan and Haidée move, paid for by

Lambro's wealth, is not unlike Gulbeyaz's over-decorated apartments, maintained by the Sultan. Having established a parallel, Byron, by emphasizing Gulbeyaz's lack of experience, proceeds to a reversal. Before Juan Gulbeyaz had encountered "nothing which had e'er/ Infected her with sympathy" (V, 119); "never having met/ In all her life with aught save prayers and praise" (V, 122), she is baffled by Juan's resistance, and even his "extremely trite" protests seem radical "to her, who ne'er had heard such things" (V, 128). By dint of this repetition Byron breaks down the distinction the reader anticipates from the difference in age and social standing and leads him to rethink his conception of innocence.

It is unnecessary to pursue through all sixteen cantos of *Don Juan* the readjustments through which Byron refines the reader's discernment. His response to Catherine will retroactively influence his attitudes to Inez, Haidée, Gulbeyaz, and Dudù, and require him to distinguish more finely the problematic pairs that Byron insistently calls to his attention: love and maternal devotion, love and lust, love and luxury, sexuality and aggression, innocence and experience, self and society, and more. When conceived as static oppositions these dualisms fragmented the tales and dramas: in *Don Juan* Byron makes their tensions into the source of ongoing poetic energy. The problems that had driven him into gigantic monologues paradoxically invoking silence and forgetfulness become the subject of enlightening conversation between writer and reader.

It is perhaps the most remarkable and least considered feature of *Don Juan* that despite the speed and arbitrariness of the action and the apparently boundless digressive license of the narrator the structure of the plot has the clarity of a geometrical figure. The shape of the poem is a magnified reflection of the complementary truths of the personality embodied in the narrator and Juan: the narrator's obsession with instability of character and the changes of time is the solvent working against Juan's fixity. Only a foundation of such simple regularity could support the extravagations: did the reader not have an intuition of the likely course of the plot to steady him, reading *Don Juan* would be a maddening exercise. The reader can confirm this hypothesis by reflecting on his response to the English cantos. He is plunged into the most elaborately detailed milieu in the poem and introduced to several new characters: Norman Abbey is the first scene in which as many as four actors other than Juan occupy the stage at once. Feelings of strangeness, however, are offset by premonitions of continuity and recognitions of familiarity. The reader's encounters with the previous heroines furnish him with rough models to gauge the new women: Inez, Julia, Gulbeyaz for Adeline (like Gulbeyaz, she is described as "imperious" [XV, 49]); Haidée for Aurora (another echo of Haidée is sounded by the pregnant country girl who appears briefly in Canto XVI); Catherine and Julia, perhaps, for Fitz-Fulke. The earlier repetitions have established a pattern, so that the reader confidently awaits the development of a Juan-Adeline-Henry triangle that will reproduce his experience of Juan-Julia-Alfonso, Juan-Haidèe-Lambro, and Juan-Gulbeyaz-Sultan.[3]

Byron reinforces the essential likeness of Juan's various confrontations with dominant women by describing each with the same cluster of images. The myth of the Fall and the network of Homeric allusions are repeated: the narrator forecasts Adeline's involvement with Juan by remarking that Henry lacks

> That undefinable *"Je ne sçais quoi,"*
> Which, for what I know, may of yore have led
> To Homer's Iliad, since it drew to Troy
> The Greek Eve, Helen, from the Spartan's bed;
> Though on the whole, no doubt, the Dardan boy
> Was much inferior to King Menelaus:—
> But thus it is some women will betray us.
>
> (XIV, 72)

Repeated images of ocean and storm which refresh the cliché "sea of life" accentuate the fundamental rhythm of the poem. The narrator refers to Juan's voyage from Spain as his entry upon "nautical existence" (II, 12); after the shipwreck the image loses its literal basis and becomes a metaphor for Byron's exploration of the relationships between men and women. Often the application is punningly suggestive, as in this comment on Gulbeyaz's frustration:

> There is a tide in the affairs of women,
> Which, taken at the flood, leads—God knows where:
> Those navigators must be able seamen
> Whose charts lay down its currents to a hair;
> Not all the reveries of Jacob Behmen
> With its strange whirls and eddies can compare:
> Men with their heads reflect on this and that—
> But women with their hearts on Heaven knows what!
>
> (VI, 2)[4]

The redirection of the image from external action to psychosexual behavior is completed in Canto XIII, when the narrator observes that "young beginners may as well commence/ With quiet cruising o'er the ocean, Woman" (XIII, 40).[5] These imagistic repetitions contribute to an increasing sense of *dèjà-vu* as the narrative advances. The pace of the English cantos slows not only because of the higher proportion of digression but also because the crowd of half-familiar figures makes the reader feel as if each earlier episode were simultaneously to be re-enacted. The rich density of these scenes is heightened by their recapitulatory nature.

The advantages of this recurrence are illustrated by the parallel between Leila's debut in society in Canto XII (which Byron calls in stanza 54 the beginning of the poem) and Juan's in Canto I. Juan's choice of the sophisticated Lady Pinchbeck to supervise his charge spares her the hypocritical education he suffered, but though Lady Pinchbeck is incontestably a more realistic tutor than Inez her teachings will hasten Leila's incorporation by a world that Byron portrays as false: the connotations of spuriousness in her name are part of his irony.[6] Leila's initiation does not return the poem to its starting point: rather, it marks the inception of the next cycle. The combination of identity and change explains why Byron's repetitiveness is intriguing instead of boring. Just as a regular meter becomes a source of poetic effect by causing even minor deviations to tell, so the sense of the basic structural pattern of *Don Juan* heightens the sensitivity to departures. The similarity of Byron's characters and situations overcomes the isolation of each picaresque incident, encouraging comparisons, and raising to significance what might have seemed an idiosyncrasy of Byron's personal history. Much of the pleasure in *Don Juan* comes from watching the dazzling permutations Byron generates from his types; much of the instruction comes from learning to distinguish among them.

Don Juan may thus be considered diachronically as a story progressing in time, and, because of Juan's relapses into the same configuration, synchronically. The narrative becomes the re-enactment of a single psychic conflict which the reader apprehends as if it were constant and it was his perspective that changed: each successive adventure seems a single event unfolding new implications as he reconsiders it in time. The duplications of Juan in Johnson and Leila, the repetitions of his own career, and the recurrent imagery together foster a sense of the plot of *Don Juan* as one infinitely expanding instant. The efflorescence of a comprehensive, finally almost static, vision surely formed no part of Byron's conscious design for the work, but it grows nonetheless in the reader's mind as a natural concomitant of the psychological materials of the poem.[7]

The repetitions thus finally serve the principle of clarity: the reader is continually asked to see more in a situation which he thought he had understood. And what may have begun as Byron's personal struggle against the obsessions reflected in Juan's career in the end constitutes one aspect only of the challenge *Don Juan* makes to notions of a fixed reality. The questions raised as *Don Juan* slithers into epistemological riddle dominate the second half of the poem. In Byron's hands a topic complex in itself becomes still more elusive, but reflexive as the rambling discussion appears it is never obscurantist. Byron provocatively weighs the ostensibly substantial world he describes against the fiction he narrates. In brief, and in terms that are crude but adequate to initiate discussion: Is the narrative a fictional imitation of a "real" world?

Byron's determination to transform his past and so emancipate himself from his fate flows into a determination to shake the reader into awareness of the problematic nature of reality, and that motive is central to the anti-illusionistic quality he cultivates in *Don Juan*. The campaign begins in the first stanza of the poem, which should be compared to the openings of its great predecessors:

> The Man, for Wisdom's various arts renown'd,
> Long exercis'd in woes, oh Muse! resound.
> > (*Odyssey*, Pope's translation)
> Achilles' wrath, to Greece the direful Spring
> Of Woes unnumber'd, heav'nly Goddess, sing!
> > (*Iliad*, Pope's translation)
> Arms and the Man I sing, who forc'd by Fate
> And haughty Juno's unrelenting Hate,
> Expell'd and exil'd, left the *Trojan* shoar....
> > (*Aeneid*, Dryden's translation)
> Of man's first disobedience, and the fruit
> Of that forbidden tree, whose mortal taste
> Brought death into the world, and all our woe
> With loss of *Eden*, till one greater Man
> Restore us, and regain the blissful Seat,
> Sing, Heav'nly Muse....
> > (*Paradise Lost*)
> I want a hero: an uncommon want,
> When every year and month sends forth a new one,

Till, after cloying the gazettes with cant,
The age discovers he is not the true one;
Of such as these I should not care to vaunt,
I'll therefore take our ancient friend Don Juan—
We all have seen him, in the pantomime,
Sent to the devil somewhat ere his time.

(*Don Juan*)

To read these lines in quick succession is to realize the extraordinary impression of wilfulness Byron deliberately creates. In all four of the earlier epics the announced subject assumes precedence over the poet. The "I," if it appears at all, does not impair objectivity because it is subordinate to the pre-existent story and the suprapersonal Muse. Byron, in contrast, begins with a statement of his needs and desires, and even points to their oddity by remarking that it is "uncommon" to want a hero when there is a plethora available. Surprising in itself, the first line of *Don Juan* is yet more so coming from Byron: how could he, who had stamped his name on the Titanic protagonist, want a hero? He easily resolves this unlooked-for dilemma by expediently "taking" a familiar figure, a pronounced difference from the grave consideration earlier writers of epic devoted to choice of subject.

Throughout *Don Juan* the narrator interposes between the reader and his nominal hero, and it is he who engrosses attention. The rigidities of Juan's behavior are never allowed to dominate the field of vision as the heroes sadly dominated the tales. The narrator misses no chance to underscore the artifice of his narrative, often by the most obvious devices: "Lambro presented, and one instant more/ Had stopped this Canto, and Don Juan's breath" (IV, 42). Byron emphasizes his authorial freedom by exaggerating the discrepancy between the erratic progress of the action and the inexhaustible proliferation of his commentary.[8] In Canto III, for example, Lambro returns in stanza 20 and reaches his house by stanza 51, when he drops from view. The remaining sixty stanzas are filled with a detailed description of the dress of Juan and Haidée, the trimmer poet, reflections on biography with particular reference to Johnson's *Life* of Milton, a contrast between the politics and diction of "the Lakers" and those of the Augustans, and an "Ave Maria" that invokes Boccaccio, imitates Sappho and Dante, and leads to an anecdote concerning Nero's death. Lest the forward movement cause the reader to miss the profusion, Byron mock-modestly highlights his achievement with the rhetorical term for this elaboration:

> But I'm digressing; what on earth has Nero,
> Or any such like sovereign buffoons,
> To do with the transactions of my hero,
> More than such madmen's fellow man—the moon's?
> Sure my *invention* must be down to zero. . . .

(III, 110; italics added)

Cantos XI and XII display Byron's freedom from the demands of narrative less flamboyantly but no less astonishingly. In ten stanzas of Canto XI Juan's reveries are interrupted by Tom the highwayman, whom he kills in self-defense—a complete drama in miniature—and in ten stanzas of Canto XII Leila is placed under Lady Pinchbeck's care. Byron fills the remaining one hundred fifty-odd stanzas of the two cantos with personal comments on England and criticism of his own poem.

If it is asked where Cantos X through XVI take place the first response is likely to be that the action has moved to England, but that is only partially true. Juan has moved to England, but the action of the poem centers in the narrator's telling, not Juan's doing. The fundamental action of *Don Juan* occurs between expatriate poet and English audience, and that relationship is constant. The imagined English reader has been an integral, solidly present part of the poem from the outset, and his attitudes the explicit target of the satire at least since the contrast between English and Spanish divorce in Canto I: the only change is that the satire is now inseparable from the narrative, has in fact become the narrative. The voice heard in the "English" cantos comes as always from Italy: Byron pointedly announces in Canto I that he is "dating from the Brenta" (I, 212), and he makes frequent reminders of his geographical location thereafter. It is a tribute to the density Byron has imparted to these scenes that we feel we are "in" England, but we misapprehend *Don Juan* if we so lose ourselves in the illusion as to forget that we are listening to a dramatic monologue and to mistake its realistic detail for realism.[9] The primary object in the English cantos is Byron's consciousness: he shows England as he remembers and imagines it.

If Byron toys with Juan's biography to demonstrate that his own life is no longer a burden, his repeated underscoring of the fictional nature of his poem also reveals that all representation is in part fictional. He frustrates the reader's desire for a tidy structure so that he can bring to prominence the subtle betrayals inherent in the notion of form. *Don Juan* exposes the inadequacy of any conventionally closed form to contain the potentially infinite meanings of experience: "But if a writer should be quite consistent,/ How could he possibly show things existent?" (XV, 87).[10] The serio-comic discussion of aesthetic questions in *Don Juan*, moreover, is meant to lead to a prior and deeper level at which the problem of form is seen to be inextricable from the patterns the mind imposes on events without even being aware that it is doing so.

The first stanza of *Don Juan* introduces the gazettes. The primacy is justified because gazettes and dispatches report major occurrences, like battles and treaties, and they claim to constitute official reality. Despite their status, however, they are the product of fallible human minds and hence susceptible to error and the aberrations of cant. Indeed, the supposed repositories of truth often confuse even the basic facts of life and death:

> Thrice happy he whose name has been well spelt
> In the despatch: I knew a man whose loss
> Was printed *Grove,* although his name was Grose.
>
> (VIII, 18)

The echo of the *Felix qui* and *Beatus ille* constructions of Latin verse illustrates once more the wealth of Byron's unobtrusive allusions. The formulae are associated with the classical ideals of retirement and throw into relief the horrors of modern war: the happy man of the Roman writers is opposed to the dead victim of contemporary aspirations. Byron makes the misprint serve as an epitome of his twofold theme: that all conceptions of reality are subjective and that many of them are life-denying.

The emergent centrality of this theme is confirmed by the stanzas on Bishop Berkeley that begin Canto XI, in which Byron eagerly misconstrues the maxim that *"esse* is *percipi"* as an idealist denial of material reality.[11] He thus enlists the bishop's authority as philosophic support for the relativism he propounds in the later cantos of the poem as a means to a positive end:

> I will not swear that black is white,
> But I suspect in fact that white is black,
> And the whole matter rests upon eye-sight:—
> Ask a blind man, the best judge. You'll attack
> Perhaps this new position—but I'm right;

> Or if I'm wrong, I'll not be ta'en aback:—
> He hath no morn nor night, but all is dark
> Within—and what seest thou? A dubious spark!
>
> (XII, 71)

Byron wittily capitalizes on the arguments of post-Lockean epistemology and the ever-dwindling external world it allowed to man
much as the metaphysical poets capitalized on the scholasticism they
inherited. Byron was well acquainted with the tradition of English
skepticism. He knew and admired the speculative works of William
Drummond and he judged David Hume "to be by far the most profound thinker and clearest reasoner of the many philosophers and
metaphysicians of the last century. . . . 'There is,' said he, 'no refuting
him . . . [he] is utterly unanswerable.' "[12] Conceits like the following
have ample roots in this tradition:

> If from great Nature's or our own abyss
> Of Thought we could but snatch a certainty,
> Perhaps Mankind might find the path they miss—
> But then 't would spoil much good philosophy.
> One system eats another up, and this
> Much as old Saturn ate his progeny;
> For when his pious consort gave him stones
> In lieu of sons, of these he made no bones.
>
> But System doth reverse the Titan's breakfast,
> And eats her parents, albeit the digestion
> Is difficult. Pray tell me, can you make fast,
> After due search, your faith to any question?
> Look back o'er ages, ere unto the stake fast
> You bind yourself, and call some mode the best one.
> Nothing more true than *not* to trust your senses;
> And yet what are your other evidences?
>
> For me, I know nought; nothing I deny,
> Admit—reject—contemn: and what know *you*,
> Except perhaps that you were born to die?
>
> (XIV, 1-3)

Hume had maintained that knowledge of the causal structure of reality could be no more than a set of internally consistent inferences, and
in *Don Juan* Byron enforces the conclusion by statement and insinuation. His allusion to the Titans neatly summarizes the triumph of the

Christian world-view over the cosmologies of Greek myth, but neither is more than a hypothetical mental construct, a model that can give no certain truth. The Christian synthesis, moreover, shatters into heresy and schism, and the brutal consequences that ensue when man believes in his system as if it were absolute truth are indicated by Byron's choice of the suddenly literal "stake." The note of outrage at the complacency with which men damn and burn each other sounds repeatedly in *Don Juan:* Byon, like Hume, holds that because it promotes tolerance skepticism is a beneficent social force. In order to enlighten man, therefore, Byron must first undermine his presumptuous faith in his convictions and persuade him that his reason is only a "dubious spark."

Sharp as the religious satire is, it is only part of Byron's effort to reveal the dangers that attend all evasions of the arduous paradoxes of man's desire to order his world and find it meaningful. " I won't describe," the narrator says in Canto X,

> —that is, if I can help
> Description; and I won't reflect,—that is,
> If I can stave off thought, which—as a whelp
> Clings to its teat—sticks to me through the abyss
> Of this odd labyrinth; or as the kelp
> Holds by the rock; or as a lover's kiss
> Drains its first draught of lips:...
>
> (X, 28)

The similes insist that thought is as natural and inescapable as man's sexual urge and his instinct for self-preservation.[13] To think, to describe, to classify, to identify, are the distinctive processes of the human consciousness, and yet the very process by which man masters the chaos that confronts him by reducing it to "system" becomes his undoing. The paradox of mind is that the power of vision on which man's intellectual dignity rests seduces him into perpetual delusion. The passage from Canto XIV quoted in the last paragraph continues:

> ... there's a courage which grows out of fear,
> Perhaps of all most desperate, which will dare
> The worst to *know* it:—when the mountains rear
> Their peaks beneath your human foot, and there

> You look down o'er the precipice, and drear
> The gulf of rock yawns,—you can't gaze a minute,
> Without an awful wish to plunge within it.
>
> (XIV, 5)

There is nothing fanciful in the implicit comparison between the suicide's wish to jump in order to end his "dread of death" (XIV, 4) and the passion to have certain knowledge of the world which dupes man into treating his constructs as reality. In both instances the cost of an inability to endure ambiguity is death: in the first, immediate physical extinction; in the second, blind belief, then cant, then their terrible products, religious persecution and self-deluding martyrs, futile and barbaric battles like Ismail. Man can protect himself against the self-destructive temptations inherent in his consciousness only by recognizing that his understanding of the world is intrinsically imperfect and learning to grant it only a provisional, "as if" status. To borrow Keats's phrase, *Don Juan* argues that healthy life can be sustained only by *"Negative Capability,* that is when man is capable of being in uncertainties, Mysteries, doubts, without any irritable reaching after fact & reason—..."[14]

Another allusion emphasizes Byron's point. "The world is all before me," exclaims the narrator four stanzas later (XIV, 9), echoing the conclusion of *Paradise Lost* (XII, 646). Milton's lines exquisitely resume the complexities of the Fall: regret for the loss of Eden, anticipation of Adam's painful growth into human choice. Byron transfers the lines from a moral to an epistemological context. The Fall has debarred man from ever possessing true knowledge of the world, but the catastrophic separation liberates his imagination. Denied access to reality, postlapsarian man—or perhaps one should say, post-Lockean—must acknowledge that even the most apparently concrete phenomena reach him as subjective impressions. "What is a lie?" Byron demands, and immediately replies:

> 'T is but
> The truth in masquerade; and I defy
> Historians—heroes—lawyers—priests, to put
> A fact without some leaven of a lie.
>
> (XI, 37)

From the vast range and disparity of men's opinions, from the very multiplicity of reflections, Byron demonstrates that perception must be creative. Even if what it creates is distortion, the distortion is itself a fertile leaven. This negative route deprives the imagination of the heuristic insight into truth the Romantics usually at least tentatively allowed it, but it results no less in its exaltation. Willy-nilly man is condemned to be an artist: even in his most unthinking, automatic perceptions of the commonplace he cannot avoid the artist's function of selection, interpretation and creation.

If all the reality man perceives is in part a "system" of his making, then the difference between ordinary "factual" description and deliberate poetic invention is one of degree only, not kind. The sole distinction between the poet and other men, but it is a momentous one, is that the poet realizes the fictional character of mental activity. What he cannot escape doing he chooses to do to the full: to create a poem like *Don Juan*, in which autobiography merges with history, is a paradigmatic human act, the supreme exercise of man's cruelly limited yet sovereign power over himself and his world. The rules of decorum and genre are superseded by Byron's will; probability and consistency likewise fall to his imperious, recondite principles of order. The most recalcitrant materials become plastic in his imagination: a monotonous, one-dimensional world metamorphoses under his direction into a multi-faceted, glittering spectacle.

Two stanzas beyond those just discussed in Canto XIV an imagined interlocutor asks Byron why in the face of public condemnation he continues to write. The interchange is typical of the relationship between poet and reader that *Don Juan* vividly includes and projects:

> But "why then publish?"—There are no rewards
> Of fame or profit when the World grows weary.
> I ask in turn,—Why do you play at cards?
> Why drink? Why read?—To make some hour less dreary.
> It occupies me to turn back regards
> On what I've seen or pondered, sad or cheery. . . .
>
> I think that were I *certain* of success,
> I hardly could compose another line:
> . . . .
> In play, there are two pleasures for your choosing—
> The one is winning, and the other losing.
>
> (XIV, 11–12)

The echo of the *Epistle to Arbuthnot* defines by contrast the motives which impel Byron to poetry.[15] He claims to write, not, like Pope, in order to join an honorific, coherent literary community, but to combat his own melancholy. The sense of emptiness and nostalgia which pervades his work becomes in *Don Juan* the starting point of an intro-spective refashioning of his own life into an unconstricted and amus-ing image. Alienated from complete emotional allegiance to the pres-ent in which he lives, Byron perceives all man's activities as games he devises to occupy and shape his life. Even the satiric theme of deceptive appearances in *Don Juan* is more accurately described as a conflict between different games, because in this poem "reality" is only an agreed-upon system, and a system, like a game, is a set of rules adopted by the players. Byron's playing with his own identity, examined earlier, dovetails with the empiricist critique of reality.[16]

Writing poetry is for Byron play at its most self-conscious, a sig-nificant mode of fulfillment; the play of unimaginative men is less rewarding. His own boredom makes him an acute observer of the boredom of others. In England men's visions of wealth and status have solidified into a formal ritual that Byron repeatedly likens to a game. "Good society is but a game" (XII, 58), he declares, and "good company's a chess board" (XII, 89). It is, however, a bad, dull game in which the participants are so lacking in individuality that type-names are adequate to describe them. In the course of the reflections on England contained in his reworking of the *ubi sunt* motif Byron re-marks that "Life's a poor player" (XI, 86), appropriating another allu-sion to imply that he is the brilliant one. The stultifying sameness of English life is a parodic version of the timelessness of Eden, monotony elevated into a "paradise of Pleasure and *Ennui*" (XIV, 17). Ennui is more than the malaise of a sterile society: it is the vacuum of existence that consciousness must fill, but which the English are too inert to resist. They act by a tedious rote, varied only by meretricious novelties and petty resentments:

> And hence high life is oft a dreary void,
> A rack of pleasures, where we must invent
> A something wherewithal to be annoyed.
> (XIV, 79)

In Canto I Byron had commented that "perfection is/ Insipid in this naughty world of ours," and wondered how Adam and Eve "got through" the day before the Fall awakened them (I, 18). Millennia later the dilemma presents itself again in debased form, another example of the paradoxical changes wrought by time. Prelapsarian Adam and Eve are so undivided from nature that they do not comprehend their state: they are happy, and it is only fallen man who perceives them as insipid. *Le grand monde* in England are so absorbed in the fallen world that they do not know it is fallen, and without irony name their streets "Paradise Row" (XI, 21). They do not know that they are only playing: because they earnestly believe in their tawdry reality they can never rise above it.

Byron's philosophical skepticism is the tactic he employs to emphasize that daily routines like these are only fictions and games, and that they are impoverished: like his contemporaries Blake and Shelley he would liberate man from bondage to "facts" which are only unimaginative preconceptions. If Byron's skeptical guard is to be effective, however, he must turn it on the duplicity of his own medium, for not since Adam in the garden have words corresponded exactly to the phenomena they name. Man's imperfect language is the base of his larger orderings—literary conventions, genres, philosophies, religions, "reality,"—for it is the preformed system from which they are constructed. The power of words to obscure the reality they articulate is a major concern of *Don Juan*. We exploit their force when we weave a socially acceptable disguise for our selfish motives, and Byron has few peers in imitating the rationalizations of "Platonic" love (e.g., II, 211-212) or the pretended diffidence in which political ambition cloaks itself (XVI, 72-76). But the force can turn against us, and the power of language becomes painful when deception of others shades into self-deception.

The cost of an insufficiently self-critical attitude toward the fictions that lend meaning to life and the words in which they are clothed is exemplified by the slaughter at the siege of Ismail. The recognition that the identical human needs issue in the antithetical occupations of war and poetry underlies a surprising juxtaposition of cannon and prosody: "The Russian batteries were incomplete,/ Because they were constructed in a hurry:/ . . . the same cause which makes a verse want feet" (VII, 26). The equivalence of art and life holds at one level and jars at all others, and the resulting incongruity is the foundation of many of Byron's most tendentious conceits. Each of these startling conjunctions makes the reader conscious that he is reading a witty poem, and so reminds him that more salutary ambitions than "glory" are available. Another instance: a decimated Russian column is said to be "reduced, as is a bulky volume/ Into an elegant extract (much less massy)/ Of heroism" (VIII, 34). The joke reveals its ominousness when it is realized that the soldiers have given their lives in hopes of being memorialized: in pursuing the chimera of fame they elevate a dubious mention by history over their flesh-and-blood actuality. In *Childe Harold* Byron despaired because he had not found "words which are things" (III, 14), but by their actions these men invest words with the worth usually accorded only to things. A pun points up the fatal consequences of the delusion: "I wonder.../... if a man's name in a *bulletin*/ May make up for a bullet in his body?" (VII, 21). Equivocation and doubt are the life-giving antidotes to the deadliness of ready belief, the signs of a perpetually renewable self.

Byron's declaration that "Heroes are but made for bards to sing" (VIII, 14) should therefore be understood in the light cast upon it by the battlefield. The soldiers' very motive is the thirst for glory which is contingent on the writers who may afterwards record their deeds, and so the siege, the most brutal assault of "fact" in *Don Juan*, ironically provides the most compelling evidence of the power of language to shape reality. If since the Fall man has been cursed by a language that no longer corresponds to the objects it denominates, he who masters language combats that loss by the influence he gains on men's *opinions* of things:

> But words are things, and a small drop of ink,
> Falling like dew, upon a thought, produces
> That which makes thousands, perhaps millions, think; ...
>   (III, 88)

The view of language in *Don Juan* is thus double, and its doubleness enlarges the poet's sphere. Byron's alternating evaluation of poetry as on the one hand lying and trivial and on the other truthful and important depends from a duality of reference he perceives inherent in language itself. When words are considered to refer to an objective reality they are seen as inevitably deceitful, and their inadequacy is an occasion for satire, comic or tragic. When they are considered rather as affecting men's actions they have potent authority, and realization of this second aspect, ambiguous as it is, frees Byron from the anxious doubts of poetry expressed in Canto III of *Childe Harold*. His satire is nerved by rage at all the writers—authors of epic, historians, gazetteers, and Wordsworth, who calls Carnage "God's daughter" (VIII, 9)—who have misused their gift to glorify war and so led men to their deaths. The task of the poet who abhors unjust war is to devalue the fantasy that nourishes it, to present "Glory's dream/ Unriddled" (VIII, 1). This sanative demythologizing, however, has the dangers suggested by Byron's invocation of *Don Quixote:*

> Cervantes smiled Spain's chivalry away;
> A single laugh demolished the right arm
> Of his own country;—seldom since that day
> Has Spain had heroes. While Romance could charm,
> The World gave ground before her bright array;
> And therefore have his volumes done such harm,
> That all their glory, as a composition,
> Was dearly purchased by his land's perdition.
>
> (XIII, 11)

Exposing the fantasy that inspires men's energies risks inducing apathy, but Byron evades the charge he somewhat disingenuously levels at Cervantes. *Don Juan* does not attack a tinsel "illusion" to replace it with a drab "reality": the poem seeks rather to enlarge the role of imagination than to deny it. The poles of *Don Juan* are self-destructive belief and liberating play: the remedy it advocates for disillusionment is self-conscious fiction.

Most men remain the prisoners of their limited vocabularies, if with less severe penalties than those exacted at Ismail. Man's linguistic confusion is explained in the Old Testament by the story of the tower of Babel, to which Byron alludes as early in *Don Juan* as the fourth stanza of the Dedication.[17] According to the myth, God determined to obstruct communication between men by entailing multiple languages upon them. The barrier between cultures doubles the flaws of each man's perception, and the cacophony of tongues is a manifestation of man's fallen nature. The shallow cosmopolitanism of the English in the later cantos of *Don Juan*, embellishing their idle chatter with chic bits of French, is a mockery of the lost unity.

The significance of French, however, exists on two levels, and the poet's employment of it should be distinguished from that of his characters:

> But Juan was received with much *"empressement":*—
> These phrases of refinement I must borrow
> From our next neighbours' land, where, like a chessman,
> There is a move set down for joy or sorrow....
>
> (XI, 42)

The unthinking English scatter French as if they had a tic, but a second language arms the conscious artist with a powerful new mode of exploring and presenting reality. The bewildering profusion of languages is not only the obstacle in the poet's path but also the arsenal at his disposal. To use Byron's own metaphor: he escapes the restrictions of any one system of "moves" by playing two games simultaneously, and thus transforms the polyglot chaos to which man is doomed into an instrument of clarity. He defines the social circle by the fatuousness of their borrowing, but he himself borrows expressions for which there is no equivalent in English, like *tact* (I, 178) and *mobilité* (XVI, 97), in order to fix his meanings more precisely. The resources of a second language enable Byron to raise to consciousness the spiritual apathy in which the English are so totally immersed that it is invisible to them:

> For *ennui* is a growth of English root,
> Though nameless in our language:—we retort
> The fact for words, and let the French translate
> That awful yawn which sleep can not abate.
> (XIII, 101)

The traditional moral principle that underlies Byron's satiric anatomizing is that a disease must be recognized before it can be cured: to name it is to begin to know it. Fluent in two languages, Byron can warn of the ills of gluttony merely by punning on the French and English significations of "gout" (XV, 72).

The poet's contest with language is a type of man's struggle to overcome the imperfections of his world, and the epitome of his endeavor to restore harmony through mastery of language is rhyme, whose consonances and dissonances mark the precariousness of his success. Byron never ceases to bemoan the constraints of rhyme, but each fresh lament is a reminder that he gratuitously assumed its burdens, willingly rendering his game more difficult in order to reap the added joy of "the sense of difficulty overcome" (the phrase is Wordsworth's). The very rigidity of the octave, enduring through sixteen cantos against the demands of common sense and customary orthography, testifies to his ability to profit from the exigencies of his materials and bring order to confusion. The names of heroes Byron says are "not at all adapted to my rhymes" (I, 3) are nonetheless made to fit; the uneuphonious Russians he declares he "cannot tune . . . into rhyme" (VII, 16) are simultaneously assimilated. Without breaking the stanza he casually dominates bastard jargons like doctors' Latin (X, 41) and highwaymen's cant (XI, 16–19), which are the very emblems of man's corrupt understanding. Byron's all-encompassing order incorporates the separate universes of French and Italian: the rhyme can comprehend "Amor Mio's" and "Addio's" (XVI, 45) as well as *"tracasserie/ agacerie"* (XIV, 41). The more alogical the rhyme, the more incompatible the linguistic environments its components inhabit—as in "Theogony/Cosmogony/mahogany" (IX, 20)—the more powerfully it witnesses the poet's effort to bind together the fragments of the world. Hence Byron directly opposes Babel when he brings words from different languages into the parlous union of rhyme: "Trecentisti/this t 'ye" (III, 86); "Κγθέρειαγ/Dian/tie an" (XVI, 109); *"quarum/* harem/spare 'em" (XIV, 21). Such exuberant playing is not equivalent to the lost prelapsarian certainty, but it demonstrates that the clumsiness of language has not entirely defeated Byron. Man sees only as his linguistic structure permits him to see, and by playing with language Byron can reveal more. "If you insist on grammar" (VII, 42), if you "pique" yourself on the niceties of spelling (VIII, 74), he warns, you warp the actuality you are trying to discern; his words may also be only approximations, but they have acquired the quicksilver nature of the phenomena they try to pinpoint.

In their innocent lovemaking on the beach Haidée and Juan have little need of words:

> though their speech
> Was broken words, they *thought* a language there,—
> And all the burning tongues the passions teach
> Found in one sigh the best interpreter
> Of Nature's oracle—first love,—that all
> Which Eve has left her daughters since her fall.
>
> (II, 189)

Once initiated into consciousness man is never again able to do without speech. Even the pure "silent, lone" Aurora Raby (XV, 47) loses her pristine quiet and is drawn into conversation: "From answering she began to question: this/ With her was rare" (XV, 81). After the Fall silence is no longer a mark of innocence: the narrator says that the mutes who strangle rebel pashas "spoke by signs—that is, not spoke at all" (V, 90), much like Juan and Haidée. Juan's comparative silence throughout *Don Juan* only betrays his helplessness before circumstances; the narrator, in contrast, fully cognizant that all his activities and reflections are merely exalted games, makes his almost obsessive playing with words into an heroic attempt to examine himself and to know his world.

Yet Byron's display of the powers of language is not always

aimed at uncovering truth: his awareness of its use to divert and deceive springs from his own adroitness at verbal camouflage. *Don Juan* seems so forthright and unmysterious that it is easy to miss the challenge it poses to conventional assumptions of reading. Words in *Don Juan* mean in various ways, and understanding of the poem depends on learning which questions to ask of them—and which not. Take, for example, the ironic praise of Donna Inez's goodness:

> In virtues nothing earthly could surpass her,
> Save thine "incomparable oil," Macassar!
>
> (I, 17)

The point of "Macassar" is merely its incongruity, which undermines Inez's conviction of rectitude. To press it further, to inquire into the particular properties of the oil, is to be led down an endless garden path of annotation and speculation. A poet who employs words with this low a density of significance fits uncomfortably with most critical canons, and unease increases when it is recognized that irrelevance often forms part of Byron's intention. His ludicrous rhymes reduce the ominousness of his materials; it is striking how many of his most outrageous couplets, such as "Oh! ye lords of ladies intellectual,/ Inform us truly, have they not hen-pecked you all?" (I, 22) involve his deepest anxieties. This surprising conjunction insists upon the fictive nature of the poem and thus minimizes the menacing reality of the couplet's subject, granting Byron a temporary mastery. The digressions that figure prominently in his style function in a similar manner. They provide the opportunity to shift the discussion, to sidle away from a topic, to avert attention from its most dangerous component, to rework it into more manageable terms. It is no coincidence that as the action of *Don Juan* returns to England digression should increase; as Juan's entanglements again come close to Byron's own in 1815–1816 the need for such breathing-spaces rises proportionately. [18]

To say that language in *Don Juan* repeatedly behaves as a kind of screen concealing Byron's obsessions is not to reduce the poem to gabble, but to set forth the most germane and fruitful terms for approaching it. Byron can compress his meaning when compression is his purpose; his customary expansions serve other, equally legitimate ends. The digressions enlarge his meaning and mark his increasing artistic self-consciousness, so that if the desire to express and re-form is the origin of Byron's poetry, it is by no means the limit of his final achievement.

The uncanniest of *Don Juan*'s successes, however, is the voice it creates of a man talking without stop, as if only by never ceasing could he prevent his words from sinking into the category of fixed and lifeless objects. The heroes of Byron's tales are distinguished rather by their eyes and looks. Of the Giaour, for example, Byron writes: "Oft will his glance the gazer rue,/ For in it lurks that nameless spell,/ Which speaks, itself unspeakable" (837–839). Conrad is still more mesmerizing:

> Too close inquiry his stern glance would quell.
> There breathe but few whose aspect might defy
> The full encounter of his searching eye;
> He had the skill, when Cunning's gaze would seek
> To probe his heart and watch his changing cheek,
> At once the observer's purpose to espy
> And on himself roll back his scrutiny. . . .
>
> (I, 214–220)

Lara too possesses the power of retorting their questions upon the curious, and so remaining opaque: "You could not penetrate his soul, but found,/ Despite your wonder, to your own he wound" (377–378). The impermeable, dominating glance is the sign of an identity which must continuously be imposed on others: the eye is paramount in the Byronic hero not because he sees but because he is seen, because by occupying center stage he forces others to acknowledge his myth as a true identity. But the role is always vulnerable to a slant perspective, a momentary inattention, as when Selim turns to look at Zuleika, and dies. In contrast to these overbearing and hidden figures the narrator of *Don Juan* appears virtually transparent. He invites the reader backstage, as it were, and so freely admits his uncertainties and inconsistencies, so quickly points out his theatrical indulgences, that he seems, paradoxically, sincere. Yet the passage from eye to voice is deceptive. *Don Juan* only seems intimate and private: it is every bit as much an attempt to construct a public self as the declamatory *Childe Harold*. Through its studied casualness Byron accomplishes the feat of establishing as his public self the seemingly spontaneous and open self he chooses to show, and thus stands more securely protected than ever. His ever-shifting, all-encompassing voice, allowing nothing to remain outside itself, enables Byron to be at once everywhere revealed and everywhere concealed, nowhere to be pinned down. Turning back upon himself and revising his themes as he advances, proceeding from confessions of personal confusion to moral argument and inclusive philosophic speculation, calling into doubt even the language through which he appears, Byron is overwhelmingly present yet forever elusive. The capriciousness of fame, the little likelihood of preservation, the universality of transience, and the treachery of memory are topics which haunt him throughout the poem, and they are all instances of the sense of futility which threatens him from within and without. Driven by unconscious motives, inserted into a network of history, culture, and language, Byron can assert identity only through a perpetual re-establishment of his difference, yet another digression. He must at every moment perform himself anew.

8

Heroes and Heroines, Artists and Readers

The insistence in *Don Juan* on the priority of language over the events it records has a crucial effect on the presentation of the hero. In the universe of the poem gazettes and bulletins impart significance equally with Homer, and Byron's recognition of their ephemeral but ubiquitous influence is a sign of the marked change in his representation of masculine power since the Oriental tales: the boy masquerading as stern and the fearsome father who together form the Byronic hero are exposed. The treatment of Suwarrow is illustrative.

The two Turkish women who escape with Juan and Johnson from the harem, accustomed to see their sultan "as a sort of god . . . with all the pomp of Power," are surprised by the respect accorded Suwarrow, who to them appears no more than an old man in a dirty shirt prosaically drilling his troops (VII, 73–74). Since his unglamorous preparations enable his men to take Ismail, their wonder seems to suggest a distinction between the trappings and the essence of power which favors the Russian general. Byron nonetheless scarcely intends any endorsement of Suwarrow himself:

244

> ... great joy unto the camp!
> To Russian, Tartar, English, French, Cossacque,
> O'er whom Suwarrow shone like a gas lamp,
> Presaging a most luminous attack;
> Or like a wisp along the marsh so damp,
> Which leads beholders on a boggy walk,
> He flitted to and fro a dancing light,
> Which all who saw it followed, wrong or right.
>
> 'T is thus the spirit of a single mind
> Makes that of multitudes take one direction,
> As roll the waters to the breathing wind,
> Or roams the herd beneath the bull's protection;
> Or as a little dog will lead the blind,
> Or a bell-wether form the flock's connection
> By tinkling sounds, when they go forth to victual;
> Such is the sway of your great men o'er little.
>
> (VII, 46, 48)

The multiple similes are characteristically deflationary, and the principle of the deflations is consistent.[1] In each instance Byron accomplishes the diminution of the leader by emphasizing the credulity and stupidity of the followers, a process which implies that leaders are known solely by their being followed. Suwarrow does not possess the personal distinction of a Lara, the gloomy magnificence Byron ascribed to the hero independently of any action in which he engaged, and which most made itself felt when he was alone. In the post-Lockean world of *Don Juan* the status of hero no longer proceeds from innate qualities of character, but is rather conferred upon an individual, and hence may be conferred even upon a nonentity by men's delusions. The resonant antitheses that describe Napoleon in *Childe Harold* (III, 36–38)—"the greatest, nor the worst of men," "Conqueror and Captive," "more or less than man,"—shrink when applied to the kindred figure of Suwarrow not only because historically the man was less. Byron now thoroughly divorces magnitude of effect from intrinsic magnitude of character:

> For the man was, we safely may assert,
> A thing to wonder at beyond most wondering;
> Hero, buffoon, half-demon, and half-dirt,
> Praying, instructing, desolating, plundering;
> Now Mars, now Momus—and when bent to storm
> A fortress, Harlequin in uniform.
>
> (VII, 55)

The distance from Manfred, "half dust, half deity" (I, ii, 40), to Suwarrow, "half-demon, and half-dirt," is a forceful indicator of the alteration in Byron's stance toward the protagonists who towered over his early works. The terrifying older man is here shrunk to a cartoon, his potency neutralized by irony. Guarded at last from the sway of figures like Suwarrow, Byron turns to liberate those still awed. He focuses not directly on the Russian general, whose barbarity he mocks into insignificance, but on the mental attitudes which sustain him. The bitterest satire is aimed at those whom glory deceives: the soldiers who kill and are killed, and the readers who share their distorted ideals. The gratuitous horror of the assault on Ismail is epitomized by a figure who stands as Suwarrow's benevolent double: the "good old Khan" who perishes in it. Neither "Priam's, Peleus', or Jove's son... but a good, plain, old, temperate man," the Khan is that rare creature in Byron's work: a loving father united with his sons. Upon seeing the last of his five boys die he gives up his life in despair. The scene recalls both the situation of Bonnivard and his brothers and the sternness of Minotti, but it is suffused with Byron's wishful fantasies as son rather than his fears and resentments. The Khan's devotion touches even the Russians who slay him, and his selfless defense of the family he cherishes earns praise wholly unqualified by Byron's usual irony (VIII, 104–119).[2]

Significantly, the paradigm of Suwarrow's essential brutality is the couplet in which he announces his victory:

> With bloody hands he wrote his first despatch;
> And here exactly follows what he said:—
> "Glory to *God* and to the Empress!" (*Powers*
> *Eternal! such names mingled!*) "Ismail's ours."
>
> (VIII, 133)

Byron's breaches of decorum serve awareness, but Suwarrow's coupling of God and the Empress, the lascivious Helen of Byron's new Troy, and his "Polar melody... duly accompanied by shrieks and groans" (VII, 135), manifest only the chaotic and destructive contradictions of his character. Suwarrow is a bad man because he does not see, and the proof that he does not see is that he is a bad poet. His solecism is the link between two strains whose co-presence contributes to the unique vitality of *Don Juan*: the traditional concept of the hero as man of action and the emerging Romantic concept of the hero as artist.

Byron's redefinition of his masculine protagonist in the later cantos of *Don Juan* is matched by an evolution in his women. Previously, women have been maternally fostering or figures who threaten the hero's independence; now—with much ironic qualification—they appear as active heroines. Byron's unease on the subject makes him in this final phase of his career a subtle observer of sexual roles. His extended portrait of the "gynocracy," the women of the aristocracy and upper middle class who rule English society, is the wonderful consequence of his gynophobia.

Byron does not scruple to remind the reader of how difficult it is to enter into the psychology of the opposite sex, yet the simultaneous bringing to the surface of his own buried attitudes commands more respect:

> But as to women—who can penetrate
> The real sufferings of their she condition?
> Man's very sympathy with their estate
> Has much of selfishness, and more suspicion.
> Their love, their virtue, beauty, education,
> But form good housekeepers—to breed a nation.
>
> All this were very well, and can't be better;
> But even this is difficult, Heaven knows,
> So many troubles from her birth beset her,
> Such small distinction between friends and foes;
> The gilding wears so soon from off her fetter,
> That—but ask any woman if she'd choose
> (Take her at thirty, that is) to have been
> Female or male? a schoolboy or a Queen?
>
> "Petticoat Influence" is a great reproach,
> Which even those who obey would fain be thought
> To fly from, as from hungry pikes a roach; . . .
>   (XIV, 24–26)

Potentially painful reflection is dissolved in irony, but the last simile indicates strongly disquieting feelings. The picture of women in the English cantos need only be compared with the degradation of Julia in Canto I to realize that Byron is now willing—and, because of the jocular manner, able—seriously to confront questions that previously he had evaded by reducing to farce.

Violently separated from Juan, Julia writes the lines which are perhaps of all Byron's verse the most famous:

"Man's love is of his life a thing apart,
'Tis woman's whole existence; man may range
The court, camp, church, the vessel, and the mart,
Sword, gown, gain, glory, offer in exchange
Pride, fame, ambition, to fill up his heart,
And few there are whom these cannot estrange;
Man has all these resources, we but one,
To love again, and be again undone.

                                                              (I, 194)

This and the surrounding stanzas (190–198) are another of Byron's
revealing accretions. They were added almost a month after the manuscript of Canto I had been despatched to London,[3] and the return to
Julia suggests the attraction of the figure of the abandoned woman.
The pathos of Julia's letter is as self-dramatizing as her tirade against
Alfonso, however, and her assertion that "to love too much has been
the only art/ I used" rings false when followed by rhetoric as exquisite
as the gilt-edged paper on which it is inscribed. The letter leads to
doubts about her sincerity, but its chief contention is confirmed by the
mechanics of the plot, which immure her in a convent while Juan
escapes with letters of credit to embark upon his adventures. Byron
extenuates Juan's involvement with his youth and passivity but
stacks the deck against Julia by making her an adulterous wife, transforming her from an appealing girl with an old husband to a shrewish
coquette who melodramatically bewails her lot when exposed. Byron's decision to maintain the comic tone by sacrificing Julia culminates in the use of her letter after the shipwreck to provide lots for
choosing the victim of cannibalism. His abrupt dismissal of Haidée's
death and the irony which often throughout that scene seems in excess
of its didactic function, similarly suggest an evasion of unassimilated
emotion (discussed above, pp. 187–88).

By the time he reached Canto XIV, more than three years after
these two episodes, Byron had achieved greater disinterestedness. In
the stanzas just quoted he takes over Julia's generalization and argues
it without the self-pleading that taints her. Although on the two
occasions it appears in the poem Byron rhymes "gynocracy" with
"hypocrisy" (XII, 66; XVI, 52), his withdrawn position enables him
wryly to enjoy the complicated protocols of the sexual chase. The
bitter ground colors but sharpens his appreciation of the myriad ruses
of mothers and daughters in determined pursuit of husbands. For

women in the world which Byron describes marriage is a necessity. Milliners outfit prospective brides in hopes of a satisfactory return on their investment when the groom is landed (see Byron's note to XI, 49); conversely, wealthy debutantes are the prey of impecunious fortunehunters. "Cash rules Love the ruler, on his own/ High ground" (XII, 14) is his precise summary of the facts that turn courtship into sordid calculation. Men and women suffer mutually in this vicious charade: as its wreck receded into the past, the defensive, wounded cynicism of Byron's preoccupation with his marriage developed into concern with the economic and class structures which shape the eternal contest between the sexes. The firm nexus between character and social context Byron establishes without impairing his fluid improvisation is one cause of the solid achievement of the English cantos.

Denied by convention any of the careers in which a man may realize himself, restricted to marriage as a goal, and trapped in loveless unions by financial constraint, women are inevitably forced to become dexterous manipulators if they are to survive at all. Two stanzas at the beginning of Canto XV particularly illuminate their situation. Emotion, the narrator declares, is "the grand Antithesis to great *Ennui*" (XV, 2): joy or misery, laughter or scorn,

> ... all are better than the sigh suppressed,
> Corroding in the cavern of the heart,
> Making the countenance a *masque* of rest
> And turning Human Nature to an art.
> Few men dare show their thoughts of worst or best;
> Dissimulation always sets apart
> A corner for herself; and, therefore, *Fiction*
> Is that which passes with least contradiction.
>
> 　　　　　　　　　　(XV, 3; italics added)

In this extended and perspicacious re-vision of the materials of Canto I Byron pursues the implications of the comment he made there that "Passion most dissembles" (I, 73). To encompass their ends even the most direct of emotions must have recourse to artifice: "a little genial sprinkling of hypocrisy/ Has saved the fame of thousand splendid sinners ... So gentle, charming, charitable, chaste—/ And all by having *tact* as well as taste" (XII, 66). The nonchalant tone is possible because Byron is only indirectly confronting the deceptions of women; the satire focuses on the social pressures of "a low, news-

paper, humdrum, lawsuit/ Country" (XII, 65) which require, and in
part, exculpate, their hypocrisy. Moreover, viewed positively, their
virtuosic self-presentation is the most immediate form of art:

> ... our notion is not high
> Of politicians and their double front,
> Who live by lies, yet dare not boldly lie:—
> Now what I love in women is, they won't
> Or can't do otherwise than lie—but do it
> So well, the very Truth seems falsehood to it.
>
> And, after all, what is a lie? 'T is but
> The truth in masquerade; ...
>
> (XI, 36–37)

The analogy between women and artists, both of whom must rely
on fictions of uncertain status, not lies but "truth in masquerade," to
cope with their fallen condition and to accomplish the purposes they
cannot effect straightforwardly, is central to these cantos. The extended discussion is a sign of the anxieties the subject of women
continued to provoke in Byron, but the terms of the discussion have
evolved. The narrator can now safely acknowledge his involvement
with the women of his story because he presents himself as the master of their wiles, guarded against the dangers they represent by his
superior knowledge; the elaborate condescension, however, belies
the calm.

Juan's reception in England fresh from his Russian triumphs
epitomizes the shifting conjunction of the concepts of hero and
heroine. At Catherine's court the narrator asked the reader to "sup-
pose" Juan "Made up by Youth, Fame, and an army tailor" (IX, 45); in
London he appears resplendently clothed by "Rumour,/ That live
Gazette" (XV, 11):

> His fame too,—for he had that kind of fame
> Which sometimes plays the deuce with Womankind,
> A heterogeneous mass of glorious blame,
> Half virtues and whole vices being combined;
> Faults which attract because they are not tame;
> Follies tricked out so brightly that they blind:—...
>
> (XV, 57)

The antithetical constructions which mark all Byron's heroes, debased in Suwarrow, pass to Juan. In actuality, however, he is as passive as ever, and his semblance of "character" is the faithful mirror of his admirers: Juan is the screen of their projections. Heroism too is in the eye of the beholder, and by clearly demonstrating its externality this epistemological satire continues the comic reduction of the conventional ideal of the hero begun in the stanzas on Suwarrow. Juan owes his prominence to the English women, who cast on his utter blandness the radiant light of their own fancy. "Romantic heads are pretty painters" (XI, 33), proclaims the narrator in mocking wonder:

> ... with Women he [Juan] was what
> They pleased to make or take him for; and their
> Imagination's quite enough for that:
> So that the outline's tolerably fair,
> They fill the canvas up—and *"verbum sat."*
> If once their phantasies be brought to bear
> Upon an object, whether sad or playful,
> They can transfigure brighter than a Raphael.
>
> (XV, 16)

The only woman not to be deluded by her vision of Juan is Aurora Raby, who looks "as if she sat by Eden's door,/ And grieved for those who could return no more" (XV, 45). The comparison suggests that she possesses a prelapsarian accuracy of perception capable of apprehending the true nature of objects, but such clarity is an instructive paradigm rather than a virtue available in the fallen world.

Byron edgily catalogues all the stratagems the infatuated English women employ in their pursuit of Juan. Foolish and manipulative as they are, their ruses point up the paradox that sincere desires must often be pursued with artifice. As the Duchess of Fitz-Fulke commences her flirtatious assault on Juan Byron informs us that "her late *performance* had been a dead set/ At Lord Augustus Fitz-Plantagenet" (XIV, 42; italics added), and the word exactly conveys the theatricality he perceives to be the necessary consequence of self-consciousness. Fitz-Fulke has the ingenuity to carry out her amorous whim by adopting the superstition of the Black Friar, another demonstration that in *Don Juan* fiction controls reality and the prize—in this case, Juan— goes to those who devise the best fictions.[4] Her disguise makes literal the inseparability of masquerade and deliberate behavior that Byron

wants the reader to see: through it he transforms the stock ghost of
Gothic melodrama that he had exploited in *Lara* into the focus of his
epistemological comedy, cleverly supplies the supernatural ma-
chinery that was a traditional feature of epic, and vindicates the
power of art and theater.

The most luminous star of the gynocracy is Lady Adeline Amundeville, whose portrait Byron built on his deep and lasting ambivalence to women. "The fair most fatal Juan ever met" (XIII, 12), her
danger is in exact proportion to the intensity beneath her scintillating
exterior:

> ... she had that lurking Demon
> Of double nature, and thus doubly named—
> Firmness yclept in Heroes, Kings, and seamen,
> That is, when they succeed; but greatly blamed
> As *Obstinacy*, both in Men and Women,
> Whene'er their triumph pales, or star is tamed:—
> And 't will perplex the casuist in morality
> To fix the due bounds of this dangerous quality.
>
> Had Buonaparte won at Waterloo,
> It had been firmness; now 't is pertinacity:
> Must the event decide between the two?
> I leave it to your people of sagacity
> To draw the line between the false and true,
> If such can e'er be drawn by Man's capacity:
> My business is with Lady Adeline,
> Who in her way too was a heroine.
>
> (XIV, 89–90)

As he begins stanza 89 the reader naturally assumes that Adeline's
"double nature" will be the familiar antithetical temperament of the
Byronic hero, but after the dash his expectations are belied. Adeline
presents the neatest instance of epistemological satire: her nature is
single, but as circumstances change impressions of its force vary. She
is no puzzle to Byron-as-narrator, however, who lampoons "people
of sagacity" in order to set off his own discernment. Adeline may be
fatal for Juan, but she is transparent to him.

The comparison between Adeline and Napoleon in stanza 90, and
the grounds of her claim to be considered "in her way ... a heroine,"
are elucidated by a remark in the next canto. Byron comments:
"Knights and Dames I sing,/ Such as the times may furnish" (XV, 25).

The theatrical metaphors of these cantos blend with others drawn from epic and heroic sources. The two are closely linked, since in planning their objectives and using their art to attain them the women resemble military commanders plotting a campaign. Through this unobtrusive analogy Byron enlarges the import of the narrow milieu of English high society and relates it to his heroic themes. "Your men of business," he says "are not apt to express/ Much passion, since the merchant-ship, the Argo,/ Conveyed Medea as her supercargo" (XIV, 76), dryly implying that the callous fortune-hunting of nineteenth-century England is the modern form of Jason's capture of the Golden Fleece. Allusion animates the depiction of a society Byron insists is "formed of two mighty tribes, the *Bores* and *Bored*" (XIII, 95; cf. XIV, 18), a society so moribund and commonplace, he immodestly notes, that no other writer has been able to describe it (XIV, 15–20). Allusion also provides the perspective for satiric evaluation. To say that Adeline is as "bright as a new napoleon from its mintage" is punningly to indicate the commercial values of contemporary society and to equate her position in it with that held by Napoleon in the vanished days of heroism.

The assertion that Napoleon can be measured only by Waterloo is a comic climax to Byron's argument that man lacks absolute knowledge and can judge only by deceptive appearances. In a world that gauges by the "event" and "truth" is merely consensus, social success is true success, and Adeline is a consummate mistress of the skills by which it is won. Her performance of the song she composed on the Black Friar displays "by one *three* talents" combined (XVI, 39), and her grandest achievement makes clear the convergence in her of the sexual and political themes of *Don Juan*. Her husband, Lord Henry, shares the cold pride of Titans like Conrad and Lara; it is as if he were the same type in a later historical manifestation. He is a member of Parliament who cultivates his constituents by lavish general dinners, the modern versions of the feasts their mock-epic menus recall. The heroic warrior has given way to the elected official whose only "contest" (XVI, 70) is at the ballot box. The linking figure in this progress is the pirate Lambro, whom Byron presents as a "sea-attorney" or "Prime Minister" (III, 14). It is Adeline who steers Henry through the Odyssean "rocks of re-elections" (XVI, 95), presiding with sublime generalship over his banquet. The guests retire at the end of the evening, "delighted with their dinner and their Host,/ But with the Lady Adeline the most" (XVI, 101).

The only one to mistrust her is Juan, who

... when he cast a glance
On Adeline while playing her grand *rôle,*
Which she went through as though it were a dance,
Betraying only now and then her soul
By a look scarce perceptibly askance
(Of weariness or scorn), began to feel
Some doubt how much of Adeline was *real;*

So well she acted all and every part
By turns—with that vivacious versatility,
Which many people take for want of heart.
They err—'t is merely what is called mobility,
A thing of temperament and not of art,
Though seeming so, from its supposed facility;
And false—though true; for, surely, they're sincerest
Who are strongly acted on by what is nearest.

This makes your actors, artists, and romancers,
Heroes sometimes, though seldom—sages never;
But speakers, bards, diplomatists, and dancers,
Little that's great, but much of what is clever; ...

                                        (XVI, 96–98)

Byron agilely characterizes Adeline while following a discursive pattern of thought that line by line leads him away from her: the train of associations enhances her significance and at the same time causes her threatening presence to recede. Juan's doubts of Adeline resonate with the narrator's exposure of the unsteadiness of notions of reality. The yearning for glory that surrounds "great" is checked by the consistently ironic contexts in which it occurs earlier in the poem: "Potemkin—a great thing in days/ When homicide and harlotry made great" (VII, 37); "Arseniew, that great son of slaughter" (VIII, 9), who leads the attack on Ismail; Suwarrow, great as is a little dog followed by the blind (VII, 48); and Tom the highwayman, "a great man,/ Who in his time had made heroic bustle," who provokes Byron's most forceful dismissal of that sort of heroism: "Heroes must die; and by God's blessing 't is/ Not long before the most of them go home" (XI, 19–20). The self-consciousness that precludes heroic concentration is the best antidote against its destructiveness to others and to the self. Byron's repudiation of heroism is a repudiation of obsessiveness; the actors and artists he twits are the company he has joined, not self-torturers like Tasso but ironic contemplators of their own condition.

Because character in *Don Juan* is not viewed as the organic growth of the self in time, to have a self is to choose a role. Adeline's protean ease is "a thing of temperament and not of art," but it issues in a "grand role": "she acted all and every part/ By turns." To explain the seeming paradox Byron again borrows from the French, appending a description of the word he naturalizes:

> In French *"mobilité."* I am not sure that mobility is English; but it is expressive of a quality which rather belongs to other climates, though it is sometimes seen to a great extent in our own. It may be defined as an excessive susceptibility of immediate impressions—at the same time without *losing* the past: and is, though sometimes apparently useful to the possessor, a most painful and unhappy attribute.
>
> (Byron's note to XVI, 97)

The uncommon tentativeness of the prose strengthens the impression that in this passage Byron is obliquely speaking of his own "painful and unhappy" tensions. The phrase "excessive susceptibility" suggests a fear that the ego is too fragilely rooted to withstand absorption by circumstance. When the sense of identity is not firm enough to provide a genuine footing in the present, actions seem no more than parts to be momentarily assumed. The recurrent theatrical metaphors in *Don Juan* are the corollary of the psychological divisions out of which Byron began to write.

Yet all is not loss. The tales record the terrible cost of trying to preserve psychic unity by rigid repression of disruptive forces. The multiple roles Byron relishes in Adeline are the sign of the more expansive view of the self in *Don Juan*. The poem is a triumphant demonstration that conflicts can be accommodated within the personae devised by imagination. Beyond and above Adeline stands Byron the narrator, who adopts the strategies of the women who beset him and beats them at their own game. Their flirtations attempt like his poetry to combat the tedium of English life: an artificial suspense, he jokes, is "the surest way for ladies and for books—/ To bait their tender—or their tenter—hooks" (XIV, 97). The contrast between their "Romances/ Reduced to practice, and performed like dances" (XIV, 79) and his abounding invention, however, is wholly to his advantage. Their imaginations transfigure Juan, but less brilliantly than his own. From the start Byron's presentation of Juan involves a double process, in that he both undercuts the hero of legend and re-establishes his interest through the fictions with which he surrounds him.

It is just this point which marks the superiority of Byron to the women in his story: he possesses the self-consciousness to recognize the fictional nature of his creativity, but they are duped by their fantasies. Juan's fame "plays the deuce with Womankind" (XV, 57; the stanza is quoted above, p. 250), but does not fool the clear-sighted narrator. In most of Byron's earlier works the Titanic protagonist overwhelms all efforts to place him in perspective: in these late cantos only the women mistake Juan for a hero. By reducing the archetype of masculine aggressiveness to the passive Juan Byron fully reveals the little boy who was inside the Titan all along. Though his anxieties persist, his emergence as the artist-narrator gives Byron a position of dominance over both the masculine and the feminine figures who darken his other works.

The transformation of the hero Byron effects is the more remarkable because the temptations of glory he was impelled to expose he keenly felt. The restlessness which drove him from Teresa to Missolonghi testifies to the continued hold of the old obsessions, maternal envelopment and masculine rivalry. His works return to the same haunting figures, but the scrutiny to which they are submitted weakens their grasp. When Byron proclaims himself "the grand Napoleon of the realms of rhyme" (XI, 55), the characteristic self-identification mocks poetic ambition but allies itself to a genuine satisfaction. Unlike his one-time idol, Byron continued to affirm in deeds and verse "that Revolution/ Alone can save the earth from Hell's pollution" (VIII, 51). In his poetry he is a hero twofold: for the sovereign power that he wields as artist over a refractory world, and for the enlightened politics his power serves.

Byron was nonetheless reluctant to give full assent to the ideal of the artist-hero at which he had arrived. The complex organization of modern society which lessened the scope of individual action increased the allure of exotic adventures and Titanic figures. Byron's recognition that the artistry of women is a defensive response to their helplessness comments ironically on his own evolution. His hostility to Wordsworth, Coleridge, and Keats for their frank if troubled acceptance of themselves as ineluctably the subject of their poetry mirrors his ambivalence toward the inward turning he too exemplifies. To accompany Juan through tempests and battles to Norman Abbey is to follow the metamorphosis of the epic into a new kind—contemporary and psychological—whose originality Byron proudly announces:

> Here the twelfth canto of our Introduction
> Ends. When the body of the Book's begun,

> You'll find it of a different construction
> From what some people say 't will be when done...
>
> And if my thunderbolt not always rattles,
> Remember, reader! you have had before,
> The worst of tempests and the best of battles....
> (XII, 87–88)

Few writers have articulated as clearly as Byron the needs which determine his adaptation of tradition. The tensions in his presentation of himself as the artist-hero, visible in his self-deprecating, improvisatory manner, strengthen *Don Juan*.

In retrospect, the opera troupe with which Juan is imprisoned on board ship in Canto IV appears as the representative emblem of *Don Juan*. In it meet Byron's two most extended metaphors for the ambiguities and uncertainties of the human condition: life as "nautical existence" (II, 12) and life as theater. The conjunction illustrates how consistently the poem develops from its co-ordinate premises of the inaccessibility of the outer world and the instability of the inner. To borrow the title of John Barth's novel, life in *Don Juan* is a Floating Opera; with the singers the concept of role is explicit. The *buffo* and tenor who "hated with a hate/ Found only on the stage" (IV, 93) make the reader reconsider the multiple relationships between the artificial and the quintessential: art, like Adeline, is "false—though true." In his long, good-humored description of the troupe's plight Raucocanti, the *buffo*, functions briefly as Juan's mentor, a part in which he is succeeded almost immediately by Johnson. The pairing typifies the familiar configuration of artist and hero: the soldier counsels stoicism, the singer, cheerfully confident that "if the Sultan has a taste for song,/ We will revive our fortunes before long" (IV, 82), knows that difficulties can also be surmounted through imagination.

In the world that *Don Juan* presents one cannot avoid "turning Human Nature to an art" (XV, 3). Passion is the core of the Byronic personality, and passions require mediated expression. "She had no prudence, but he had," Byron remarks of Gulbeyaz and the eunuch Baba, the "old black enchanter" who by his mastery of disguise first aids in her attempted seduction of Juan and then argues against her self-consuming wish to kill him when it is frustrated (V, 83–84; VI, 115). Their relationship is a comic version of the necessary interplay of passion and deliberation. Our own needs and the conflicting reality of others lead us into playing roles, and the self we construct must be imaginatively shaped if it is not to repress our essential nature. Juan, by contrast, never matures, never goes beyond mere compliance with his surroundings. His lack of character becomes pernicious when, pervaded by the thirst of glory (VIII, 52), he joins the aggressors at Ismail:

> But Juan was quite "a broth of a boy,"
> A thing of impulse and a child of song;
> Now swimming in the sentiment of joy,
> Or the *sensation* (if that phrase seem wrong),
> And afterward, if he must needs destroy,
> In such good company as always throng
> To battles, sieges, and that kind of pleasure,
> No less delighted to employ his leisure;
>
> But always without malice: if he warred
> Or loved, it was with what we call "the best
> Intentions," . . .
>
> (VIII, 24–25)

Byron duly credits Juan for rescuing Leila, but because the act springs from the same thoughtlessness as his fighting rejects the praise heaped on such sentimental anecdotes by "these ambrosial, Pharisaic times,/ With all their pretty milk-and-water ways" (VIII, 90): "What's this in one annihilated city,/ Where thousand loves, and ties, and duties grew?" (VIII, 124).

The process of bringing the forces of the psyche under the direction of the ego requires the diligent self-examination that is also the only possible means of unilluded perception. The conjunction of psychology and epistemology can be illuminated by the example of Hume. In the section "Of personal identity" in the *Treatise of Human Nature* he observes:

> There are some philosophers, who imagine we are every moment intimately conscious of what we call our SELF; that we feel its existence; and are certain, beyond the evidence of a demonstration, both of its perfect identity and simplicity. The strongest sensation, the most violent passion, say they, instead of distracting us from this view, only fix it the more intensely, and make us consider their influence on *self* either by their pain or pleasure. . . . Unluckily all these positive assertions are contrary to that very experience, which is pleaded for them, nor have we any idea of *self*, after the manner it is here explain'd. . . . For my part, when I enter most intimately into what I call *myself*, I always stumble on some particular perception or other, of heat or cold, light or shade, love or hatred, pain or pleasure. I never can catch *myself* at any time without a

perception, and never can observe any thing but the perception.... If any one upon serious and unprejudic'd reflection thinks he has a different notion of *himself,* I must confess that I can reason no longer with him. All I can allow him is, that he may be in the right as well as I, and that we are essentially different in this particular.... But setting aside some metaphysicians of this kind, I may venture to affirm of the rest of mankind, that they are nothing but a bundle or collection of different perceptions, which succeed each other with an inconceivable rapidity, and are in a perpetual flux and movement.[5]

Hume's philosophical challenge to the unity of the self is a reminder that the view of it Byron exhibits is not a psychological aberration peculiar to him; indeed, the popularity of his works suggests that even the specific oral and oedipal conflicts in Byron's work are in unison with tensions at the heart of Western culture. Hume confesses that there is no logical escape from the "forelorn solitude" in which his all-encompassing skepticism places him, but he finds relief in a way which is Byron's as well. In the next section of his essay he continues: "Most fortunately it happens, that since reason is incapable of dispelling these clouds, nature herself suffices to that purpose, and cures me of this philosophical melancholy and delirium... I dine, I play a game of backgammon, I converse, and am merry with my friends...."[6]

Don Juan is likewise stabilized by its firm anchor in mundane reality. Though the narrator's intellectual speculations tend to dissolve this reality, the increasing emphasis on indigestion and death in the latter part of the poem is a reassurance that Byron's anti-materialism has not obscured the common elements of human experience. The more doubting the narrator becomes the more the poem asserts the abrasive actuality of existence, and counters the pull towards fantasy and wish-fulfillment by stress on man's physical weakness. The consciousness of death is the basis of the poem's affirmation of life. Materials that locate *Don Juan* squarely within the ordinary universe of the reader oppose the threat of solipsism. Byron castigates Wordsworth for his radically private innovations and writes in a traditional form, however altered. Despite its vaunted license he provides his poem with the paraphernalia of authenticity: a fastidious respect for accurate detail, verifiable dates, indications of factual sources. Most important, *Don Juan* is crammed with the familiar names and objects, the current controversies and the proverbial wisdom, that the reader knows from his everyday life outside the poem: clichés about English weather, schoolboy Latin tags, hoary *sententia*, Napoleon, Castlereagh, Wellington, Wordsworth, Coleridge, Southey, Malthus, Wilberforce, and the price of corn, the suspension of habeas corpus, parliamentary maneuvers, teachers of mnemonics, makers of ships' pumps, macassar oil, miners' lamps— the list is practically endless and extraordinarily diverse. There are moments when *Don Juan* seems a combination topography and inventory: topical reference by topical reference the poem builds up the comfortable landscape the narrator philosophically denies until it acquires the particularity of life itself. Byron had earned his boast to Kinnaird: "... confess—confess—you dog—and be candid—that it is the sublime of *that there* sort of writing—it may be bawdy—but is it not good English?—it may be profligate—but it is not *life*, is it not *the thing?*" (*BLJ* 6: 232). The narrator's consciousness of things mitigates the alienation that festers in Byron's other protagonists. The self in isolation was fragmented, but in *Don Juan* the self is in the world, defining its contours by voraciously incorporating, manipulating, and remembering.

The most powerfully steadying element in *Don Juan* is Byron's relationship to his audience. *Don Juan* baffled contemporaries and incurred accusations of cynicism because its first readers did not realize that Byron had transferred the locus of meaning from within the poem outside to them. Pope draws his audience into a compact of solidarity against the fools he presents—the Dunces, the Timons, the Sir Balaams. In Byron, however, the object of satire is not a fictive, representative character, but the false assumptions in the individual reader that his reactions to the poem bring to the surface. Once the reader is admitted as a necessary consideration it can be appreciated how the actions of the poem complete themselves in his consciousness. To repeat two instances: the carnage and grim humor of the siege of Ismail would be as perverse as early critics charged were it not that Byron wants to awaken by them the unthinking "Cockneys of London" and "Muscadins of Paris" (VIII, 124) whose jingoism is the fuel of such slaughters. Similarly, Byron makes us see that it is sentimentalism that causes over-valuation of Juan's rescue of Leila, and jadedness that makes us wish to indulge in the melodrama of Haidée's idyll and death. His abrupt deflations force into the open these underlying escapist and self-deluding impulses.

Each time Byron shifts the context in which events are viewed he reinforces the reader's respect for his knowledgeability. His reflections on his story illustrate the importance of the question of "real" order, and in discoursing so learnedly and lucidly about the impossibility of ever achieving it Byron allays the fears of incoherence and nihilism that he raises. Over the arbitrary and chaotic world of Juan's experience stands a perceptive intelligence determined "to show things really as they are" (XII, 40). By the end of the first stanza the reader has already been enticed into partnership with Byron and invited to share in the freedom of self-consciousness.

"Invited" is too weak a word: Byron compels the reader to participate in his cleansing of error. Towards the close of Canto XIV he begs "all men to forbear/ Anticipating . . . They'll only make mistakes" (XIV, 99), but he therapeutically induces and exorcises such miscalculations. Therefore an "outline is the best,—/ A lively reader's fancy does the rest" (VI, 98). Byron reiterates that understanding requires alert co-operation from the reader, not passive absorption of the printed page:

> Oh, reader! if that thou canst read,—and know,
> 'T is not enough to spell, or even to read,
> To constitute a reader—there must go
> Virtues of which both you and I have need;—...
>
> (XIII, 73)

Through the technique of *Don Juan* Byron carries the reader along on the sinuous mental processes requisite to pursue the elusive windings of truth:

> If people contradict themselves, can I
> Help contradicting them, and everybody,
> Even my veracious self?—But that's a lie:
> I never did so, never will—how should I?
> He who doubts all things nothing can deny:
> Truth's fountains may be clear—her streams are muddy,
> And cut through such canals of contradiction,
> That she must often navigate o'er fiction.
>
> Apologue, Fable, Poesy, and Parable,
> Are false, but may be rendered also true,
> By those who sow them in a land that's arable:
> 'T is wonderful what Fable will not do!
> 'T is said it makes Reality more bearable:
> But what's Reality? Who has its clue?
>
> (XV, 88–89)

In the playful manner that is the delight of the poem these stanzas point its final lesson. Contradictions can be surmounted only by fiction, by an art sufficiently flexible and self-critical to catch them and give them expression. Byron knows that words never precisely enclose reality, and only an artist who thus humbly accepts the limits of "Man's capacity" can imitate a world in which "the same things change their names at such a rate" (III, 6).

These stanzas also bring the resolving modulation of Byron's ocean imagery. In *Childe Harold* III Byron compared himself to a weed flung from a rock, and in the fourth canto to a swimmer on a tempestuous ocean. *Don Juan* employs the same metaphor to describe the hazardous "nautical existence" on which all men embark and the especial dangers of "the ocean, Woman." Byron now amplifies the affirmative tone sounded with the shipborne opera troupe by coming forth himself as a skilled "navigator." In an earlier stanza he announced his purpose in similar language:

> . . . Truth is always strange—
> Stranger than fiction: if it could be told,
> How much would novels gain by the exchange!
> How differently the World would men behold!
> How oft would Vice and Virtue places change!
> The new world would be nothing to the old,
> If some Columbus of the moral seas
> Would show mankind their Soul's antipodes.
>
> What "antres vast and deserts idle," then,
> Would be discovered in the human soul!
> What icebergs in the hearts of mighty men,
> With self-love in the centre as their Pole!
> What Anthropophagi are nine of ten
> Of those who hold the kingdoms in control!
> Were things but only called by their right name,
> Caesar himself would be ashamed of Fame.
>
> (XIV, 101–102)

By indirectly announcing himself the "Columbus of the moral seas" who will show "mankind their Soul's antipodes" Byron claims for psychological exploration the magnitude that had previously belonged to narratives of heroic adventure. The interiorization of the heroic is emphasized by the echoes of *Othello*.

It is important to note that for Byron these inner seas are still *moral* seas. The heightened interest in the recesses of the self does not lead him to abandon the public, normative scales of judgment. Byron will not permit an inner world so private that it is exempt from criticism, and by insisting that men are responsible for their actions he preserves the definition of man as a social being in saving contact with his fellows. "I hate a motive," Byron declares in Canto XIV, but chiefly because the motives attached to actions obfuscate and gloss over what they pretend to explain, like "a Laureate's Ode, or servile Peer's 'content'" (XIV, 58). As the pricking of these two self-serving fictions demonstrates, his appreciation of the mystery of the personality in no way weakens his satire. He continues:

> 'T is sad to hack into the roots of things,
> They are so much intertwisted with the earth;
> So that the branch a goodly verdure flings,
> I reck not if an acorn gave it birth.
> To trace all actions to their secret springs
> Would make indeed some melancholy mirth;...
>
> (XIV, 59)

If the lines jokingly express an aversion to analysis which is the vestige of Byron's resistance to tracing the springs of his own character, they nonetheless manifest the enormous progress he had made since *Childe Harold* I. The melancholy mirth he had risked in the self-exploration of a decade and a half brought its rewards: the unruffled gaze at the iceberg Titans and the Caesars is the mark of the emancipation he had achieved. This steady, worldly-wise voice and its resilient but responsible commentary is the *cantus firmus* of the scene in England.

Don Juan shows that fictions are necessary to organize reality, and that they can do so only when seen as fictions. For Byron this recognition is to be shared between author and audience: if objective truth is unavailable there is all the more need for free and open intercourse between our isolated selves. In Canto XII he ironically apostrophizes as "your only poet" the miser devoted to "Money, that most pure imagination," perhaps because the miser realizes the dream of wealth that inspires human energy in the commercial nineteenth century (XII, 2-12). The miser is a pure type of the self formed by withdrawal and reduction: he becomes his role, sacrificing his life to his hoarding. Byron exercises a like absolute control over his world through his poetry, but he is the vital opposite of the miser in his dramatically multiplied selves and inexhaustible giving. The growth of *Don Juan* filled the late nights and early mornings of Byron's last years. Living in a foreign land, hearing all day a foreign language, Byron elaborated his inner life in those solitary hours of composition often mellowed by gin and water. "Donny Johnny" became his most intimate companion, and what he found in its writing he gave liberally to his readers. The "arable land" in which Byron sows and which in turn renders his fictions true (XV, 89) is the consciousness of his audience. The partnership of the unilluded poet and the reader whom he has brought to participate in his awareness is a generous image of the victory of self-consciousness over its own divisions.

Notes

Introduction

1. *Byron's Letters and Journals* (London: John Murray, 1973–1976), ed. Leslie Marchand, 1: 79. The volumes of this edition which have thus far appeared are hereafter cited as *BLJ*. My epigraph is quoted from *BLJ*, 3: 179. The other collections of Byron's letters are R. E. Prothero, ed., *The Works of Lord Byron: Letters and Journals*, 6 vols. (London: John Murray, 1898–1901), cited as *LJ*, and *Lord Byron's Correspondence*, ed. John Murray, 2 vols. (London: John Murray, 1922), cited as *LBC*.

2. The quotations in this paragraph are taken from Thomas Moore, *Letters and Journals of Lord Byron: with Notices of His Life*, 2 vols. (London: John Murray, 1830), 1: 8–9. Cited throughout also is the standard biography by Leslie Marchand, *Byron: A Biography*, 3 vols. (New York: Alfred Knopf, 1957), hereafter cited as "Marchand."

3. Of the figures who have increased psychoanalytic knowledge of the pre-oedipal stages (Mahler, Bowlby, Jacobson, Spitz, and others), I have made most use of the writings of D. W. Winnicott: *Through Paediatrics to Psycho-Analysis* (1958; rpt. with an introduction by Masud Khan, New York: Basic Books, 1975); *The Maturational Processes and the Facilitating Environment* (New York: International Univ. Press, 1965); *Playing and Reality* (New York: Basic Books, 1971). An introduction to the area which emphasizes the connection Winnicott suggests between these stages and the "cultural field" is Arnold H. Modell, *Object Love and Reality* (New York: International Univ. Press, 1968). From the readings in ego psychology which have contributed to the assumptions of this essay I cite only works of particular relevance by two authors: Erik H. Erikson, *Childhood and Society*, 2nd. ed. rev. and enl. (New York: Norton, 1963), and "Identity and The Life Cycle: Selected Papers," *Psychological Issues* 1 (1959); Ernst Kris, *Psychoanalytic Explorations in Art* (1952; rpt. New York: Schocken, 1964).

4. Unless otherwise noted, all quotations from Byron's verse are taken from the edition of E. H. Coleridge, *The Works of Lord Byron: Poetry*, 7 vols. (London: John Murray, 1898–1904), hereafter cited as *Poetry*. *Byron's Don Juan: A Variorum Edition*, ed. T. G. Steffan and W. W. Pratt, 2nd. ed., 4 vols. (Austin: Univ. of Texas Press, 1971), was also consulted, but for the sake of uniformity quotations are from the Coleridge edition except in cases of significant difference.

5. Robert F. Gleckner has persuasively argued this theme in *Byron and the Ruins of Paradise* (Baltimore: Johns Hopkins Univ. Press, 1967).

6. In thus insisting upon the primacy of Byron's self-dramatizing qualities this study aligns itself with Jerome J. McGann's *Fiery Dust: Byron's Poetic Development* (Chicago: Univ. of Chicago Press, 1968) and his *DON JUAN in Context* (Chicago: Univ. of Chicago Press, 1976), which, however, appeared after this manuscript was completed.

Though I reach the conclusion by different routes, my concurrence with previous critics of Byron in the sections of Part III concerned with the narrator's stance and techniques should be acknowledged. My assessment of Byron's "counter-heroic values," as Michael G. Cooke aptly terms them, is not unlike that which he puts forward in *The Blind Man Traces the Circle: On the Patterns and Philosophy of Byron's Poetry* (Princeton: Princeton Univ. Press, 1969), yet there is a substantial difference between a view of Byron as an ethical and philosophical poet, and a study which finds its inception in a certain psychological congeries.

7. I stress here the amplitude of Byron's revelation rather than any presumed adaptation. The polemics of Jacques Lacan and his followers against the conformist bias of American ego psychology are instructive; the contrasting mode of the French school is exemplified in Serge Leclaire, *Psychanalyser* (Paris: Editions du Seuil, 1968): "Au terme de l'analyse, le patient ne saura pas plus qui il est, mais seulement à quoi il est assujetti, de quel 'chiffre' . . . il est le répondant" (p. 174).

Chapter 1

1. An omnibus footnote will prevent cumbersome repetition. In addition to the works already cited, the following discussions are useful: W. P. Elledge, *Byron and the Dynamics of Metaphor* (Nashville: Vanderbilt Univ. Press, 1968); M. K. Joseph, *Byron The Poet* (London: Gollancz, 1964); Karl Kroeber, *Romantic Narrative Art* (1960; rpt. Madison: Univ. of Wisconsin Press, 1966); William H. Marshall, *The Structure of Byron's Major Poems* (Philadelphia: Univ. of Pennsylvania Press, 1962).

2. Byron's affair with Mrs. Spencer Smith is narrated in Marchand, 1: 199–228; 264–272.

3. "A Special Type of Choice of Object Made by Men," *The Standard Edition of the Complete Psychological Works of Sigmund Freud*, ed. James Strachey (London: The Hogarth Press, 1957), 11: 163–175. Hereafter cited as *Standard Edition*.

4. The fullest discussion of the revisions of *Childe Harold* is given by Jerome J. McGann in *Fiery Dust*.

5. Jerome J. McGann, *Fiery Dust*.

6. A corrective to Byron's view of Elgin is William St. Clair, *Lord Elgin and the Marbles* (London: Oxford Univ. Press, 1967).

7. Wingfield was thus celebrated as "Alonzo" in Byron's "Childish Recollections," *Poetry* 1: 96–97.

8. Byron's response to news of Edleston's death is given by Marchand, 1: 295–297.

9. The account of his mother's death is taken from Marchand, 1: 284–285.

10. Cited by Marchand, 1: 277.

11. The matriarchal dominance which Philip Slater shows in *The Glory of Hera* (1968; rpt. Boston: Beacon Press, 1971) to have been a pronounced element of classical Greek culture perhaps contributes to Byron's interest in Greece and brings these two statements together.

12. The additions are surveyed by Michael Sundell, "The Development of *The Giaour*," *SEL*, 9 (1969), 587–599.

13. In a note to line 690 E. H. Coleridge cites *Judges* V: 28. The parallel reinforces the threatening undertones of the scene: Sisera, defeated general of the forces of Jabin, is treacherously killed by a Kenite woman, Jael, with whom he had taken refuge. The conflation of the dangerous love object and the dominating mother is evident in line 699: "Why sends not the Bridegroom his promised gift?" The question seems more appropriate to Hassan's intended than to his mother: the momentary confusion it causes tends to blend the two figures.

14. Freud developed these assumptions in *The Interpretation of Dreams, Standard Edition*, vols. 4 and 5. See also the essays by Freud collected in *On Creativity and the Unconscious*, ed. Benjamin Nelson (New York: Harper, 1958).

15. Ernest J. Lovell, Jr., ed., *Medwin's "Conversations of Lord Byron"* (Princeton: Princeton Univ. Press, 1966), 55–57. Hereafter referred to as "Medwin."

16. Byron told Medwin: "I lost my father when I was only six years of age." In fact Byron was three and a half years old when his father died on August 2, 1791; the confusion in dates suggests repression and an unconscious desire to make their relationship more prolonged than it was.

17. Charles Brenner, *An Elementary Textbook of Psychoanalysis* (1955; rpt. Garden City: Doubleday, 1971), p. 117: "Indeed the period of life from about two and a half to six years is called the oedipal phase or the oedipal period as often as it is called the phallic stage or phase. The object relations which comprise the oedipus complex are of the greatest importance both to normal and to pathological mental development. Freud considered the events of this phase of life to be crucial, in fact (Freud, 1924a), and although we now know that still earlier events may be crucial to some individuals, so that the events of the oedipal period are of less importance in their lives than those of the pre-oedipal or prephallic period, it still seems probable that the events of the oedipal period are of crucial significance for most persons and of very great significance for nearly all." The essay referred to by Brenner is "The Passing of the Oedipus-complex," *Standard Edition*, 19. A full discussion of the oedipus-complex with the appropriate references may be found in Otto Fenichel, *The Psychoanalytic Theory of Neurosis* (New York: Norton, 1945), hereafter cited as "Fenichel."

18. See Fenichel, p. 94.

19. The relationship in Byron's mind between his title and the loss of his father is apparent in "Childish Recollections," *Poetry* 1: 95:

> Stern Death forbade my orphan youth to share
> The tender guidance of a Father's care;
> Can Rank, or e'en a Guardian's name supply
> The love, which glistens in a Father's eye?
> For this, can Wealth, or Title's sound atone,
> Made, by a Parent's early loss, my own?   (219–224)

The emphases in this passage are suggestive. Although "orphan" can be used to mean bereft of one parent only, it is in that case a strong term; those Byron calls orphans in *Don Juan*, Leila and Aurora, have lost both parents (but see Canto 17). Captain Byron, who never saw his son after he was two years and seven months old, was not the ideal father of this description. The distortions mark the intensity of Byron's feelings of deprivation.

20. Comparison of this scene with one of its precursors, the abandonment of Dido by Aeneas in *Aeneid* IV, points up the self-doubt of the Byronic hero.

21. Francesca's husband, Giovanni Malatesta, was a cripple; if Byron saw in him an image of his own physical defect it would have increased his interest in the story.

22. P. L. Thorslev, Jr., *The Byronic Hero: Types and Prototypes* (Minneapolis: Univ. of Minnesota Press, 1962). Byron's infusion into tradition of his own psychological imperatives is always a nice critical question. "This breathing world" in line 315, for example, is an echo of the opening soliloquy of Shakespeare's *Richard the Third* (I, i, 21): the deformed monarch is one of Byron's deepest identifications.

23. Cited by E. H. Coleridge, *Poetry* 3: 367–369.

24. Text as given by W. D. Ross, *Aristotle: Selections* (New York: Scribners, 1938), pp. 287–288.

Chapter 2

1. Cf. Paul West, *Byron and the Spoiler's Art* (London: Chatto and Windus, 1960): "Reduce everything Byron ever wrote, and you will find an essential act of repulsion: either self-emptying into a *persona,* or a repudiation" (p. 12).

2. Medwin, p. 194.

3. The "Epistle to Augusta", written at Diodati, begins with an apostrophe to "My Sister! my sweet Sister!" and continues with memories of Newstead:

7.
I feel almost at times as I have felt
In happy childhood; trees, and flowers, and brooks,
Which do remember me of where I dwelt,
Ere my young mind was sacrificed to books,
Come as of yore upon me, and can melt
My heart with recognition of their looks;
And even at moments I could think I see
Some living thing to love—but none like thee.
8.
Here are the Alpine landscapes which create
A fund for contemplation;—to admire
Is a brief feeling of a trivial date;
But something worthier do such scenes inspire:
Here to be lonely is not desolate,
For much I view which I could most desire,
And, above all, a Lake I could behold
Lovelier, not dearer, than our own of old.
9.
Oh that thou wert but with me!—but I grow

The fool of my own wishes, and forget
The solitude which I have vaunted so
Has lost its praise in this but one regret;
There may be others which I less may show;—
I am not of the plaintive mood, and yet
I feel an ebb in my philosophy,
And the tide rising in my altered eye.
                        10.
I did remind thee of our own dear Lake,
By the old Hall which may be mine no more.
Leman's is fair; but think not I forsake
The sweet remembrance of a dearer shore:
Sad havoc Time must with my memory make,
Ere that or thou can fade these eyes before;
Though, like all things which I have loved, they are
Resigned for ever, or divided far.
                        11.
The world is all before me; I but ask
Of Nature that with which she will comply—
It is but in her Summer's sun to bask,
To mingle with the quiet of her sky,
To see her gentle face without a mask,
And never gaze on it with apathy.
She was my early friend, and now shall be
My sister—till I look again on thee.

The long quotation is necessary to illustrate one of Byron's characteristic fusions. The address to Augusta seems to grow out of the recollections of "happy childhood" in stanza 7; the invocation of "our own" lake in stanza 8 thus seems to refer to a time spent with Augusta at Newstead before Byron's "mind was sacrificed to books"—that is, before his schooldays. The differences between the biographical evidence and the poetic creation illuminate a particular element of Byron's fictions. Marchand declares that Augusta "did not see her half-brother until he went to Harrow [April, 1801], and then only rarely" (*BLJ* 1: 273); he was then thirteen. Elsewhere Marchand comments that although their correspondence in 1804 presumes some previous meeting, it was "possibly during Byron's holidays spent in London" (1: 81). The first reference in Marchand placing Byron and Augusta together at Newstead occurs when they were snowbound there in January, 1814 (1: 432). The lines therefore both connect Byron's response to landscape with Augusta and reveal the earlier feelings invested in her: that Byron should have conflated his memories of childhood with those of his much later affair with Augusta is further confirmation of the argument of this chapter.

4. On this subject see Richard J. Onorato, *The Character of The Poet: Wordsworth in THE PRELUDE* (Princeton: Princeton Univ. Press, 1971).

5. E.g., stanza 113: "I have not loved the World, nor the World me; / I have not flattered its rank breath," to which E. H. Coleridge compares *Coriolanus:*

"For the mutable, rank-scented many, let them/ Regard me as I do not flatter" (III, i, 66–67).

6. *Poetry*, 4: 82.

7. *The Romantic Ventriloquists* (Seattle: Univ. of Washington Press, 1963).

8. *Byron: A Critical Study* (1961; rpt. Edinburgh: Oliver and Boyd, 1965), pp. 89–90.

9. E.g., David Eggenschwiler, "The Tragic and Comic Rhythms of *Manfred*," *SiR* 13 (1974), 63–77.

10. See K. M. Luke, "Lord Byron's *Manfred*: A Study of Alienation from Within," *UTQ*, 40 (1970), 15–26.

11. A paraphrase of Harold Bloom, *The Visionary Company*, rev. and enl. edition (Ithaca: Cornell Univ. Press, 1971), p. 252.

12. The most comprehensive discussion of Byron's treatment of nature in *Manfred* is that of E. J. Lovell, Jr., "The Wordsworthian Note and the Byronic Hero," *Byron: The Record of a Quest* (1949; rpt. Hamden, Conn.: Archon, 1966).

13. For example, by E. J. Lovell in the work just cited: "This is, of course, pictorial composition with the emphasis on the picturesque as it was understood by Byron" (p. 177). G. Wilson Knight is an exception; although his cryptic comment does not explore the significance of the passage, he pointed to it as long ago as 1939 in "The Two Eternities": "the phrases go deep into the acceptances and revolts of Byron's work." The essay is reprinted as "Byron: The Poetry, " in *Poets of Action* (London: Methuen, 1967), p. 199.

14. Noted by Bostetter, p. 275, and Gleckner, p. 232.

15. The original third act is printed in *Poetry* 4: 121–130. The two versions are compared by M. H. Butler, "An Examination of Byron's Revisions of *Manfred*, Act III, " *SP*, 60 (1963), 627–636.

16. For example, Ward Pafford, "Byron and the Mind of Man: *Childe Harold* III–IV and *Manfred*," *SiR*, 1 (1962), 105–127. Yet in "Byron's *Manfred* and Zoroastrianism," *JEGP*, 57 (1958), 726–738, M. J. Quinlan points out that Astarte, a deity of the early Canaanites, was both bride and mother of Tammuz: the name of this incestuous goddess of sexual love is appropriate for the sister Manfred loves. Quinlan believes that Byron did not have the pagan figure in mind, but took the name rather from Montesquiou's *Persian Letters*, where it is found in a loving brother-sister relationship; the maternal aspects, however, are also relevant. Quinlan notes too that "Ashtaroth," the demon who carries off the Abbot in the original third act, is a variant form of "Astarte," inferring therefrom that Byron must have been ignorant of that fact; it would be a nice touch, however, and consistent with his characteristic patterns, if Byron had used a representative of female sexuality to overcome the

chief male authority of his drama. P. L. Thorslev, Jr., discusses the range of the incest motif in "Incest as Romantic Symbol," *CLS* 2 (1965), 41–58.

17. The incantation was published before the drama, on December 5, 1816. Leslie Marchand has challenged the assumption that it reflects Byron's sense of guilt, arguing in *Byron's Poetry* (Boston: Houghton Mifflin, 1965) that it is "obviously directed" against Lady Byron (p. 77). The allusions to the "brotherhood of Cain," however, seem to suggest a male rather than a female subject.

18. *The Blind Man Traces the Circle*, p. 65.

19. On the connection between this phenomenon and "identity diffusion," a useful term for consideration of *Manfred*, see Erik H. Erikson, "The Problem of Ego Identity," *Identity and the Life Cycle.*

20. The allusions to *Hamlet* are especially suggestive in the light of the oedipal content found there by Freud and Ernest Jones, *Hamlet and Oedipus* (1949; rpt. Garden City: Doubleday, 1954).

21. *Byron and the Dynamics of Metaphor*, pp. 81–94.

22. The terms are drawn from Margaret S. Mahler. The most inclusive theoretical statement of her work is to be found in Margaret S. Mahler, Fred Pine, and Anni Bergman, *The Psychological Birth of the Human Infant* (New York: Basic Books, 1975).

23. Use is made here of the work of D. W. Winnicott on early parent-infant relations, particularly "Mirror-role of Mother and Family in Child Development," *Playing and Reality*, and of the concept of the *stade du miroir* in the thought of Jacques Lacan, whose theoretical speculations here Winnicott's observations corroborate: see *The Language of the Self*, tr. Anthony Wilden (1968; rpt. New York: Delta, 1975).

24. This account converges with that of Stuart M. Sperry, "Byron and the Meaning of *Manfred*," *Criticism*, 16 (1974), 189–202, insofar as the play is seen as "Byron's confrontation with his own persona, his latent realization of the danger of personal domination by the character of his own creating." Sperry's essay is one of the best the play has received, but it is perhaps slightly idealizing. *Manfred* is not quite *"Man Freed"* or "Byron's renunciation" of his Titanic hero, as Sperry suggests: while Byron's exposure of his hero undoubtedly points in that direction, his psychological victories were never that clear-cut.

25. Medwin, p. 70. Byron's murmuring against the influence "all women" gained over him is a representative instance of the fear of maternal dominance that runs throughout his life. Compare the remark of his valet Fletcher about his marriage: "It is very odd, but I never yet knew a lady that could not manage my Lord, *except* my Lady" (quoted by Marchand, 2: 547).

26. Marchand, 1: 404n. John S. Chapman, in *Byron and the Honourable Mrs. Leigh* (New Haven: Yale Univ. Press, 1975), has queried this conclusion, but his reconsideration seems insufficient to reverse the consensus. It is, in any event, the *image* that Byron constructed out of Augusta and earlier strata which matters to his poetry, and its significance cannot be approached through literal facts alone.

27. Moore's recollection of Byron's burnt *Memoirs,* quoted by Marchand, 2: 505. Byron's fatalistic sense that he would repeat the conduct of his father is apparent in a confession made years later to Medwin, part of which has already been quoted: "I was not so young when my father died, but that I perfectly remember him; and had very early a horror of matrimony, from the sight of domestic broils: this feeling came over me very strongly at my wedding. Something whispered me that I was sealing my own death-warrant" (p. 55).

28. It is impossible to fix the precise degree of consciousness that attends this process. The exigencies of discursive prose must on occasion lead me to seem to attribute intentionality to Byron when such an inference is, at best, moot. I have treated the problem as delicately as I know how.

29. The typological aspects are discussed by Jerome J. McGann in *Fiery Dust,* pp. 40–49.

30. Princess Charlotte died November 6, 1817; for a full discussion of the addition of the stanzas to *Childe Harold* IV, see *Fiery Dust.*

31. Quoted in *Poetry* 2: 315.

32. Well discussed in *Romantic Narrative Art,* pp. 145–146.

33. Given by Marchand, 2: 708.

34. It is uncertain whether Byron knew the story recounted by Coleridge (*Poetry* 4: 202) of the historical Mazeppa's *affaire du coeur* while in his sixties with his god-daughter; it is so consonant with his own themes that it would surely have reinforced his interest.

Chapter 3

1. Byron's plays and their relation to the theater of his day are discussed by Samuel Chew, *The Dramas of Lord Byron* (1915; rpt. New York: Russell and Russell, 1964). In addition to the essay by G. Wilson Knight already cited the

reader should consult his chapter on Byron in *The Golden Labyrinth* (New York: Norton, 1962). Michael G. Cooke, W. P. Elledge, R. F. Gleckner, M. K. Joseph, Jerome J. McGann, and Paul West all have chapters on the plays in their studies of Byron.

2. Byron's ambivalence toward the stage of his day is explored by David Erdman, "Byron's Stage Fright," *ELH*, 6 (1939), 219–245. The attraction of Kean is set forth in my "Edmund Kean and Byron's Plays," *KSJ*, 21–22 (1972–1973), 188–206.

3. George M. Ridenour analyzes Byron's employment of Pegasus similes in *The Style of DON JUAN*, Yale Studies in English, No. 144 (New Haven: Yale Univ. Press, 1960).

4. Byron the pure, controlled neoclassical poet is another of his ideal visions of himself, but the question of his neoclassicism has been much mooted: e.g., William Calvert, *Byron: Romantic Paradox* (1935; rpt. New York: Russell and Russell, 1962). A thorough survey of the reputation of the Augustans in the Romantic period may be found in Upali Amarasinghe, *Dryden and Pope in the Early Nineteenth Century* (Cambridge: Cambridge Univ. Press, 1962). There is a good article on the form of the dramas by James R. Thompson, "Byron's Plays and *Don Juan*: Genre and Myth," *Bucknell Review*, 15, No. 3 (Dec. 1967), 22–38.

5. See E. D. H. Johnson, "A Political Interpretation of Byron's *Marino Faliero*," *MLQ*, 3 (1942), 417–425, and T. L. Ashton, "*Marino Faliero*: Byron's 'Poetry of Politics,'" *SiR*, 13 (1974), 1–13.

6. *Romanticism and Revolt: Europe 1815–1848* (New York: Harcourt, 1967), p. 9.

7. Not the opinion of Chew: "Byron is thoroughly in sympathy with the conspirators; here, as always, he is the poet of revolution" (p. 91). The manuscript, now in the Pierpont Morgan Library, New York, makes clear that the last scene, implying the justice of Faliero's cause, was an afterthought on Byron's part, and it remains unintegrated in the play.

8. One might note in this connection that in 1819 a performance of Alfieri's *Mirra*, a tragedy concerning a daughter's incestuous love for her father, threw Byron "into convulsions.—I do not mean by that word—a lady's hysterics—but the agony of reluctant tears—and the choaking shudder which I do not often undergo for fiction" (*BLJ* 6: 206). Two weeks later he was still complaining that he had "never been quite well since the night of the representation of Alfieri's Mirra" (*BLJ* 6: 217).

9. *LJ* 5: 95. Cited in *Poetry* 4: 366n.

10. Byron wrote Moore, September 19, 1818: "I could have forgiven the dagger or the bowl, any thing, but the deliberate desolation piled upon me, when I stood alone upon my hearth, with my household gods shivered around me"

(*BLJ* 6: 69). Compare the description of Don José's plight in *Don Juan:* "It was a trying moment that which found him/ Standing alone beside his desolate hearth,/ Where all his household gods lay shivered round him" (I, 36). The closeness of Byron and José is discussed in Chapter 5.

11. "Byron and the Byronic in History," introduction to *The Selected Letters of Lord Byron* (New York: Farrar, 1953), p. xiv.

12. Byron's habitual self-presentation in Shakespearean terms is traced by G. Wilson Knight, *Byron and Shakespeare* (London: Routledge and Kegan Paul, 1966).

13. *Marino Faliero* appeared April 25 amidst a flurry of injunctions against performance issued by the Lord Chancellor and protesting handbills distributed in the theater by Murray. The play had been severely cut to bring it within the acting time; the *Times* commented: "we have said that Lord Byron's *tragedy* was performed, but we ought rather to have stated, that fragments, violently torn from that noble work, were presented to the audience." Byron's opposition had relented only once, when he wistfully expressed the hope that Drury Lane "might have the grace to wait for Kean's return" from America before attempting production (*LJ* 5: 278); by the time he wrote, however, the role had already been entrusted to Cooper. The *European Magazine and London Review* commented that he "did his best in a part quite out of his line, but Macready and Kean are the only two who could do it justice." Byron understandably described the treatment of his play less charitably: "the manner in which it was got up was shameful! All the declamatory parts were left, all the dramatic ones struck out; and Cooper, the new actor, was the murderer of the whole" (Medwin, p. 120). For a full account of the first production, drawing upon the acting copy of the play now in the Huntington Library, see T. L. Ashton, "The Censorship of Byron's *Marino Faliero,*" *HLQ,* 36 (1972), 27–44.

14. Medwin, p. 135.

15. Two examples of his identification with the Roman chosen from many in his letters will suffice. In 1814 Byron echoes Coriolanus in order to declare his independence of popularity (*BLJ* 4: 61): "I have never courted it, nor, I may add, in the general sense of the word, enjoyed it—and 'there is a world elsewhere!'" (*Coriolanus,* III, iii, 133). Years later Coriolanus's distaste for the plebeians serves as the model for his own expression of integrity (*BLJ* 6: 105–106): "I have not written for their pleasure;—if they are pleased—it is that they chose to be so,—I have never flattered their opinions—nor their pride—nor will I.—Neither will I make 'Ladies books' *'al dilettar le femine e la plebe'* —I have written from the fullness of my mind, from passion—from impulse—from many motives—but not for their 'sweet voices'" (*Coriolanus,* II, iii, 107).

16. The phrase is Michael Cooke's; he compares *Marino Faliero* to *Venice Preserved* in "The Restoration Ethos of Byron's Classical Plays," *PMLA,* 79 (1964),

569–579. Byron's specific debts to *Venice Preserved* include the tolling bell in Act IV and Calendaro's spitting at Bertram.

17. Teresa's account may conveniently be found in *His Very Self and Voice: Collected Conversations of Lord Byron*, ed. E. J. Lovell, Jr. (New York: Macmillan, 1954), pp. 247–248.

18. In the article just cited he argues that the same "special honor-in-love is reserved for the lovers" in both plays. A view nearer my own is that of Robert Fricker, "Shakespeare und das Englische Romantische Drama," *Shakespeare Jahrbuch*, 95 (1959), 63–82.

19. See, for example. E. H. Coleridge's comment on the word "pavilion" and the allusion to the "Queen's wrongs" in I, ii: "Unquestionably if the play had been put on stage at this time, the pit and gallery would have applauded the sentiment to the echo. There was, too, but one 'pavilion' in 1821, and that was not on the banks of the Euphrates, but at Brighton" *(Poetry* 5: 15 n. 1).

20. Semiramis is so styled as early as I, i, 43; in contrast, Beleses calls the king *"she* Sardanapalus" (II, i, 404). In "Byron: The Poetry" G. Wilson Knight argues for the ideal bisexuality of the monarch, but I am unpersuaded by his assertion that "Sardanapalus is conceived as, in essence, a saint" (p. 228).

21. Jerome J. McGann notes the ominous implications of this condensation, but the perspective in which he views Sardanapalus, indicated by the title of his essay, "The Prince of Peace," is, like Knight's, one which I cannot share.

22. Paul West believes that Foscari "takes a poisoned cup from Loredano, the most vindictive of the plotters, and dies instantly" *(Byron and the Spoiler's Art*, p. 101), but whether the Doge dies from grief or from poison seems indeterminable.

Chapter 4

1. The intellectual background of *Cain* is surveyed by M. K. Joseph, *Byron The Poet*, pp. 116–125. A brief account of the pamphlets and lawsuits provoked by *Cain* and a list of reviews is given in *Poetry* 5: 202–204; a fuller discussion may be found in R. W. Babcock, "The Inception and Reception of Byron's *Cain*," *SAQ*, 26 (1927), 178–189. This material has been collected in the edition of the drama by T. G. Steffan: *Lord Byron's CAIN* (Austin: Univ. of Texas Press, 1969). See also Murray Roston, *Biblical Drama in England* (London: Faber and Faber, 1968), pp. 198–215.

2. On Byron's ironic mode in this play see Leonard Michaels, "Byron's *Cain,*" *PMLA,* 84 (1969), 71–79. Michaels' point, however, that Cain becomes the Cain of legend, as if acting out a pre-existent criminal fate, can be put in deeper psychoanalytic terms: cf. Freud's "Criminality from a Sense of Guilt," Part III of "Some Character-Types Met With in Psycho-Analytic Work," *Standard Edition* 14: 332–336, conveniently reprinted in *On Creativity and the Unconscious.*

3. The idealism is unquestioningly endorsed by Samuel Chew (*The Dramas of Lord Byron,* p. 133): "On the one hand is verity and freedom, accompanied by hardship and perhaps despair, on the other placid conformity, submission to comfortable illusion at the sacrifice of intellectual freedom. Cain's choice is Byron's choice. He exhibits the same integrity, candor, and 'fierce intrepid scorn of compromise and comfort,' which informs the poetry of Byron with its 'splendid and imperishable excellence of sincerity and strength.' Is not this the final message of *Cain?* Is it not an inspiring one?"

4. The Biblical account (King James version) is as follows: "And Cain said unto the LORD, My punishment *is* greater than I can bear. Behold, thou hast driven me out this day from the face of the earth; and from thy face shall I be hid; and I shall be a fugitive and a vagabond in the earth; and it shall come to pass, *that* every one that findeth me shall slay me. And the LORD said unto him, Therefore, whosoever slayeth Cain, vengeance shall be taken on him sevenfold. And the LORD set a mark upon Cain, lest any finding him should kill him. And Cain went out from the presence of the LORD, and dwelt in the land of Nod, on the east of Eden" (Genesis IV: 13–16).

5. Letter of April 10, 1822; quoted in *Poetry* 5: 204.

6. Jerome J. McGann rates the play more highly: see the essay "Contentious Worlds" in *Fiery Dust.*

7. Given by Medwin, p. 157.

8. Medwin, p. 258.

9. Medwin, p. 258. The 1815 draft is printed in *Poetry* 5: 453–466.

10. The stage history was first presented by T. H. Vail Motter, "Byron's *Werner* Re-estimated," *Essays in Dramatic Literature,* ed. Hardin Craig (Princeton: Princeton Univ. Press, 1935). Macready gave the first performance of *Werner* in England on January 25, 1830, and it remained a prominent feature of his repertory until his retirement in 1851. It was his fifth most frequently performed role in London, and in the provinces where his spectacular Shakespearean productions were unfeasible the proportion was probably higher. Dickens and G. H. Lewes thought Werner the foremost of his interpretations, and in 1850 the *Theatrical Journal* placed it at the head of his roles listed "in order of excellence." Macready, however, damagingly ex-

panded the lachrymose elements of the drama in order to capitalize on his forte—the expression of domestic tenderness. The *Examiner* neatly and approvingly epitomized his emphasis, which was scarcely the author's: "Byron makes us think only of the *theft of a purse;* Macready of the *love of a father.*" Alan Downer discusses this sentimental interpretation in *The Eminent Tragedian* (Cambridge: Harvard Univ. Press, 1966). Samuel Phelps also played *Werner* in the provinces at the outset of his career, and produced it during eleven of his eighteen seasons as manager at Sadler's Wells. One is intrigued to discover, considering the themes of the drama, that Phelps chose it to introduce his son Edmund to London audiences in 1860 as Ulric to his own Werner. Phelps's career is considered by Shirley Seifried Allen, *Samuel Phelps and Sadler's Wells Theatre* (Middletown, Conn.: Wesleyan Univ. Press, 1971). The last actor to take up the drama was Henry Irving, who appeared once as Werner on June 1, 1887, in a benefit for Westland Marston. Irving employed a four-act redaction by Frank Marshall, retaining the mawkish interpolations of Macready and destroying the suspense by depicting Ulric's murder of Stralenheim.

11. *Standard Edition* 11: 172–173.

12. Medwin, p. 260.

13. Discussed in the next chapter, pp. 189–190.

14. A description of his childhood recorded in 1823 by Lady Blessington emphasizes the autobiographical components Byron reworked in *The Deformed Transformed.* I quote from *Lady Blessington's "Conversations of Lord Byron"*, ed. E. J. Lovell, Jr. (Princeton: Princeton Univ. Press, 1969): "'My poor mother was generally in a rage every day, and used to render me sometimes almost frantic; particularly when, in her passion, she reproached me with my personal deformity, I have left her presence to rush into solitude, where, unseen, I could vent the rage and mortification I endured, and curse the deformity that I now began to consider as a signal mark of the injustice of Providence. Those were bitter moments: even now, the impression of them is vivid in my mind; and they cankered a heart that I believe was naturally affectionate, and destroyed a temper always disposed to be violent. It was my feelings at this period that suggested the idea of "The Deformed Transformed.'"... As Byron had said that his own position had led to his writing 'The Deformed Transformed,' I ventured to remind him that, in the advertisement to that drama, he had stated it to have been founded on the novel of 'The Three Brothers.' He said that both statements were correct, and then changed the subject...." (pp. 80–81). Elizabeth French Boyd, *Byron's DON JUAN* (1945; rpt. New York: Humanities Press, 1958), p. 172 n. 107, directs the reader to the *Autobiography of John Galt* (London: Cochrane and M'Crone, 1833), II, 355–367, for a comparison between Pickersgill's novel and Byron's play. See also the next note.

15. See the article by Charles Robinson, "The Devil as Doppelgänger in *The Deformed Transformed*," *BNYPL*, 74 (1970), 177–202. Interesting light is shed by

the celebrated essay of Otto Rank, *The Double,* trans. Harry Tucker, Jr. (Chapel Hill: Univ. of North Carolina Press, 1971).

Chapter 5

1. *Standard Edition* 12: 150–151.

2. The relationship between repetition and recollection is described by Kierkegaard on the first page of *Repetition,* his "essay in experimental psychology": "repetition and recollection are the same movement, only in opposite directions; for what is recollected has been, is repeated backwards, whereas repetition properly so called is recollected forwards" (*Repetition,* trans. Walter Lowrie [1941; rpt. New York: Harper, 1964], p. 33).

3. The resentments emerge openly in Byron's comment to Murray on the "Remarks on *Don Juan*" in *Blackwood's Edinburgh Magazine*: "Your Blackwood accuses me of treating women harshly—it may be so—but I have been their martyr.—My whole life has been sacrificed *to* them and *by* them" (*BLJ* 6: 257). His anger at the review eventually spilled over into a formal reply, "Some Observations upon an article in Blackwood's Magazine" (*LJ* 4: 474–495).

Psychoanalytically-oriented criticism is no novelty in the history of responses to *Don Juan,* and it is prefigured in the earliest (and usually nastiest) evaluations by Byron's contemporaries. The treatment of Byron by Arthur Wormhoudt in *The Demon Lover* (1949; rpt. Freeport, New York: Books for Libraries Press, 1968) is insufficiently responsive to the complexities and particularities of literature; more sensitive and informative is Mabel P. Worthington, "Byron's *Don Juan*: Certain Psychological Aspects," *Literature and Psychology,* 7 (1957), 50–56.

Freud's essay "Creative Writers and Day-Dreaming," *Standard Edition* 9: 142–153 (reprinted in *On Creativity and the Unconscious*), illuminates Byron's presentation of himself and his life through Juan, José, and Inez: "We may say that [a phantasy] hovers, as it were, between three times—the three moments of time which our ideation involves. Mental work is linked to some current impression, some provoking occasion in the present which has been able to arouse one of the subject's major wishes. From there it harks back to the memory of an earlier experience (usually an infantile one) in which this wish was fulfilled; and it now creates a situation relating to the future which represents a fulfilment of the wish. What it thus creates is a day-dream or phantasy, which carries about it traces of its origin from the occasion which provoked it and from the memory. Thus past, present and future are strung together, as it were, on the thread of the wish that runs through them" (pp. 147–148).

4. A substantial gathering of Don Juaniana, usefully presented, is *The Theatre of Don Juan,* ed. Oscar Mandel (Lincoln: Univ. of Nebraska Press, 1963). See also Leo Weinstein, *The Metamorphoses of Don Juan,* Stanford Studies in Language and Literature, No. 18 (1959; rpt. New York: AMS Press, 1967). F. L. Beaty discusses pantomime versions of the legend Byron might have known in "Harlequin Don Juan," *JEGP,* 67 (1968), 395–405.

5. This point will be resumed in a consideration of Byron's imagery in Chapter 7.

6. *Anatomy of Criticism* (Princeton: Princeton Univ. Press, 1957), p. 44.

7. Harold Bloom, for example: "Byron's paradoxes concerning sexual love are shallow, and finally irksome. It is not enlightening to be told that 'pleasure's a sin, and sometimes sin's a pleasure'" (*The Visionary Company,* p. 261).

8. Neuha's miraculous preservation of Torquil in the secret grotto in *The Island* is a still more striking presentation of Byron's characteristic pattern, but this late work (1823), while corroborating the speculations of this study, is less compelling than Byron's other narratives. On this tale, however, see Bernard Blackstone, "The Pilgrim of Eternity," *The Lost Travellers* (London: Longman's, 1962), and Robert D. Hume, "*The Island* and the Evolution of Byron's 'Tales,'" *Romantic and Victorian,* eds. W. P. Elledge and R. L. Hoffman (Rutherford: Fairleigh Dickinson Univ. Press, 1971).

9. The phrase is from *Beppo* (40). Byron described his training as a *cavalier servente* to Hoppner: "I am drilling very hard to learn how to double a shawl, and should succeed to admiration if I did not always double it the wrong side out; and then I sometimes confuse and bring away two, so as to put all the *Serventi* out, beside keeping their *Servite* in the cold till every body can get back their property. But it is a dreadfully moral place, for you must not look at anybody's wife except your neighbour's,—if you go to the next door but one, you are scolded, and presumed to be perfidious. And then a *relazione* or an *amicizia* seems to be a regular affair of from five to fifteen years, at which period, if there occur a widowhood, it finishes by a *sposalizio;* and in the mean time it has so many rules of its own, that it is not much better. A man actually becomes a piece of female property . . ." (*LJ* 4: 400–401). Three months earlier he had complained to Hobhouse: "I am not tired of Italy—but a man must be a Cicisbeo and a singer in duets and a Connoisseur of opera—or nothing here—I have made some progress in all these accomplishments—but I can't say that I don't feel the degradation.—Better be a[n] unskilful planter—an awkward settler—better be a hunter—or anything than a flatterer of fiddlers—and a fan-carrier of a woman.—I like women—God he knows—but the more their system here develops upon me—the worse it seems—after Turkey too—here the *polygamy* is all on the female side.—I have been an intriguer, a husband, and now I am a Cavalier Servente.—by the holy! it is a strange sensation" (*BLJ* 6: 226).

10. And yet one should not ignore the literary sources of Byron's typical configuration. F. L. Beaty, "Byron's Imitations of Juvenal and Persius," *SiR,*

15 (1976), 333–355, notes the similarity of this scene to the portrait of the lustful Messalina in Juvenal's Satire X, and suggests that Byron was indebted to the commentary of the Rev. Martin Madan, *A New and Literal Translation of Juvenal and Persius; with Copious Explanatory Notes,* which Byron seems to have drawn on also in depicting Johnson. For a discussion of the allusive texture of Byron's language, see Chapter 6.

11. Dudù of course vanishes before she can become threatening.

12. Medwin, p. 101.

13. Leila is referred to as an infant at VIII, 96 and 102; X, 51, 55, and 75; and XII, 41—more than half the occurrences of the word in the poem. Byron's ambivalence towards sexual relationships with women is seen in XIV, 93: "No friend like to a woman Earth discovers,/ So that you have not been nor will be lovers." The same sentiment is expressed in a letter to Lady Hardy: "I have always laid it down as a maxim, and found it justified by experience, that a man and a woman make far better friendships than can exist between two of the same sex; but *these* with this condition, that they never have made, or are to make, love with each other. Lovers may, and, indeed, generally *are* enemies, but they never can be friends; because there must always be a spice of jealousy and something of self in all their speculations" (*LJ* 6: 137).

14. Medwin, p. 165.

15. One wonders, upon learning in the same stanza that Inez has married again, whether she has gained her ends and snared Alfonso after all.

16. Byron wrote Murray in 1821: "I meant to have made him a *Cavalier Servente* in Italy, and a cause for a divorce in England, and a Sentimental 'Werther-faced man' in Germany, so as to show the different ridicules of the society in each of those countries, and to have displayed him gradually *gâté* and *blasé* as he grew older, as is natural" (*LJ* 5:24).

17. *Four Archetypes,* trans. R. F. C. Hull (Princeton: Princeton Univ. Press, 1970), pp. 19–21. Extracted from Vol. 9, Part I, of Bollingen Series XX, *The Collected Works of C. G. Jung,* ed. Herbert Read, Michael Fordham, and Gerald Adler. The essay develops and places in a more hopeful light the analysis made by Freud in "A Special Type of Choice of Object Made by Men."

Chapter 6

1. "The Augustan Mode of English Poetry," *Hateful Contraries* (Lexington: Univ. of Kentucky Press, 1965).

2. There has been much debate over the transformations of the Augustan mode in the later eighteenth century. Some provocative studies: B. H. Bronson, "The Pre-Romantic or Post-Augustan Mode," *ELH,* 20 (1953), 15–28; Ian Watt, "Two Historical Aspects of the Augustan Tradition," *Studies in the Eighteenth Century,* ed. R. F. Brissenden (Canberra: Australian National Univ. Press, 1968); W. J. Bate, *The Burden of the Past and the English Poet* (Cambridge: Harvard Univ. Press, 1970).

3. The time of the narrator writing is also occasionally different from the time of the narrator experiencing: e.g., I, 59.

4. An omnibus note here will serve to indicate works which have contributed to the assumptions of this chapter. This point is made about the writing of history by R. G. Collingwood, *The Idea of History* (1946; rpt. New York: Oxford Univ. Press, 1970). It is also often observed about time in *Remembrance of Things Past,* and I have found fertile stimulus to thinking about Byron from much criticism of Proust, notably Samuel Beckett, *Proust* (1931; rpt. New York: Grove Press, n.d.), Leo Bersani, *Marcel Proust: The Fictions of Life and Art* (New York: Oxford Univ. Press, 1965), and Germaine Brée, *Marcel Proust and Deliverance From Time,* trans. C. J. Richards and A. D. Truitt (1955; rpt. New York: Grove Press, n.d.). See also the essay by Paul de Man, "The Rhetoric of Temporality," *Interpretation: Theory and Practice,* ed. Charles S. Singleton (Baltimore: Johns Hopkins Univ. Press, 1969).

5. The relationship of *Don Juan* to previous epics is discussed by Brian Wilkie, *Romantic Poets and Epic Tradition* (Madison: Univ. of Wisconsin Press, 1965), John Lauber, "*Don Juan* as Anti-Epic," *SEL,* 8 (1968), 607–621, and Arthur D. Kahn, "Byron's 'Single Difference' with Homer and Virgil—The Redefinition of the Epic in *Don Juan,*" *Arcadia,* 5 (1970), 143–162. The doubleness of Byron's stance toward the literary matrix from which he develops his meaning has nonetheless been insufficiently appreciated; even G. M. Ridenour, who, in *The Style of DON JUAN,* better than any other has revealed the elaborate networks of metaphor that organize the poem, underestimates the function of allusion.

A model study of the functions of allusion is Herman Meyer, *The Poetics of Quotation in the European Novel,* trans. Theodore and Yetta Ziolkowski (Princeton: Princeton Univ. Press, 1968).

6. *N&Q,* NS. No. 14 (1967), 302–303; supplemented in NS. No. 17 (1970), 385.

7. These stanzas are extensively analyzed by Ridenour.

8. Text as given in *Paradise Lost,* ed. Merritt Hughes (New York: Odyssey Press, 1935). Other echoes of Milton's lines occur in I, 123:

> 'T is sweet to be awakened by the lark,
> Or lulled by falling waters; sweet the hum
> Of bees, the voice of girls, the song of birds,
> The lisp of children, and their earliest words.

9. The most accessible modern editions: *Poetry* 6; L. I. Bredvold, ed., *Lord Byron: Don Juan and Other Satirical Poems* (New York: Odyssey Press, 1935); Leslie Marchand, ed., *Don Juan* (Boston: Houghton, 1958); Paul Elmer More, ed., *Complete Poetical Works of Byron* (1905; rpt. Cambridge: Houghton, 1952); *Byron: Poetical Works*, ed. Frederick Page, new ed. corr. John Jump (New York: Oxford Univ. Press, 1972); T. G. Steffan and W. W. Pratt, eds., *Byron's DON JUAN: A Variorum Edition*, 2nd. ed. (Austin: Univ. of Texas Press, 1971); T. G. Steffan, E. Steffan, and W. W. Pratt, eds., *Lord Byron: Don Juan* (Baltimore: Penguin, 1973).

The relationship of Byron and Milton is studied by Jerome J. McGann, "Milton and Byron," *KSMB*, 25 (1974), 9–25.

10. Discussed by Wilkie in the study cited above.

11. "Epistle to Burlington," 150. Unannotated in the first edition, but picked up by most subsequent ones, including *Poetry* 6: 358 n. 2.

12. VI, 293–294. See the commentary on this line in *The Odyssey of Homer*, ed., Maynard Mack, in *The Twickenham Edition of the Poems of Alexander Pope*, 9 (London: Methuen, 1967), 225.

13. Some of these parallels are briefly noted by Bernard Blackstone in "Guilt and Retribution in Byron's Sea Poems," *RES*, 2 (1961), 58–69, reprinted in *Byron: A Collection of Critical Essays*, ed. Paul West (Englewood Cliffs: Prentice-Hall, 1963). E. J. Lovell commented in reviewing that volume: "In Blackstone's view, finally, Lambro becomes 'this Old Man of the Sea,' and at the end of the episode, 'We are in the midst of complex Fall symbolism: the Old Man of the Sea [Proteus] is Ulysses, is God the Father, is also Satan,' entering Eden while the lovers sleep. This is interesting, to consider only one aspect of it, for if Lambro is Ulysses come home, then Blackstone's 'maternal' Haidée must be his wife and Juan the successful suitor is in love with his mother, which makes him Oedipus. 'Sed veritati interea invigilandum est, modusque servandus, ut certa ab incertis, diem a nocte, distinguamus'" (*KSJ*, 14 [1965], 90). The eclectic critic here seems closer to the mark than the distinguished editor.

14. Byron's relationship to the speculative mythography of his day is an area deserving exploration. See on the general subject Edward B. Hungerford, *The Shores of Darkness* (1941; rpt. Cleveland: World Publishing Co., 1963), and Earl Wasserman, *Shelley's PROMETHEUS UNBOUND* (Baltimore: Johns Hopkins Univ. Press, 1965). The myth of Prometheus in the Romantic Period is discussed by Harold Bloom, "Napoleon and Prometheus," *YFS*, 26 (1960–1961), 79–83; Albert Guerard, Jr., "Prometheus and the Aeolian Lyre," *YR*, 33 (1943–1944), 482–497; and Christian Kreutz, *Das Prometheussymbol In Der Englischen Romantik* (Gottingen, 1963). The myth is the subject of a brilliant monograph by C. Kerenyi, *Prometheus: Archetypal Image of Human Existence*, trans. Ralph Manheim (New York: Bollingen/Pantheon, 1963).

15. The progressive interpretation Ridenour gives these lines in his excellent discussion underestimates Byron's melancholy: "In his [Byron's] eyes gas

and steam and turn-tables are legitimate and even important means for the diminution of the traces of Original Sin.' They are civilization's way of contending with and rising above a fallen nature. Scientific advance of the kind represented by Newton is 'A thing to counterbalance human woes'" (*The Style of DON JUAN*, p. 31).

16. *The Visionary Company*, p. 262.

17. *Politics In English Romantic Poetry* (Cambridge: Harvard Univ. Press, 1970), chapter 1.

Chapter 7

1. The terms are those of Barbara Herrnstein Smith, *Poetic Closure* (Chicago: Univ. of Chicago Press, 1968).

2. The poem's first readers would of course have encountered Cantos I and II in isolation, since Canto III was not published until more than two years later.

3. Michael G. Cooke, in an essay which appeared just as this manuscript was completed, reaches conclusions parallel to my own from a more formalist perspective: "Byron's *Don Juan:* The Obsession and Self-Discipline of Spontaneity," *SiR*, 14 (1975), 285–302.

4. The variant readings emphasize the genital pun: "Man's pensive part is (now and then) the head,/ Woman's the heart or anything instead" (*Poetry* 6: 269, i).

5. Another example chosen from many of Byron's use of ocean imagery to characterize women is the description of the "amphibious sort of harlot" (XII, 62), the English tease:

> Such is your cold coquette, who can't say "No,"
> And won't say "Yes," and keeps you on and off-ing
> On a lee shore, till it begins to blow—
> Then sees your heart wrecked, with an inward scoffing.
> (XII, 63)

Consider also the description of Gulbeyaz's anger: "A storm it raged, and like the storm it passed" (V, 137). Behind these furies stands Byron's memory of his mother's bouts of temper; the imagery is so unremarkable that one should not base too much on it, but it is the same Byron employed to describe Mrs. Byron to Augusta: "The more I see of her the more my dislike augments nor can I so entirely conquer the appearance of it, as to prevent her from perceiving my opinion, this so far from calming the Gale, blows it into a *hurricane,* which threatens to destroy every thing, till exhausted by its own violence, it is lulled into a sullen torpor, which, after a short period, is again roused into fresh and renewed phrenzy, to me most terrible, and to every other Spectator astonishing" (*BLJ* 1: 75–76).

6. *Webster's New International Dictionary,* 2nd. edition, gives this definition of "Pinchbeck": "After the inventor, Christopher *Pinchbeck,* a London watchmaker. *a* An alloy of copper and zinc, used to imitate gold in cheap jewelry, etc. It ordinarily contains 10–15 per cent of zinc. *b* Hence, that which is counterfeit or spurious."

7. Even after one makes due allowance for the vast difference in tone and cause there remains an interesting relationship between the structure of *Don Juan* and the nontheological *aeternitas* sought by other Romantics, best expressed by Coleridge: "The common end of all *narrative,* nay, of all Poems is to convert a series into a *Whole:* to make those events, which in real or imagined History move on in a *strait* Line, assume to our Understandings a *circular* motion—the snake with it's Tail in it's Mouth . . . Doubtless, to *his* eye, which alone comprehends all Past and all Future in one eternal Present, what to our short sight appears strait is but a part of the great Cycle—just as the calm Sea to us *appears* level, tho' it be indeed only a part of the *globe.* Now what the *globe* is in Geography, *miniaturing* in order to *manifest* the Truth, such is a Poem to that Image of God . . ." (*Collected Letters of Samuel Taylor Coleridge,* ed. Earl Leslie Griggs, 4 [Oxford: Clarendon Press, 1959]: 956).

8. The narrator's digressive mode is well discussed by M. K. Joseph, "The Artist and the Mirror," *Byron the Poet.*

9. As do, for example, John Speirs, *Poetry Towards Novel* (London: Faber and Faber, 1971), and, to some extent, Karl Kroeber, *Romantic Narrative Art.*

10. Comparison is often made to Sterne: see Andras Horn, *Byron's "Don Juan" and the Eighteenth Century English Novel,* Swiss Studies in English, No. 51 (Bern: Francke Verlag, 1962). On Byron's relationship to other English forebears (Butler, Pope, Swift, and Fielding) see A. B. England, *Byron's Don Juan and Eighteenth-Century Literature* (Lewisburg: Bucknell Univ. Press, 1975).

11. Byron's skepticism is a commonplace of criticism, but there is room for an extended consideration of his acquaintance with eighteenth-century British philosophy. Two studies whose purposes are indicated by their titles are Edward Wayne Marjarum, *Byron as Skeptic and Believer,* Princeton Studies in English, No. 16 (Princeton: Princeton Univ. Press, 1938), and "The Limits of Skepticism: The Byronic Affirmation," the final chapter of Michael G. Cooke's *The Blind Man Traces the Circle.* Other helpful works are: George Boas, "The Romantic Self: An Historical Sketch," *SiR,* 4 (1964), 1–17; Kenneth MacLean, *John Locke and English Literature of the Eighteenth Century* (1936; rpt. New York: Russell and Russell, 1962); C. E. Pulos, *The Deep Truth* (Lincoln: Univ.

of Nebraska Press, 1954); Leslie Stephen, *History of English Thought in the Eighteenth Century* (1876; rpt. New York: Harcourt, 1962); Colin Turbayne, *The Myth of Metaphor* (New Haven: Yale Univ. Press, 1962); Ernest Tuveson, *The Imagination as a Means of Grace* (Berkeley: Univ. of California Press, 1960); and Earl Wasserman, "The English Romantics: The Grounds of Knowledge," *SiR*, 4 (1964), 17–35.

12. *His Very Self And Voice*, p. 418.

13. The similes hint too at the kind of gratification the self-reflection which produced *Don Juan* provided Byron. The image of the lover's kiss seems to contain a buried memory of a baby at the breast: compare this passage with a comment prompted by Haidée and quoted already on p. 185: "A child the moment when it drains the breast" (I, 196). The maternal undertones are consonant with the explicit reference to the whelp clinging to its teat. A more doctrinaire psychoanalytic critic than I might insist that the intake of the world which is so prominent a feature of *Don Juan* is a form of oral incorporation; the equation words = milk is a common one in classical Freudian studies (cf. Wormhoudt). As argued in the next chapter, the world in *Don Juan* remains healthily external, not assimilated by the encompassing self but a means of self-definition. On this subject, however, see the last paragraph of this book where that same critic might well wish to make more of the contrast between the anality of the miser and the orality of the poet.

14. *The Letters of John Keats*, ed. Hyder Edward Rollins (Cambridge: Harvard Univ. Press, 1958), 1: 193.

15.

> But why then publish? *Granville* the polite,
> And knowing *Walsh*, would tell me I could write;
> Well natur'd *Garth* inflam'd with early praise
> And *Congreve* lov'd, and *Swift* endur'd my Lays;
> The courtly *Talbot, Somers, Sheffield* read,
> Ev'n mitred *Rochester* would nod the head,
> And *St. John's* self (great *Dryden's* friends before)
> With open arms receiv'd one Poet more.

> (135–142)

16. In addition to Winnicott's *Playing and Reality* cited in n. 3 of the introduction, the following works have contributed to the notions of play in this study: Johan Huizinga, *Homo Ludens* (1950; rpt. Boston: Beacon Press, 1955), and *Game, Play, Literature*, ed. Jacques Ehrmann (Boston: Beacon Press, 1971).

17. The importance of this myth in *Don Juan* is argued by Rachel Mayer Brownstein, "Byron's *Don Juan*: Some Reasons for the Rhymes," *MLQ*, 28 (1967), 177–192. Though I reach different conclusions, the discussion of the following pages is indebted to her and to an article upon which she also

draws: W. K. Wimsatt, "One Relation of Rhyme to Reason," *The Verbal Icon* (Lexington: Univ. of Kentucky Press, 1954).

18. The table presented by M. K. Joseph as Appendix C of *Byron The Poet* reveals the proportion of digression in the first five cantos of *Don Juan* to be roughly 25 percent; in the last five cantos it has grown to about 42 percent. It is interesting that the canto with by far the highest proportion of digression (72 percent), according to Joseph's analysis, is XII, where the gynocracy is introduced; the canto with the second highest proportion (59 percent) is IX, which is dominated by Catherine.

Chapter 8

1. These stanzas are also analyzed by Michael G. Cooke, *The Blind Man Traces the Circle*, pp. 189–192, and M. K. Joseph, *Byron The Poet*, pp. 212–214.

2. Byron's closeness to the scene is suggested by his description of the Khan's youngest son:

> The fifth, who, by a Christian mother nourished,
> Had been neglected, ill-used, and what not,
> Because deformed, yet died all game and bottom,
> To save a Sire who blushed that he begot him.
>   (VIII, 110)

Though the episode of the Khan and his five sons occurs in the *Histoire de la Nouvelle Russie* which Byron was using as his source, this characteristic detail of the deformed, unloved son is his own invention. The scene suggests Byron's characteristic themes in other ways as well: note the satire on the eldest son whose bravery is inspired by visions of black-eyed houris, as compared with the father's devotion.

3. I quote this stanza in Byron's revised version, as set forth by Jerome J. McGann, "The Correct Text of *Don Juan* I, 190–198," *TLS*, August 13, 1976.

4. It is uncertain who is the ghost on his first appearance (XVI, 20 ff.)— perhaps the ruse is Adeline's?

5. *A Treatise of Human Nature*, ed. Ernest C. Mossner (Baltimore: Penguin, 1969), pp. 299–300.

6. *Treatise of Human Nature*, p. 315.

Select Bibliography: Literary Works; Historical, Philosophical, and Psychoanalytic Works

i. Literary Works

Allen, Shirley Seifried. *Samuel Phelps and Sadler's Wells Theatre.* Middletown, Conn.: Wesleyan Univ. Press, 1971.

Amarasinghe, Upali. *Dryden and Pope in the Early Nineteenth Century.* Cambridge: Cambridge Univ. Press, 1962.

Ashton, T. L. "The Censorship of Byron's *Marino Faliero.*" *HLQ,* 36 (1972), 27–44.

———"Marino Faliero: Byron's 'Poetry' of Politics,'" *SiR,* 13 (1974), 1–13.

Babcock, R. W. "The Inception and Reception of Byron's *Cain.*" *SAQ,* 26 (1927), 178–189.

Barzun, Jacques. "Byron and the Byronic in History." Intro. to *The Selected Letters of Lord Byron.* New York: Farrar, 1953.

Bate, Walter Jackson. *The Burden of the Past and the English Poet.* Cambridge: Harvard Univ. Press, 1970.

Beaty, F. L. "Byron's Imitations of Juvenal and Persius." *SiR,* 15 (1976), 333–355.

———"Harlequin Don Juan." *JEGP,* 67 (1968), 395–405.

Beckett, Samuel. *Proust.* 1931; rpt. New York: Grove Press, n. d.

Bersani, Leo. *Marcel Proust: The Fictions of Life and Art.* New York: Oxford Univ. Press, 1965.

Blackstone, Bernard. "Guilt and Retribution in Byron's Sea Poems." *RES,* 2 (1961), 58–69.

———*The Lost Travellers.* London: Longman's, 1962.

Bloom, Harold. "Napoleon and Prometheus." *YFS,* 26 (1960–1961), 79–83.

————*The Visionary Company*. rev. and enl. edition. Ithaca: Cornell Univ. Press, 1971.

Bostetter, E. E. *The Romantic Ventriloquists*. Seattle: Univ. of Washington Press, 1963.

Boyd, Elizabeth French. *Byron's DON JUAN*. 1945; rpt. New York: Humanities Press, 1958.

Brée, Germaine. *Marcel Proust and Deliverance From Time*, trans. C. J. Richards and A. D. Truitt. 1955; rpt. New York: Grove Press, n. d.

Bronson, Bertrand H. "The Pre-Romantic or Post-Augustan Mode." *ELH*, 20 (1953), 15–28.

Brownstein, Rachel Mayer. "Byron's *Don Juan*: Some Reasons for the Rhymes." *MLQ*, 28 (1967), 177–192.

Butler, M. H. "An Examination of Byron's Revisions of *Manfred*, Act III." *SP*, 60 (1963), 627–636.

Byron, George Gordon, Lord. *Byron's Don Juan*: A Variorum Edition, ed. T. G. Steffan and W. W. Pratt. 4 vols. 2nd. ed., Austin: Univ. of Texas Press, 1971.

————*Byron's Letters and Journals*, ed. Leslie Marchand. Vols. 1–6. London: John Murray, 1973–1976.

————*Lord Byron's CAIN*, ed. T. G. Steffan. Austin: Univ. of Texas Press, 1969.

————*Lord Byron's Correspondence*, ed. John Murray. 2 vols. London: John Murray, 1922.

————*The Works of Lord Byron: Letters and Journals*, ed. R. E. Prothero. 6 vols. London: John Murray, 1898–1901.

————*The Works of Lord Byron: Poetry*, ed. E. H. Coleridge. 7 vols. London: John Murray, 1898–1904.

Calvert, William. *Byron: Romantic Paradox*. 1935; rpt. New York: Russell and Russell, 1962.

Chapman, John S. *Byron and the Honourable Mrs. Leigh*. New Haven: Yale Univ. Press, 1975.

Chew, Samuel. *The Dramas of Lord Byron*. 1915; rpt. New York: Russell and Russell, 1964.

Cooke, Michael G. *The Blind Man Traces the Circle: On the Patterns and Philosophy of Byron's Poetry*. Princeton: Princeton Univ. Press, 1969.

————"Byron's *Don Juan*: The Obsession and Self-Discipline of Spontaneity." *SiR*, 14 (1975), 285–302.

————"The Restoration Ethos of Byron's Classical Plays." *PMLA*, 79 (1964), 569–579.

deMan, Paul. "The Rhetoric of Temporality." *Interpretation: Theory and Practice*, ed. Charles S. Singleton. Baltimore: Johns Hopkins Univ. Press, 1969.

Downer, Alan. *The Eminent Tragedian: William Charles Macready*. Cambridge: Harvard Univ. Press, 1966.

Eggenschwiler, David. "The Tragic and Comic Rhythms of *Manfred*." *SiR*, 13 (1974), 63–77.

Elledge, W. P. *Byron and the Dynamics of Metaphor*. Nashville: Vanderbilt Univ. Press, 1968.

England, A. B. *Byron's Don Juan and Eighteenth-Century Literature*. Lewisburg: Bucknell Univ. Press, 1975.

Erdman, David. "Byron's Stage Fright." *ELH,* 6 (1939), 219–245.
Fricker, Robert. "Shakespeare und das Englische Romantische Drama." *Shakespeare Jahrbuch,* 95 (1959), 63–82.
Frye, Northrop. *Anatomy of Criticism: Four Essays.* Princeton: Princeton Univ. Press, 1957.
———"Lord Byron." *Fables of Identity: Studies in Poetic Mythology.* New York: Harcourt, 1963.
Galt, John. *The Autobiography of John Galt.* 2 vols. London: Cochrane and M'Crone, 1833.
Gleckner, Robert F. *Byron and the Ruins of Paradise.* Baltimore: Johns Hopkins Univ. Press, 1967.
Guerard, Albert, Jr. "Prometheus and the Aeolian Lyre." *YR,* 33 (1943–1944), 482–497.
Horn, Andras. *Byron's "Don Juan" and the Eighteenth-Century English Novel.* Swiss Studies in English, No. 51. Bern: Francke Verlag, 1962.
Hume, Robert D. "*The Island* and the Evolution of Byron's 'Tales.'" *Romantic and Victorian,* ed. W. P. Elledge and R. L. Hoffman. Rutherford: Fairleigh Dickinson Univ. Press, 1971.
Hungerford, Edward B. *The Shores of Darkness.* 1941; rpt. Cleveland: World Publishing Co., 1963.
Johnson, E. D. H. "A Political Interpretation of Byron's *Marino Faliero.*" *MLQ,* 3 (1942), 417–425.
Joseph, M. K. *Byron The Poet.* London: Gollancz, 1964.
Kahn, Arthur D. "Byron's 'Single Difference' with Homer and Virgil—The Redefinition of the Epic in *Don Juan.*" *Arcadia,* 5 (1970), 143–162.
Knight, G. Wilson. *Byron and Shakespeare.* London: Routledge and Kegan Paul, 1966.
———*The Golden Labyrinth.* New York: Norton, 1962.
———*Poets of Action.* London: Methuen, 1967.
Kreutz, Christian. *Das Prometheussymbol In Der Englischen Romantik.* Göttingen, 1963.
Kroeber, Karl. *Romantic Narrative Art.* 1960; rpt. Madison: Univ. of Wisconsin Press, 1966.
Lauber, John. "*Don Juan* as Anti-Epic." *SEL,* 8 (1968), 607–621.
Lovell, Ernest J., Jr. *Byron: The Record of a Quest.* 1949; rpt. Hamden, Conn.: Archon, 1966.
———ed. *His Very Self and Voice: Collected Conversations of Lord Byron.* New York: Macmillan, 1954.
———ed. *Lady Blessington's "Conversations of Lord Byron."* Princeton: Princeton Univ. Press, 1969.
———ed. *Medwin's "Conversations of Lord Byron."* Princeton: Princeton Univ. Press, 1966.
Luke, K. M. "Lord Byron's *Manfred:* A Study of Alienation from Within." *UTQ,* 40 (1970), 15–26.
McGann, Jerome J. "The Correct Text of *Don Juan,* I, 190–198." *TLS,* August 13, 1976.
———*DON JUAN in Context.* Chicago: Univ. of Chicago Press, 1976.
———*Fiery Dust: Byron's Poetic Development.* Chicago: Univ. of Chicago Press, 1968.

————"Milton and Byron." *KSMB*, 25 (1974), 9–25.

Mandel, Oscar, ed. *The Theatre of Don Juan*. Lincoln: Univ. of Nebraska Press, 1963.

Manning, Peter J. "Edmund Kean and Byron's Plays." *KSJ*, 21–22 (1972–1973), 188–206.

Marchand, Leslie. *Byron: A Biography*. 3 vols. New York: Alfred Knopf, 1957.

————*Byron's Poetry*. Boston: Houghton Mifflin, 1965.

Marjarum, Edward Wayne. *Byron As Skeptic and Believer*. Princeton Studies in English, No. 16. Princeton: Princeton Univ. Press, 1938.

Marshall, William H. *The Structure of Byron's Major Poems*. Philadelphia: Univ. of Pennsylvania Press, 1962.

Meyer, Herman. *The Poetics of Quotation in the European Novel*, trans. Theodore and Yetta Ziolkowski. Princeton: Princeton Univ. Press, 1968.

Michaels, Leonard. "Byron's *Cain*." *PMLA*, 84 (1969), 71–79.

Moore, Thomas. *Letters and Journals of Lord Byron: with Notices of His Life*. 2 vols. London: John Murray, 1830.

Motter, T. H. Vail. "Byron's *Werner* Re-Estimated." *Essays in Dramatic Literature*, ed. Hardin Craig. Princeton: Princeton Univ. Press, 1935.

Onorato, Richard J. *The Character of The Poet: Wordsworth in THE PRELUDE*. Princeton: Princeton Univ. Press, 1971.

Pafford, Ward. "Byron and the Mind of Man: *Childe Harold* III–IV and *Manfred*." *SiR*, 1 (1962), 105–127.

Quinlan, M. J. "Byron's *Manfred* and Zoroastrianism." *JEGP*, 57 (1958), 726–738.

Ridenour, George M. *The Style of DON JUAN*. Yale Studies in English, No. 144. New Haven: Yale Univ. Press, 1960.

Robinson, Charles. "The Devil as Doppelgänger in *The Deformed Transformed*." *BNYPL*, 74 (1970), 177–202.

Roston, Murray. *Biblical Drama in England*. London: Faber and Faber, 1968.

Rutherford, Andrew. *Byron: A Critical Study*. 1961; rpt. Edinburgh: Oliver and Boyd, 1965.

Smith, Barbara Herrnstein. *Poetic Closure*. Chicago: Univ. of Chicago Press, 1968.

Speirs, John. *Poetry Towards Novel*. London: Faber and Faber, 1971.

Sperry, Stuart M. "Byron and the Meaning of *Manfred*." *Criticism*, 16 (1974), 189–202.

Sundell, Michael. "The Development of *The Giaour*." *SEL*, 9 (1969), 587–599.

Thompson, James R. "Byron's Plays and *Don Juan*: Genre and Myth." *Bucknell Review*, 15 no. 3 (Dec. 1967), 22–38.

Thorslev, Peter L., Jr. *The Byronic Hero: Types and Prototypes*. Minneapolis: Univ. of Minnesota Press, 1962.

————"Incest as Romantic Symbol." *CLS*, 2 (1965), 41–58.

Wasserman, Earl. *Shelley's PROMETHEUS UNBOUND*. Baltimore: Johns Hopkins Univ. Press, 1965.

Watt, Ian. "Two Historical Aspects of the Augustan Tradition." *Studies in the Eighteenth Century*, ed. R. F. Brissenden. Canberra: Australian National Univ. Press, 1968.

Weinstein, Leo. *The Metamorphoses of Don Juan*. Stanford Studies in Language and Literature, No. 18. 1959; rpt. New York: AMS Press, 1967.

West, Paul, ed. *Byron: A Collection of Critical Essays.* Englewood Cliffs: Prentice-Hall, 1963.

———*Byron and The Spoiler's Art.* London: Chatto and Windus, 1960.

Wilkie, Brian. *Romantic Poets and Epic Tradition.* Madison: Univ. of Wisconsin Press, 1965.

Wimsatt, William K. *Hateful Contraries.* Lexington: Univ. of Kentucky Press, 1965.

———*The Verbal Icon.* Lexington: Univ. of Kentucky Press, 1954.

Woodring, Carl. *Politics In English Romantic Poetry.* Cambridge: Harvard Univ. Press, 1970.

Wormhoudt, Arthur. *The Demon Lover: A Psychoanalytical Approach To Literature.* 1949; rpt. Freeport, N. Y.: Books for Libraries Press, 1968.

Worthington, Mabel P. "Byron's *Don Juan:* Certain Psychological Aspects." *Literature and Psychology,* 7 (1957), 50–56.

ii. Historical, Philosophical, and Psychoanalytic Works

Aristotle. *Aristotle: Selections,* ed. W. D. Ross. New York: Scribners, 1938.

Boas, George. "The Romantic Self: An Historical Sketch." *SiR,* 4 (1964), 1–17.

Brenner, Charles. *An Elementary Textbook of Psychoanalysis.* 1955; rpt. Garden City: Doubleday, 1971.

Collingwood, R. G. *The Idea of History.* 1946; rpt. New York: Oxford Univ. Press, 1970.

Ehrmann, Jacques, ed. *Game, Play, Literature.* Boston: Beacon Press, 1971.

Erikson, Erik H. *Childhood and Society.* 2nd. ed. rev. and enl. New York: Norton, 1963.

———"Identity and The Life Cycle: Selected Papers." *Psychological Issues,* 1 (1959).

Fenichel, Otto. *The Psychoanalytic Theory of Neurosis.* New York: Norton, 1945.

Freud, Sigmund. *On Creativity and the Unconscious,* ed. Benjamin Nelson. New York: Harper, 1958.

———*The Standard Edition of the Complete Psychological Works of Sigmund Freud,* ed. James Strachey. 24 vols. London: The Hogarth Press, 1957.

Huizinga, Johan. *Homo Ludens.* 1950; rpt. Boston: Beacon Press, 1955.

Hume, David. *A Treatise of Human Nature,* ed. Ernest C. Mossner. Baltimore: Penguin, 1969.

Jones, Ernest. *Hamlet and Oedipus.* 1949; rpt. Garden City: Doubleday, 1954.

Jung, C. G. *Four Archetypes,* trans. R. F. C. Hull. Princeton: Princeton Univ. Press, 1970.

Kerenyi, C. *Prometheus: Archetypal Image of Human Existence,* trans. Ralph Manheim. New York: Bollingen/Pantheon, 1963.

Kierkegaard, Soren. *Repetition,* trans. Walter Lowrie. 1941; rpt. New York: Harper, 1964.

Kris, Ernst. *Psychoanalytic Explorations in Art.* 1952; rpt. New York: Schocken, 1964.

Lacan, Jacques, *Écrits.* Paris: Éditions du Seuil, 1966.

————*The Language of the Self,* tr. and ed. Anthony Wilden. 1968; rpt. New York: Delta, 1975.

Leclaire, Serge. *Psychanalyser: Essai sur l'ordre de l'inconscient et la pratique de la lettre.* Paris: Éditions du Seuil, 1968.

MacLean, Kenneth. *John Locke and English Literature of the Eighteenth Century.* 1936; rpt. New York: Russell and Russell, 1962.

Mahler, Margaret S., Pine, Fred, and Bergman, Anni. *The Psychological Birth of the Human Infant.* New York: Basic Books, 1975.

Modell, Arnold H. *Object Love and Reality.* New York: International Univ. Press, 1968.

Pulos, C. E. *The Deep Truth.* Lincoln: Univ. of Nebraska Press, 1954.

Rank, Otto. *The Double,* trans. Harry Tucker. Chapel Hill: Univ. of North Carolina Press, 1971.

St. Clair, William. *Lord Elgin and The Marbles.* London: Oxford Univ. Press, 1967.

Siater, Philip. *The Glory of Hera.* 1968; rpt. Boston: Beacon Press, 1971.

Stephen, Leslie. *History of English Thought in the Eighteenth Century.* 2 vols. 1876; rpt. New York: Harcourt, 1962.

Talmon, J. L. *Romanticism and Revolt: Europe 1815-1848.* New York: Harcourt, 1967.

Turbayne, Colin. *The Myth of Metaphor.* New Haven: Yale Univ. Press, 1962.

Tuveson, Ernest L. *The Imagination as a Means of Grace.* Berkeley: Univ. of California Press, 1960.

Wasserman, Earl. "The English Romantics: The Grounds of Knowledge." *SiR,* 4 (1964), 17-35.

Winnicott, D. W. *The Maturational Processes and the Facilitating Environment.* New York: International Univ. Press, 1965.

————*Playing and Reality.* New York: Basic Books, 1971.

————*Through Paediatrics to Psycho-Analysis.* 1958; rpt. with an introduction by Masud Khan. New York: Basic Books, 1975.

Index

Peter J. Manning is an associate professor of
English at the University of Southern California
(Los Angeles). He holds a B.A. (1963) from
Harvard, and an M.A. (1965) and Ph.D. (1968) from
Yale University. He is a frequent contributor to
scholarly journals.

The manuscript was edited by Jean Spang.
The book was designed by Don Ross. The
typeface for the text and display is Palatino, designed by Hermann Zapf about 1950.

The text is printed on Glatfelter's Litho
paper; and the book is bound in Holliston's Kings-
ton natural finish cloth over binder's boards.
Manufactured in the United States of America.